HIGH COURT CASE SUMMARIES

CRIMINAL LAW

Keyed to Kaplan's Casebook on Criminal Law, 7th Edition

WEST®

Mat #41305656

© West, a Thomson business, 2005
© 2010 Thomson Reuters
© 2013 LEG, Inc. d/b/a West Academic Publishing
      610 Opperman Drive
      St. Paul, MN 55123
      1-800-313-9378

Printed in the United States of America

ISBN:978–0–314–28244–6

Table of Contents

Alphabetical Table of Cases VII

Chapter One. The Purposes and Limits of Punishment 1
Kansas v. Hendricks 3
Graham v. Florida 5
Kennedy v. Louisiana 9
Ewing v. California 11
Apprendi v. New Jersey 15

Chapter Two. The Criminal Act 17
Proctor v. State 21
Jones v. United States 23
United States v. Maldonado 25
State v. Barger 27
Lawrence v. Texas 29
People v. Newton 31
Martin v. State 33
People v. Grant 35
Robinson v. California 37
Johnson v. State 39
Keeler v. Superior Court 41
United States v. Hudson and Goodwin 43
Rogers v. Tennessee 45
Chicago v. Morales 49

Chapter Three. The Guilty Mind 51
People v. Dillard 55
United States v. Wulff 57
Lambert v. California 59
Regina v. Faulkner 61
Regina v. Prince 63
People v. Ryan 65
People v. Bray 67
United States v. Baker 69
Cheek v. United States 71
Commonwealth v. Twitchell 73
Hendershott v. People 75
State v. Cameron 77
Montana v. Egelhoff 79

Chapter Four. Causation 81
Regina v. Martin Dyos 83
R. v. Benge 85
Hubbard v. Commonwealth 87
Commonwealth v. Rhoades 89
Commonwealth v. Root 91
United States v. Hamilton 93
Stephenson v. State 95
People v. Kevorkian 97
Commonwealth v. Levesque 99

Chapter Five. Intentional Homicide 101
Francis v. Franklin 103
United States v. Watson 107
People v. Walker 109

Ex Parte Fraley 111
Rowland v. State 113
People v. Berry 115
People v. Wu 117

Chapter Six. Unintentional Homicide **121**
Commonwealth v. Welansky 123
State v. Williams 125
Mayes v. The People 127
State v. Martin 129
People v. Hickman 131
People v. Gladman 133
People v. Cavitt 135
State v. Shock 137

Chapter Seven. Capital Murder and the Death Penalty **139**
Olsen v. State 141
Tison v. Arizona 145
McCleskey v. Kemp 149

Chapter Eight. Defensive Force, Necessity, and Duress **151**
People v. La Voie 153
People v. Gleghorn 155
State v. Leidholm 157
People v. Goetz 159
Tennessee v. Garner 161
People v. Ceballos 163
The Queen v. Dudley & Stephens 165
People v. Unger 167
State v. Warshow 169
State v. Crawford 171
State v. Hunter 173

Chapter Nine. Mental Illness as a Defense **175**
People v. Serravo 177
Smith v. State 181

Chapter Ten. Attempt **185**
State v. Lyerla 187
People v. Stone 191
People v. Murray 193
McQuirter v. State 195
People v. Rizzo 197
People v. Staples 199
People v. Lubow 201
Booth v. State 203
People v. Dlugash 205
People v. Thousand 207

Chapter Eleven. Complicity **209**
State v. Ochoa 211
State v. Tally 213
State v. Formella 215
People v. Beeman 217
Wilson v. People 219
State v. Etzweiler 221
State v. Christy Pontiac—GMC, Inc. 223
United States v. Hilton Hotels Corp. 225

Chapter Twelve. Conspiracy **227**
State v. Verive 229
Griffin v. State 231
United States v. Recio 233
People v. Lauria 235
United States v. Diaz 237
United States v. Neapolitan 239

Chapter Thirteen. Rape **241**
Brown v. State 243
People v. Dorsey 245
People v. Barnes 247
State v. Smith 249
In the Interest of M.T.S. 251
State v. Moorman 253
Commonwealth v. Mlinarich 255
Boro v. People 257
Commonwealth v. Fischer 259

Chapter Fourteen. Theft Offenses **261**
Commonwealth v. Mitchneck 263
The Case of the Carrier Who Broke Bulk Anon v. The Sheriff of London 265
Rex v. Chisser 267
The King v. Pear 269
People v. Sattlekau 271
Durland v. United States 273
People v. Dioguardi 275
McCormick v. United States 277
Lear v. State 279
State v. Colvin 281

Chapter Fifteen. Perjury, False Statements, and Obstruction of Justice **283**
Bronston v. United States 285
United States v. Moore 287
Brogan v. United States 289
United States v. Aguilar 291
United States v. Cueto 293
Arthur Andersen LLP v. United States 295

Alphabetical Table of Cases

Cases

Adcock v. Commonwealth ----------------- 88
Apprendi v. New Jersey ---------------- 15
Arthur Andersen LLP v. United States 295
Booth v. State -------------------- 203, 206, 208
Boro v. People -------------------------- 257
Bouie v. City of Columbia ------------------ 46
Bowers v. Hardwick------------------- 29
Brogan v. United States ------------------ 289
Bronston v. United States ---------------- 285
Brown v. State-------------------------243, 279
Callins v. Collins---------------------- 150
Cheek v. United States ------------------ 71
Chicago v. Morales ----------------------- 49
Commonwealth v. Fischer -----------259, 260
Commonwealth v. Karenbauer ---------- 108
Commonwealth v. Levesque---------------- 99
Commonwealth v. Mitchneck -------263, 266
Commonwealth v. Mlinarich -------------- 255
Commonwealth v. Osachuk ---------------- 90
Commonwealth v. Rhoades----------------- 89
Commonwealth v. Root ------------------ 91
Commonwealth v. Twitchell---------------- 73
Commonwealth v. Welansky -------------- 123
Commonwealth v. Williams -------------- 260
Denham v. State ------------------------- 114
Durland v. United States---------------- 273
Enmund v. Florida ---------------------- 146
Ewing v. California------------------------ 11
Ex Parte Fraley ----------------------- 111
Francis v. Franklin---------------------- 103
Fuller v. Decatur Public School Board of
    Education ---------------------------- 50
Graham v. Florida-------------------------5
Gregg v. Georgia ------------------------- 150
Griffin v. State------------------------- 231
Harmelin v. Michigan --------------------- 12
Heard v. State -------------------------- 104
Hendershott v. People-------------------- 75
Holdridge v. United States ---------------- 57
Hubbard v. Commonwealth ------- 87, 92, 94
Hyde v. U.S. ---------------------------- 197
In the Interest of M.T.S. ----------------- 251
Johnson v. State ------------------------ 39
Jones v. United States ------------------- 16, 23
Kansas v. Hendricks-----------------------3
Keeler v. Superior Court -------------- 41, 46
Kennedy v. Louisiana ----------------------9
Lambert v. California ------------------- 59
Lambert v. State ------------------------ 22
Lawrence v. Texas ----------------------- 29
Lear v. State--------------------------- 279
M'Naghten's Case ----------------------- 178
Martin v. State ------------------------- 33
Mayes v. The People -------------------- 127
McCleskey v. Kemp --------------------- 149
McCormick v. United States ------------- 277
McQuirter v. State -------------------195, 198
Montana v. Egelhoff --------------------- 79
Olsen v. State ------------------------141, 282
People v. Akins ------------------------ 110

People v. Arnold ----------------------------- 56
People v. Barnes -------------------------- 247
People v. Beeman -------------------------- 217
People v. Berry --------------------------- 115
People v. Bissett------------------------109, 112
People v. Bray ----------------------------- 67
People v. Cavitt---------------------------- 135
People v. Ceballos ------------------------ 163
People v. Cole ---------------------------- 116
People v. Dillard ------------------------- 55
People v. Dioguardi ------------------275, 280
People v. Dlugash -------------------------- 205
People v. Dorsey---------------------------- 245
People v. Espenscheid ---------------------- 36
People v. Gladman ------------------------- 133
People v. Gleghorn ------------------------- 155
People v. Goetz --------------------------- 159
People v. Grant---------------------- 35, 38, 40
People v. Hickman -------------------------- 131
People v. Kacer ---------------------------- 278
People v. Kevorkian ------------------------ 97
People v. La Voie -------------------------- 153
People v. Lauria --------------------------- 235
People v. Leichtweis ----------------------- 206
People v. Lovercamp ------------------------ 168
People v. Lubow---------------------------- 201
People v. Miller--------------------------- 193
People v. Murray--------------------------193, 196
People v. Newton -------------------------- 31
People v. Rizzo---------------------------197, 200
People v. Roberts------------------------- 97, 98
People v. Ryan ---------------------------- 65
People v. Sattlekau---------------------271, 274
People v. Serravo -------------------------177, 182
People v. Snyder -------------------------- 68
People v. Staples -------------------------- 199
People v. Stone --------------------------- 191
People v. Thousand ------------------------ 207
People v. Unger---------------------------- 167
People v. Vanrees-------------------------- 76
People v. Walker -------------------------109, 112
People v. Wu ------------------------------ 117
Proctor v. State -------------------------- 21
R. v. Benge------------------------------- 85
Regina v. Collin -------------------------- 204
Regina v. Faulkner------------------------ 61, 64
Regina v. Martin Dyos -------------------- 83, 86
Regina v. Prince -------------------------- 63
Rex v. Chisser---------------------------- 267
Robinson v. California-------------------- 37, 40
Rogers v. Tennessee ----------------------- 45
Rowland v. State ------------------------- 113
Rummel v. Estelle ------------------------ 11
Smith v. State---------------------------181, 272
Solem v. Helm --------------------------- 12
Stanley v. Turner ------------------------ 58
State v. Barger -------------------------- 27
State v. Bauman -------------------------- 78
State v. Bland--------------------------108, 112
State v. Brown -------------------------- 80
State v. Cameron ------------------------- 77
State v. Christy Pontiac–GMC, Inc. ---- 223
State v. Colvin -------------------------- 281

State v. Crawford ---------------------------- 171
State v. Davis ------------------------------- 263
State v. Etzweiler--------------------------- 221
State v. Finch -------------------------------- 142
State v. Formella --------------------------- 215
State v. Hunter------------------------------- 173
State v. Leidholm --------------------------- 157
State v. Lyerla ------------------------------ 187
State v. Martin ------------------------------ 129
State v. Medibus–Helpmobile, Inc. ------ 224
State v. Moorman--------------------------- 253
State v. Ochoa ------------------------------ 211
State v. Shock------------------------------- 137
State v. Smith------------------------------- 249
State v. Tally-------------------------------- 213
State v. Urbina ------------------------------ 28
State v. Verive ------------------------------ 229
State v. Warshow --------------------------- 169
State v. Williams---------------------------- 125
Stephenson v. State------------------------- 95
Tennessee v. Garner------------------------- 161
The Case of the Carrier Who Broke Bulk
   Anon v. The Sheriff of London ---265, 267
The King v. Pear ----------------------------- 269
The Queen v. Dudley & Stephens ------- 165
Tison v. Arizona----------------------------- 145
United States v. Aguilar-------------------- 291
United States v. Atkinson-------------------- 72
United States v. Baker----------------------- 69
United States v. Coleman ------------------- 33
United States v. Cueto --------------------- 293
United States v. Diaz------------------------ 237
United States v. Hamilton ------------- 93, 96
United States v. Hilton Hotels Corp. --- 225
United States v. Hooker --------------------- 69
United States v. Hudson and Goodwin -- 43
United States v. Liranzo --------------------- 26
United States v. Maldonado---------------- 25
United States v. Meade --------------------- 60
United States v. Moore--------------------- 287
United States v. Murdock ------------------- 72
United States v. Neapolitan--------------- 239
United States v. Nieves---------------------- 16
United States v. Recio---------------------- 233
United States v. Watson------------------- 107
United States v. Wulff ---------------------- 57
Vulcan Last Co. v. State------------------- 226
Wilson v. People----------------------------- 219
Young v. U.S. ex rel. Vuitton et Fils S.A. 44

CHAPTER ONE

The Purposes and Limits of Punishment

Kansas v. Hendricks

Instant Facts: A repeat sexual predator was involuntarily committed following criminal convictions for sexual assaulting children.

Black Letter Rule: Where a civil commitment statute does not seek retribution or deterrence, it does not establish punitive criminal proceedings necessary to uphold double jeopardy and ex post facto claims.

Graham v. Florida

Instant Facts: After a juvenile violated his probation, he was found guilty of the two crimes that underlay his probation sentence, as well as violating his probation, and was sentenced to life in prison without parole; he challenged his sentence as violating the Eighth Amendment's prohibition on cruel and unusual punishment.

Black Letter Rule: For a juvenile offender who did not commit homicide, the Eighth Amendment forbids the sentence of life without parole.

Kennedy v. Louisiana

Instant Facts: Kennedy (D) was found guilty of the aggravated rape of his eight-year-old stepdaughter and was sentenced to death; he challenged the constitutionality of his sentence.

Black Letter Rule: The Eighth Amendment prohibits the death penalty in child rape cases where the crime did not result, and was not intended to result, in the death of the victim.

Ewing v. California

Instant Facts: Ewing (D) was sentenced to twenty-five years to life following his conviction for grand theft under California's three-strikes law.

Black Letter Rule: Imposing a sentence of twenty-five years to life in prison on the conviction of felony grand theft under the three-strikes law is not grossly disproportionate and does not violate the Eighth Amendment's prohibition on cruel and unusual punishment.

Apprendi v. New Jersey

Instant Facts: Apprendi (D) fired into the home of a black family that had recently moved into a white neighborhood; finding that Apprendi (D) acted on racial motives, the court sentenced him under a hate crime act providing for stricter punishment.

Black Letter Rule: The due process considerations of the Fifth Amendment, applied to the states through the Fourteenth Amendment, require that any increase in the maximum prison sentence must be based on facts found by a jury beyond a reasonable doubt.

Kansas v. Hendricks

(State Government) v. (Committed Sex Offender)

521 U.S. 346 (1997)

STATES MAY INVOLUNTARILY COMMIT SEXUAL PREDATORS WITHOUT VIOLATING THEIR CONSTITUTIONAL RIGHTS

He's not "mentally ill"-- He just needs a really long time-out.

stus.com

■**INSTANT FACTS** A repeat sexual predator was involuntarily committed following criminal convictions for sexual assaulting children.

■**BLACK LETTER RULE** Where a civil commitment statute does not seek retribution or deterrence, it does not establish punitive criminal proceedings necessary to uphold double jeopardy and ex post facto claims.

■ **PROCEDURAL BASIS**

Certiorari to review a decision of the Kansas Supreme Court invalidating a state statute.

■ **FACTS**

Hendricks (D), a convicted criminal with a history of sexually molesting children, was the first person committed under the Kansas Sexual Violent Predator Act. Under the statute, persons may be committed upon a showing that, due to a "mental abnormality" or "personality disorder," they are likely to commit predatory acts of sexual violence. Hendricks (D) admitted that he suffered an uncontrollable personality disorder that caused him to molest children, but claimed that the statute violated his substantive due process rights and the Double Jeopardy and Ex Post Facto Clauses of the Constitution. Agreeing with Hendricks (D), the Kansas Supreme Court invalidated the statute, holding that the statute violated the Due Process Clause by permitting involuntary commitment of a person not suffering from a "mental illness." The State (P) appealed to the Supreme Court, and Hendricks (D) cross-appealed on double jeopardy and ex post facto grounds. After determining that the statute does not offend due process concerns by allowing commitment for less than a mental illness, the Court considered Hendricks's (D) claims.

■ **ISSUE**

Does a state statute permitting involuntary civil commitment of one who suffers mental abnormalities not arising to mental illness violate the Double Jeopardy and Ex Post Facto Clauses of the Constitution?

■ **DECISION AND RATIONALE**

(Thomas, J.) No. Where a civil commitment statute does not seek retribution or deterrence, it does not establish punitive criminal proceedings necessary to uphold double jeopardy and ex post facto claims. The statute here implicates neither retribution nor deterrence. It does not seek retribution for prior criminal conduct, but rather uses that conduct as evidentiary support

---

for the enforcement of the statute. In fact, a prior criminal conviction is not even a statutory prerequisite, for one can be involuntarily committed without any criminal culpability for his actions. Because culpability is not required, the statute cannot seek retribution. Likewise, the statute does not act as a deterrent. The statute commits only persons who, by definition, are unable to control their actions because of mental abnormalities or personality disorders. Because of their conditions, these persons are unlikely to be deterred by the threat of civil commitment. Without these punitive objectives, the statute does not establish a criminal proceeding and cannot run afoul of the double jeopardy and ex post facto prohibitions. Reversed.

Analysis:

Constitutional critics of civil commitment question the lengths States may go to to confine their citizens. For instance, under the Kansas civil commitment statute, the State may civilly commit one who is incapable, because of mental abnormality or personality disorder, of refraining from committing sexual abuse against minors. Yet other mental "abnormalities," such as alcoholism and drug addition, could cause an individual's inability to refrain from driving drunk or committing drug-related crimes. Given the States' interests in protecting its citizens, reliance on mental abnormalities to justify civil commitment appears to be a broad expansion of governmental authority.

■ **CASE VOCABULARY**

CIVIL COMMITMENT: A commitment of a person who is ill, incompetent, drug-addicted, or the like, as contrasted with a criminal sentence.

DETERRENCE: The act of process of discouraging certain behavior, particularly by fear; especially, as a goal of criminal law, the prevention of criminal behavior by fear of punishment.

DOUBLE JEOPARDY: The fact of being prosecuted twice for substantially the same offense.

EX POST FACTO LAW: A law that applies retroactively, especially in a way that negatively affects a person's rights, as by criminalizing an action that was legal when it was committed.

RETRIBUTION: Punishment imposed as repayment or revenge for the offense committed; requital.

Graham v. Florida

(Juvenile) v. (Prosecuting Authority)

130 S. Ct. 2011 (2010)

JUVENILES MUST BE GIVEN A MEANINGFUL CHANCE AT REHABILITATION

No, grounding a teenager is not "cruel and unusual" since it's not LWOP.

KEEP OUT

stus.com

■**INSTANT FACTS** After a juvenile violated his probation, he was found guilty of the two crimes that underlay his probation sentence, as well as violating his probation, and was sentenced to life in prison without parole; he challenged his sentence as violating the Eighth Amendment's prohibition on cruel and unusual punishment.

■**BLACK LETTER RULE** For a juvenile offender who did not commit homicide, the Eighth Amendment forbids the sentence of life without parole.

■ **PROCEDURAL BASIS**

Certiorari to review the juvenile defendant's challenge to his criminal sentence.

■ **FACTS**

When Graham (D) was sixteen years old, he and three other youths attempted to rob a restaurant. One of the youths worked there, and he left the back door unlocked just before closing. Graham (D) and another youth entered through the back door, wearing masks, and came upon the manager. The other youth hit the restaurant manager in the back of the head with a metal bar, but when the man started yelling Graham (D) and his accomplice ran out without taking anything. The manager's injuries required stitches. Graham pleaded guilty to armed burglary with assault or battery, a first-degree felony, and attempted armed robbery, a second-degree felony. The court withheld adjudication of guilt and sentenced Graham (D) to two concurrent three-year terms of probation, but he had to spend twelve months of his probation in the county jail. Less than six months after his release, Graham (D) was again arrested. The court found Graham guilty of violating his probation, as well as the two earlier charges, and sentenced him to the maximum allowable: life in prison. Florida has abolished its parole system, which meant that Graham could not be released from prison during his lifetime unless granted executive clemency. Graham filed a motion in the trial court challenging his sentence as a violation of the Eighth Amendment's prohibition on cruel and unusual punishment. The court denied the motion, the appellate court affirmed, and the state supreme court denied review. The United States Supreme Court granted certiorari.

■ **ISSUE**

Does the Constitution permit a juvenile offender to be sentenced to life in prison without parole for a nonhomicide crime?

■ **DECISION AND RATIONALE**

(Kennedy, J.) No. For a juvenile offender who did not commit homicide, the Eighth Amendment forbids the sentence of life without parole. According to the Eighth Amendment, no cruel or usual punishment may be inflicted. Embodied in this ban on cruel and unusual

---

punishment is the precept of justice that punishment for crime should be graduated and proportioned to the offense. The concept of proportionality is central to an Eighth Amendment analysis. In order to determine whether punishment is cruel and unusual, courts must look beyond historical perceptions to the evolving standards of decency that mark the progress of a maturing society.

The Court has considered Eighth Amendment challenges to the length of particular defendants' sentences and to the death penalty, but has not yet considered a categorical challenge to a term-of-years sentence as applied to an entire class of offenders, as in this case. Six jurisdictions do not allow life-without-parole sentences for any juvenile offenders, and seven jurisdictions permit such a sentence only for homicide crimes. Thirty-seven jurisdictions permit life-without-parole sentences for juveniles only under certain circumstances. The state argues that there is no national consensus against the type of sentence imposed in this case, such that the sentence is appropriate, but the state's argument is unavailing. The judicial exercise of independent judgment requires consideration of the culpability of offenders in light of their crimes and characteristics, along with the severity of the punishment in question. This inquiry includes a consideration of whether the sentence serves legitimate penological goals. Juveniles have lessened culpability, and defendants who do not kill or intend to kill are less deserving of the most serious punishments than are murderers. Life without parole is an especially harsh punishment for a juvenile, and the need for retribution is not as strong with regard to a minor as it is with regard to an adult. The same characteristics that render a juvenile less culpable than an adult suggest that they are less susceptible to deterrence, so that penological goal does not justify the sentence imposed here. And although incapacitation is a legitimate reason for imprisonment, it does not justify life in prison for a juvenile who did not kill. Moreover, life in prison without the possibility of parole destroys the goal of rehabilitation, especially in minors where the chance at rehabilitation exists. Penological theory is not adequate to justify life without parole for juvenile nonhomicide offenders. The limited culpability of juvenile nonhomicide offenders and the severity of life without parole sentences lead to the conclusion that the sentencing practice under consideration here is cruel and unusual. The state must give defendants like Graham (D) a meaningful opportunity to obtain release based on demonstrated maturity and rehabilitation. Reversed and remanded.

Analysis:

As the Court notes in this case, the concept of proportionality, which is central to the Eighth Amendment, is viewed less through a historical prism than according to the evolving standards of decency that mark the progress of a maturing society. The clearest and most reliable evidence of contemporary values, for purposes of an Eighth Amendment challenge, is the legislation enacted by the country's legislatures, but there are measures of consensus other than legislation, and actual sentencing practices are an important part of the Court's inquiry into consensus. Community consensus, while entitled to great weight, is not determinative of whether a punishment is cruel and unusual. A sentence lacking any legitimate penological justification is, by its nature, disproportionate to the offense and in violation of the Eighth Amendment.

■ CASE VOCABULARY

CULPABILITY: Blameworthiness; the quality of being culpable. Except in cases of absolute liability, criminal culpability requires a showing that the person acted purposely, knowingly, recklessly, or negligently with respect to each material element of the offense.

DETERRENCE: The act or process of discouraging certain behavior, particularly by fear; especially, as a goal of criminal law, the prevention of criminal behavior by fear of punishment.

REHABILITATION: The process of seeking to improve a criminal's character and outlook so that he or she can function in society without committing other crimes.

RETRIBUTION: Punishment imposed as repayment or revenge for the offense committed; requital.

Kennedy v. Louisiana

(Criminal Defendant) v. (Prosecuting State)

554 U.S. 407 (2008)

THE COURT SAYS CHILD RAPE IS NOT HEINOUS ENOUGH TO JUSTIFY THE DEATH PENALTY

Constitutionality? Proportionality? This job used to be so easy.

■**INSTANT FACTS** Kennedy (D) was found guilty of the aggravated rape of his eight-year-old stepdaughter and was sentenced to death; he challenged the constitutionality of his sentence.

■**BLACK LETTER RULE** The Eighth Amendment prohibits the death penalty in child rape cases where the crime did not result, and was not intended to result, in the death of the victim.

■ **PROCEDURAL BASIS**

U.S. Supreme Court review of the state supreme court's upholding of the defendant's death sentence.

■ **FACTS**

Kennedy (D) called 911 to report that his eight-year-old stepdaughter had been raped. She was transported to the hospital, where she underwent emergency surgery to treat her injuries. The child's injuries were later described by an expert in pediatric forensic medicine as the most severe he had ever seen from a sexual assault in four years of practice. Kennedy (D) was charged with the crime. His stepdaughter testified at trial that she woke up on the morning of the rape and Kennedy (D) was on top of her. Kennedy (D) was found guilty and was sentenced to death pursuant to a Louisiana statute that authorized the death penalty in cases involving the rape of a child under twelve years of age.

■ **ISSUE**

Was the Louisiana statute imposing the death penalty in child rape cases unconstitutional?

■ **DECISION AND RATIONALE**

(Kennedy, J.) Yes. The Eighth Amendment prohibits the death penalty in child rape cases where the crime did not result, and was not intended to result, in the death of the victim. Capital punishment must be limited to those offenders who commit a narrow category of the most serious crimes, and whose extreme culpability makes them the most deserving of execution. When the law punishes by death, it risks its own sudden descent into brutality. Although thirty-seven jurisdictions have the death penalty, only six of them authorize the death penalty for the rape of a child. There are, of course, measures of consensus other than legislation. The number of executions carried out in recent years may indicate whether execution for child rape is regarded as acceptable by our society. Louisiana is the only state since 1964 that has sentenced an individual to death for the crime of child rape. There is obviously no national consensus in favor of capital punishment for this crime.

Capital punishment is excessive when it is grossly out of proportion to the crime or it does not fulfill the two purposes served by the death penalty: retribution and deterrence. It is possible that these purposes would be served by imposition of the death penalty in child rape cases. But the incongruity between the crime of child rape and the harshness of the death penalty poses too great a risk of over-punishment, and counsels against a constitutional ruling that the death penalty can be expanded to include this offense. One other important consideration is whether the death penalty would balance the wrong to the victim. It is not at all evident that a child rape victim's hurt is lessened when the law permits the death of the perpetrator. Asking the child victim to be part of a process that inflicts capital punishment forces a moral choice on a child who is not mature enough to make that choice. The death penalty may also increase the risk of non-reporting. Under-reporting is already a concern. We conclude that the death penalty is not a proportional punishment for the rape of a child. Reversed.

Analysis:

It is hard to imagine a more gruesome crime than that described in this case. Although the Court's opinion notes that it could not possibly capture on paper the full hurt, horror, and revulsion of Kennedy's (D) crime, it goes on to describe the child's injuries as including a laceration to the vaginal wall so severe that it separated her cervix from the back of her vagina, causing her rectum to protrude into the vaginal structure. Her entire perineum was torn, from front to back. Even so, Kennedy (D) did not fit into that category of offenders who commit the most serious crimes, and whose extreme culpability makes them the most deserving of execution. Nor, per the Court's opinion, would the death penalty be deemed to balance the wrong to the victim in this case. Accordingly, the state court decision upholding the defendant's death sentence was reversed.

Ewing v. California

(Golf Club Thief) v. (Prosecuting State)

538 U.S. 11, 123 S. Ct. 1179 (2003)

A HARSH "THREE-STRIKES" SENTENCE IS NOT UNCONSTITUTIONAL

■**INSTANT FACTS** Ewing (D) was sentenced to twenty-five years to life following his conviction for grand theft under California's three-strikes law.

■**BLACK LETTER RULE** Imposing a sentence of twenty-five years to life in prison on the conviction of felony grand theft under the three-strikes law is not grossly disproportionate and does not violate the Eighth Amendment's prohibition on cruel and unusual punishment.

■ **PROCEDURAL BASIS**

Not provided.

■ **FACTS**

Gary Ewing (D) was on parole from a nine-year prison term. He entered the pro shop at the El Segundo Golf Course in Los Angeles County and stole three golf clubs valued at $399 each. Ewing (D) had previously been convicted of multiple misdemeanor and felony offenses and was in prison nine separate times. Most of his crimes were committed while on parole for previous infractions. Ewing's (D) previous "strikes" were serious felonies that included residential burglaries. For stealing the golf clubs, Ewing (D) was charged with felony grand theft. As part of the formal complaint, the prosecutor alleged the requisite previous convictions under the "Three Strikes Law" and Ewing (D) was sentenced to twenty-five years to life in prison.

■ **ISSUE**

Does the Eighth Amendment prohibit California courts from sentencing repeat felons to a prison term of twenty-five years to life under the state's "Three Strikes and You're Out" law?

■ **DECISION AND RATIONALE**

(O'Connor, J.) California adopted a "three strikes" law targeting repeat offenders. Under the law, if a defendant had a prior "serious" or "violent" felony conviction, on conviction of another felony he must be sentenced to twice the prison term that would be imposed without the conviction. If the defendant had two "serious" or "violent" felony convictions, he must be sentenced to an indeterminate "life" sentence. Under the "life" sentence, a defendant would be eligible for parole after serving a *minimum of* (1) three times the sentence a first-time offender would receive; (2) twenty-five years or (3) a term decided by the trial court.

In addition to the prohibition of cruel and unusual punishment, the Eighth Amendment also requires that noncapital offenses be punished in proportion to the seriousness of the crime. In

Rummel v. Estelle, 445 U.S. 263 (1980), however, the Court determined the Eighth Amendment did not prevent a three-time offender from being sentenced to a life term with the possibility of parole. In *Rummel*, the defendant was sentenced to a lengthy prison term under an antirecidivism statute. Rummel's previous convictions involved fraudulent use of a credit card to obtain $80 worth of services and passing a forged check in the amount of $28.36. His last arrest involved obtaining $120.75 by false pretenses. The court upheld the stiff punishment, holding that "Texas was entitled to place upon Rummel the onus of one who is simply unable to bring his conduct within the social norms . . . of the State." After *Rummel*, in *Solem v. Helm*, 463 U.S. 277 (1983), the Court determined that the Eighth Amendment prohibited imposing a sentence of life without parole for multiple nonviolent felonies. In *Solem*, the underlying offense was passing a bad check. The Court took note of three factors relevant to a determination of proportionality: (1) the gravity of the offense and harshness of the penalty, (2) the sentences imposed on other criminals in that jurisdiction, and (3) the penalties imposed in other jurisdictions for the same violations. The Court found the circumstances in *Solem* sufficiently differed from those in *Rummel*, and declined to uphold the penalty imposed. The question was again raised in *Harmelin v. Michigan*, 501 U.S. 957 (1991). *Harmelin* did not involve a recidivism statute; instead, it involved a life sentence for a defendant convicted of possessing 672 grams of cocaine. The Court declined to find the sentence was disproportionate to the crime, but could not articulate the basis for this finding, with some of the justices stating that proportionality is an argument specifically reserved for death penalty cases. Ultimately, the Court held that the Eighth Amendment did not require strict proportionality; rather, it simply prohibited gross disproportionality. *Harmelin* provides the current guidance on proportionality.

The Court has a long tradition of deferring to the states in matters of sentencing. A sentence may be imposed for one of many reasons, including incapacitation, rehabilitation, and retribution, any combination of which comes into play in a state's sentencing scheme. When California adopted the "three-strike rule," it made a decision that public safety would be advanced by the law. Applying *Harmelin* to Ewing's (D) sentence, the record supports the punishment. The sentence is long but it reflects considered legislative judgment that those who commit serious felonies must be incapacitated. The sentence is not grossly disproportionate to the crime.

■ **CONCURRENCE**

(Scalia, J.) Proportionality is a notion that is tied to the concept of retribution; however, it is difficult to speak of proportionality once the criminal law goals of deterrence and rehabilitation are given the weight they are due. A laudable goal of the criminal justice system is also incapacitation, and it is furthered by the imposition of the "three-strikes law." The Constitution does not mandate that states adopt a specific theory of criminal punishment and it does not require proportionality. Whatever goal a state chooses to emphasize must be respected. Proportionality represents just a part of the punishment scheme. A proper assessment should not stop with whether the crime fits the punishment; it should also decide whether the punishment fits the stated goals of the state's criminal law.

Analysis:

The compounded penalty here is imposed on the commission of a criminal's third violent or serious felony. Whether or not an offense can be characterized as violent is obvious in most cases. Here, Ewing's (D) stealing of golf clubs was not violent; there is no indication he took the clubs at gunpoint or even threatened the staff at the pro shop. Accordingly, his qualification for punishment under the three-strikes law was based on the state's characterization of his crime as "serious." While all crime may be considered serious by its victims, stealing $1200 in golf clubs is not as serious as a crime involving a deadly weapon or threatening physical violence. In the long string of California cases that have come after *Ewing*, the courts have been quick to point out that what makes many of these defendants worthy of punishment as serious offenders is their inability to conform their behavior to social requirements, as demonstrated by their tendency to repeat their offenses.

■ **CASE VOCABULARY**

CRUEL AND UNUSUAL PUNISHMENT: Punishment that is torturous, degrading, inhuman, grossly disproportionate to the crime in question, or otherwise shocking to the moral sense of the community.

DETERRENCE: The act or process of discouraging certain behavior, particularly by fear; especially as a goal of criminal law, the prevention of criminal behavior by fear of punishment.

DETERRENT PUNISHMENT: Punishment intended to deter others from committing crimes by making an example of the offender so that like-minded people are warned of the consequences of crime.

PROPORTIONALITY REVIEW: An appellate court's analysis of whether a death sentence is arbitrary or capricious by comparing the case in which it was imposed with similar cases in which the death penalty was approved or disapproved.

RECIDIVISM: A tendency to relapse into a habit of criminal activity or behavior.

REHABILITATION: The process of seeking to improve a criminal's character and outlook that he or she can function in society without committing other crimes.

RETRIBUTION: Punishment imposed as repayment or revenge for the offense committed; requital.

SERIOUS OFFENSE: An offense not classified as a petty offense and usually carrying at least a six-month sentence.

VIOLENT OFFENSE: A crime characterized by extreme physical force, such as murder, forcible rapes, and assault and battery with a dangerous weapon.

FACTUAL DETERMINATIONS RESULTING IN AN INCREASED SENTENCE MUST BE SUPPORTED BY PROOF BEYOND A REASONABLE DOUBT

■INSTANT FACTS Apprendi (D) fired into the home of a black family that had recently moved into a white neighborhood; finding that Apprendi (D) acted on racial motives, the court sentenced him under a hate crime act providing for stricter punishment.

■BLACK LETTER RULE The due process considerations of the Fifth Amendment, applied to the states through the Fourteenth Amendment, require that any increase in the maximum prison sentence must be based on facts found by a jury beyond a reasonable doubt.

■ PROCEDURAL BASIS

On appeal from a decision by the New Jersey Supreme Court affirming the court's determination that the hate crime act applied to impose enhanced punishment for Apprendi's (D) crime.

■ FACTS

Apprendi (D) fired several shots into the home of an African-American family that recently moved into an all-white neighborhood. Apprendi (D) admitted firing the shots. During questioning, he stated that he did not know the home's occupants; he simply did not want them in the neighborhood because of their color. He later retracted that statement. Apprendi (D) then pleaded guilty to, among other charges, second-degree possession of a firearm for an unlawful purpose. At an evidentiary hearing on Apprendi's (D) purpose for shooting, testimony was offered by a psychologist and seven character witnesses who stated that Apprendi (D) did not have a reputation as a racial bigot. Apprendi (D) also testified that his acts were the result of too much alcohol rather than of bias. He further claimed that his statement to the police was not accurately reported. The judge found that the testimony of the police was credible and that the evidence supported a conclusion that Apprendi's (D) crime was racially motivated. Based on a preponderance of the evidence, the judge concluded that the purpose of the defendant's actions was to intimidate the occupants of the house; hence, the provision of the hate crime law allowing for enhanced punishment was applicable. Apprendi (D) argued that the finding of a racial motive for the crime must be rendered by a jury on evidence beyond a reasonable doubt.

■ ISSUE

Does the Due Process Clause require that a factual determination of racial motivation that authorizes an increase in the maximum prison sentence for the underlying offense be made by a jury and based on proof beyond a reasonable doubt?

■ **DECISION AND RATIONALE**

(Stevens, J.) Yes. A New Jersey law classifies the crime of possession of a firearm for an unlawful purpose as a second-degree offence. That law calls for punishment to include imprisonment for a term of between five and ten years. A separate statute, deemed a "hate crime" law by New Jersey's Supreme Court, provides for a defendant to receive an increased punishment when a trial judge finds a defendant acted to intimidate a person or group of individuals because of their "race, color, gender, handicap, religion, sexual orientation or ethnicity." The increased punishment for a hate crime ranges between ten and twenty years' imprisonment.

In *Jones v. United States*, 526 U.S. 227 (1999), the Court held that increases in maximum penalties must be charged in an indictment, submitted to a jury, and proven beyond a reasonable doubt to satisfy the combination of interests protected by the Fifth Amendment due process and the Sixth Amendment jury trial guarantees. The Fourteenth Amendment will require the same from a state. The essence of a trial by jury has been understood to include proof of each accusation, proven to the satisfaction of twelve individuals beyond a reasonable doubt. Distinguishing between an element of the underlying offense and a factor in sentencing was not historically done. Just as the circumstances of the crime and intent of the defendant are important elements that must be alleged in the indictment to allow the defendant to prepare his defense accordingly, so must the allegations relative to the sentencing be provided. Judges may retain discretion in the area of sentencing, but their discretion is confined to the range of limits provided by the legislature. Simply because the New Jersey legislature placed the hate crime provisions in the sentencing portions of their criminal code does not make the elements of the crime any less a part of the charge. Reversed.

Analysis:

In the cases that have followed *Apprendi*, the courts have been asked to distinguish between those sentencing factors that must be shown to exist based on a preponderance of the evidence and those that are subject to the "beyond a reasonable doubt" standard of proof. For example, in *U.S. v. Nieves*, 322 F.3d 51 (1st Cir. 2003), the trial court took into account a number of factors when imposing sentence on Nieves, a drug dealer, including the quantity of drugs she possessed. Some of the factors were not stated in her indictment. The court declined to find that the omitted factors were among the elements that needed to be stated in the indictment, since the sentence imposed in that case was within the range of acceptable penalties.

■ **CASE VOCABULARY**

DEGREE: An incremental measure of guilt or negligence; a level based on the seriousness of an offense.

DEGREE OF CRIME: A division or classification of a single crime into several grades of guilt, according to the circumstances surrounding the crime's commission, such as aggravating factors present or the type of injury suffered; a division of crimes generally, such as felonies or misdemeanors.

EVIDENTIARY HEARING: A hearing at which evidence is presented, as opposed to a hearing at which only legal argument is presented.

HATE CRIME: A crime motivated by the victim's race, color, ethnicity, religion, or national origin. Certain groups have lobbied to expand the definition by statute to include a crime motivated by the victim's disability, gender, or sexual orientation.

CHAPTER TWO

The Criminal Act

Proctor v. State

Instant Facts: Proctor (D) was accused of violating a law that made it illegal to keep a building intending to use it to offer liquor.

Black Letter Rule: A statute that seeks to impose criminal sanctions simply for an intent when it is coupled with an otherwise lawful act, and that does not require proof of any overt act, is unconstitutional.

Jones v. United States

Instant Facts: Jones (D) took Green's kids into her home, and one later died from malnutrition; Jones (D) was found guilty of involuntary manslaughter, but she argued that the court erred in failing to instruct the jury that she first had to have a legal duty to care for the kids before she could be charged with breaching that duty.

Black Letter Rule: The failure to instruct the jury on a critical element of the crime charged is plain error.

United States v. Maldonado

Instant Facts: Zavala (D) was convicted of possessing cocaine with the intent to distribute it in violation of 21 U.S.C. § 841.

Black Letter Rule: Actual possession need not be established in order to find possession under 21 U.S.C. § 841; constructive possession is sufficient.

State v. Barger

Instant Facts: Barger (D) was convicted of possessing or controlling child pornography based on evidence that incriminating images were in the temporary Internet file cache on his home computer, but he argued that such evidence did not support the conclusion that he "possessed" or "controlled" the pornographic images as required by the Oregon statute under which he was charged.

Black Letter Rule: The requirement of "possession" or "control" of child pornography requires more than simply accessing and looking at such material on one's computer.

Lawrence v. Texas

Instant Facts: Lawrence (D) was convicted of deviate sexual intercourse with another man in violation of a state statute.

Black Letter Rule: State laws criminalizing homosexual relations violate substantive due process.

People v. Newton

Instant Facts: Due to an unscheduled landing, Newton (D), who had boarded a flight with a revolver and ammunition, was charged with violating a New York law prohibiting possession of an unregistered firearm.

Black Letter Rule: An individual may not be charged with violating a law when he has done no voluntary act to commit it.

Martin v. State

Instant Facts: Martin (D) was arrested for a public display of drunkenness after the arresting officers transported Martin (D) to a highway, where he became loud and obnoxious.

Black Letter Rule: A statute prohibiting intoxicated persons from appearing in any public place is not violated when an intoxicated individual is involuntarily taken into public; a violation presumes that the public appearance was voluntary.

People v. Grant

Instant Facts: Grant (D) ran through a crowd and hurled himself at the police, who were arresting another man, injuring one of the officers; following his arrest, Grant (D) was taken to the hospital and treated for several days for a grand mal seizure.

Black Letter Rule: A conviction for battery and obstructing a police officer cannot be sustained when the defendant's allegedly criminal actions were involuntary.

Robinson v. California

Instant Facts: Robinson (D) was convicted of violating a statute that made it illegal to be addicted to narcotics.

Black Letter Rule: It is unconstitutional, as cruel and unusual punishment, to prosecute a defendant for a crime based not on any voluntary act, but on his or her status or illness.

Johnson v. State

Instant Facts: Johnson (D) gave birth and admitted to using illegal drugs prior to going into labor.

Black Letter Rule: Delivering an illegal drug by way of the blood passing through the umbilical cord is not a violation of the statutory prohibition against delivery by an adult of a controlled substance to minor.

Keeler v. Superior Court

Instant Facts: Keeler (D) assaulted his pregnant ex-wife so violently that the fetus died, and he was charged with murder; he appealed, arguing that "murder" can only relate to a live human being, not a fetus.

Black Letter Rule: Under the California Penal Code, "murder" is the unlawful killing of a "human being," which means a person who has been born alive.

United States v. Hudson and Goodwin

Instant Facts: A newspaper was indicted for libel based on an article it printed on the President's true motives for a treaty.

Black Letter Rule: The courts of the United States have no common law jurisdiction in criminal cases absent a grant of authority in the U.S. Constitution or a grant under a specific congressional enactment.

Rogers v. Tennessee

Instant Facts: Rogers (D) stabbed Bowdery, causing injuries that led to cardiac arrest and brain damage and culminated in Bowdery's death fifteen months after Rogers' (D) attack; Rogers (D) was convicted of murder.

Black Letter Rule: The constitutional prohibition of ex post facto laws is directed at legislative bodies, not courts, as the very nature of the common law permits a court to overrule or abandon existing precedent.

Chicago v. Morales

Instant Facts: A Chicago ordinance banned loitering in public places in an effort to discourage gang members from intimidating law-abiding people who seek to make use of public areas.

Black Letter Rule: An ordinance that seeks to impose criminal penalties for conduct that is vaguely defined and for which violations are deemed to have been committed at the discretion of law enforcement officers will not be enforced as in contravention of due process.

UNEXECUTED CRIMINAL INTENT DOES NOT TRANSFORM A LEGAL ACT INTO AN ILLEGAL ONE

■INSTANT FACTS Proctor (D) was accused of violating a law that made it illegal to keep a building intending to use it to offer liquor.

■BLACK LETTER RULE A statute that seeks to impose criminal sanctions simply for an intent when it is coupled with an otherwise lawful act, and that does not require proof of any overt act, is unconstitutional.

■ **PROCEDURAL BASIS**

None provided.

■ **FACTS**

The plaintiff was convicted of owning "a two-story building, with the intent and for the purpose of unlawfully selling . . . liquor." The defendant demurred to the charge on the ground that the information did not charge a public offense. He argued that the provision of the Oklahoma law that he was charged with violating was unconstitutional.

■ **ISSUE**

Is a combination of two non-criminal acts (owning a building with an intention to sell alcohol on the premises) sufficient to constitute a criminal act without proof of a related, overt act on the intention?

■ **DECISION AND RATIONALE**

(Galbraith, Spec. J.) No. Proctor (D) was charged with violating a statute that makes it a crime to keep a place or rent it to other persons when it will be used to manufacture, sell, barter, give, or otherwise furnish wine, spirits, or malt liquor. The statute provides for punishment by a fine of between $50 and $2000 and imprisonment for a term of thirty days to five years. Proctor (D) argues that the statute was improper since it made simply having "an intention" a crime. It also makes the doing of a legal act, "the keeping of a place," a violation of the law when coupled with proof of the intent, and did not require proof of any act to put the intention into effect. As a result, Proctor (D) argues, the statute should be void.

The Attorney General insists that this is not a case of punishing illegal thought. Under the statute, the combination of obtaining a place combined with the intent to later use it to sell illegal liquor constitutes the overt act. The prosecutor argues that this statute was enacted by the state in the exercise of its police power, so that while ownership of property is innocent in and of itself, the legislature has the authority to declare such action, when coupled with the proscribed intent, illegal. The prosecution insists that it need not wait until a defendant actually begins selling liquor to find he has done something illegal. But this argument is incorrect. Some overt act must be proven beyond the simple thought. There is no evidence that Proctor (D) obtained liquor. Therefore, the information charges two innocent acts and attempts to make them a crime; the legislature may not do this. Since keeping a place is not illegal, and having criminal thoughts is not illegal, there has been no crime committed here. The law as written lacks an essential element to declare the existence of a crime. It fails to connect a bad intent with an overt act. Judgment vacated and cause remanded with instructions to discharge the accused.

Analysis:

The problems associated with laws like the one at issue here are potentially endless. A person who legally owns a firearm and has an illicit thought to kill a coworker, family member, or acquaintance could be found guilty of attempted murder. Might the order in which events unfold make a difference in this type of case? Would it have made a difference if Proctor (D) first had the intention to sell illegal liquor and then went out and bought the building? In *Lambert v. State*, 374 P.2d 783 (Okla. Crim. App. 1962), the defendant made the mistake of buying the liquor first. In holding against the defendant, the court in *Lambert* held the possession of the liquor was sufficient to constitute the "act."

■ CASE VOCABULARY

DEMURRER: A pleading stating that although the facts alleged in a complaint may be true, they are insufficient for the plaintiff to state a claim for relief and for the defendant to frame an answer. In most jurisdictions, such a pleading is now termed a *motion to dismiss*, but the demurrer is still used in a few states, including California, Nebraska, and Pennsylvania.

INFORMATION: A formal criminal charge made by a prosecutor without a grand-jury indictment.

INTENT: The state of mind accompanying an act, especially a forbidden act. While motive is the inducement to do some act, intent is the mental resolution or determination to do it. When the intent to do an act that violates the law exists, motive becomes immaterial.

MENS REA: [Latin, "guilty mind."] The state of mind that the prosecution, to secure a conviction, must prove that a defendant had when committing a crime; criminal intent or recklessness. *Mens rea* is the second of two essential elements of every crime at common law, the other being the *actus reus*.

OVERT ACT: An outward act, however innocent in itself, done in furtherance of a conspiracy, treason, or criminal attempt.

POLICE POWER: The inherent and plenary power of a sovereign to make all laws necessary and proper to preserve the public security, order, health, morality and justice. It is a fundamental power essential to government, and it cannot be surrendered by the legislature or irrevocably transferred away from government.

(Criminal Defendant) v. (Prosecuting Authority)

308 F.2d 307 (D.C. Cir. 1962)

THERE'S NO CRIMINAL LIABILITY FOR BREACHING A DUTY UNLESS IT'S FIRST ESTABLISHED THAT A DUTY ACTUALLY EXISTS

She was sitting on the egg.

It's not my egg.

Without "duty", there's no "guilty".

stus.com

■**INSTANT FACTS** Jones (D) took Green's kids into her home, and one later died from malnutrition; Jones (D) was found guilty of involuntary manslaughter, but she argued that the court erred in failing to instruct the jury that she first had to have a legal duty to care for the kids before she could be charged with breaching that duty.

■**BLACK LETTER RULE** The failure to instruct the jury on a critical element of the crime charged is plain error.

■ **PROCEDURAL BASIS**

Federal appellate court review of a district court judgment against the defendant.

■ **FACTS**

After Green gave birth to an out-of-wedlock child in 1958, Jones (D) took the child into her home to spare the Green family from embarrassment. Jones (D) made a few futile efforts toward adopting the child. Green provided her with limited expense money. Green became pregnant again in 1960, and that child was released from the hospital into Jones's (D) custody. When Green herself was released from the hospital, she, too, spent three weeks in Jones's (D) home, after which she moved back in with her parents, leaving the two children with Jones (D). Jones appeared to have ample means to provide support for the children. At one point, she called a doctor to the home to examine Anthony, the younger child. The doctor told Jones (D) she should inform the child's mother that he needed to be seen at the hospital, but this never happened. On another day, two gas company employees had occasion to go into the basement of Jones's (D) home, and they saw the older boy in a crib lined with stained and feces-covered newspapers, as well as the younger boy, who they said looked like a small baby monkey. Roaches were crawling over both boys. The gas company employees later returned with the police. The boys were taken to the hospital, where young Anthony died just hours later from malnutrition. Jones (D) was charged with involuntary manslaughter for her failure to perform her legal duty to care for Anthony, which resulted in his death. Jones (D) was found guilty and appealed.

■ **ISSUE**

Did the trial court commit plain error in failing to instruct the jury that it must first find that Jones (D) was under a legal obligation to provide food and necessities to Anthony, before finding her guilty of manslaughter for failing to provide them?

■ DECISION AND RATIONALE

(Wright, J.) Yes. The failure to instruct the jury on a critical element of the crime charged is plain error. A breach of the duty of care may arise from a failure to act only in certain defined circumstances: when a statute imposes a legal duty to care for another, when one stands in a certain relationship status to another, when one has assumed a contractual duty to care for another, or when one has voluntarily assumed the care of another and so secluded the helpless person as to prevent others from rendering aid. The government contends that either the third or fourth situation is present here, but the evidence is conflicting. Jones (D) says that Green was living with her and should have been taking care of the child herself, but Green says she was living with her parents and paying Jones (D) to care for the kids. In spite of this conflict, the jury instructions failed to even suggest the necessity for finding a legal duty of care. Although we disagree with the appellant's argument that there was insufficient evidence to warrant a finding of breach of duty (if one existed), we agree that the court failed to properly instruct the jury. A finding of legal duty is a critical element of the crime charged, and the failure to instruct the jury was plain error. Reversed and remanded.

Analysis:

Neglect on the part of one charged with the duty of providing another with necessary food, clothing, and shelter, resulting in the charge'sdeath, renders the person upon whom the duty rests guilty of culpable homicide. The crime charged may be murder when the neglect is willful or malicious, such as when a person intentionally withholds the food necessary to sustain an infant's life. The crime charged may be manslaughter when, by contrast, the omission is not malicious but arises out of negligence,such as when the caregiver, having the means at his or her command, negligently fails to provide a child with food, clothing, or shelter and the child dies as a result. But the element of duty is present in all cases; where there is no duty, there is no crime.

■ CASE VOCABULARY

PLAIN ERROR: An error that is so obvious and prejudicial that an appellate court should address it even despite the parties' failure to raise a proper objection at trial. A plain error is often said to be so obvious and substantial that failure to correct it would infringe a party's due-process rights and damage the integrity of the judicial process.

REVERSIBLE ERROR: An error that affects a party's substantive rights or the case's outcome, and thus is grounds for reversal if the party properly objected at trial.

CONSTRUCTIVE POSSESSION REQUIRES ACCESS AND AN INTENT TO EXERCISE CONTROL

■**INSTANT FACTS** Zavala (D) was convicted of possessing cocaine with the intent to distribute it in violation of 21 U.S.C. § 841.

■**BLACK LETTER RULE** Actual possession need not be established in order to find possession under 21 U.S.C. § 841; constructive possession is sufficient.

■ **PROCEDURAL BASIS**

On appeal from Zavala's (D) conviction for possession of cocaine with intent to distribute.

■ **FACTS**

In January 1992, the M/V Euro Colombia was docked in Cartagena, Columbia, when Santos, a seaman on the ship, accepted sixteen packages of cocaine weighing eight kilograms each from a drug dealer. He was instructed to deliver the cocaine to another party when the ship docked in Puerto Rico. He took the cocaine with the knowledge of American drug enforcement agents, who intended to work with Santos to track the drugs. On arrival in Puerto Rico, Santos did as he had been instructed. He went to the Hotel Melia and asked to see Palestino, the man the Cartagena dealer told him to see. A man named Zavala (D) arrived in the hotel lobby and took Santos to a room to wait for Palestino. When Santos refused to turn over the cocaine to anyone other than Palestino, Zavala (D) supposedly called Palestino and summoned him to the hotel. Santos and Zavala (D), growing impatient for Palestino's arrival, left the cocaine in Zavala's (D) room and went to have a soda. As the men left the room, the supervising customs agent detained them. When the customs agent was told Palestino had not shown up, the men returned to the room with other agents. More calls were received, allegedly from Palestino. Each time a call was received, Santos told the caller that Zavala (D) was unable to come to the phone. After the last call, the agents arrested Zavala and two men in the room believed to be Palestino and his driver. Only Zavala (D) was charged and convicted of violating 21 U.S.C. § 841 for possessing cocaine with the intent to distribute. Zavala (D) argued his conviction was improper since there was insufficient evidence offered at trial to prove he was in possession of the cocaine.

■ **ISSUE**

Under the facts presented here, did Zavala (D) possess the cocaine brought by Santos to the hotel room?

■ DECISION AND RATIONALE

(Boudin, J.) Yes. Under the ordinary meaning of the word "possess," Zavala (D) probably did not have possession of the cocaine Santos delivered to the hotel. Under the drug statutes, however, possession has been found to include not only physical possession, but also constructive possession, and joint, as well as exclusive, possession. Under these definitions, a court can find an individual in possession of an article even though it is at home hidden in a closet, secured in a safe deposit box, or held by an agent. The problem with constructive possession is in carrying it too far. When Santos and Zavala (D) were first in the room together, it is unlikely Zavala would have been considered to be in possession of the cocaine. Santos was steadfastly refusing to turn the drugs over to anyone other than Palestino. However, once the two men decided to leave the room, the situation changed. Santos surrendered his possession of the drugs, and they were left secured in Zavala's (D) room. At that point, Zavala (D) had both the power to control the cocaine and the intent to exercise the power. The power could be inferred by the fact the drugs were in his room, awaiting arrival of his accomplice to pay for them. Despite the fact the room was registered to Palestino, Zavala (D) had been occupying the room and intended to return to it. When an item is located in a place accessible to the defendant and the defendant knows of the existence of the item, possession can be found. Certainly Zavala's (D) possession was diluted by the fact that Santos may have resisted the transfer pending payment; but the drugs could still be inferred to be in their joint possession. And intent could also be determined from the facts presented here. Zavala (D) knew the drugs were there, and he was not likely to let them be taken from the room. He repeatedly told Santos that Palestino would be there soon, and he suggested storing the drugs. His presence at the hotel was clearly to facilitate the transfer of the drugs. While his purpose may be limited to the effective transfer of the drugs and not their eventual control, that argument makes too fine a distinction that Congress did not intend. Affirmed.

Analysis:

While actual, physical possession seems to be at issue here, the more important issue is often whether the defendant had the intention to exercise dominion over the drugs. Physical possession can sometimes result from trickery, mistake, or ignorance, but constructive possession can result from something less than actual ownership. In *U.S. v. Liranzo*, 385 F.3d 66 (1st Cir. 2004), the court explained that possession is not to be confused with "ownership."

■ CASE VOCABULARY

CONSTRUCTIVE POSSESSION: Control or dominion over a property without actual possession or custody of it.

EXCLUSIVE POSSESSION: The exercise of exclusive dominion over property, including the use and benefit of the property.

POSSESSION: The fact of having or holding property in one's power; the exercise of dominion over property; the right under which one may exercise control over something to the exclusion of all others; the continuing exercise of a claim to the exclusive use of a material object.

(Prosecuting Authority) v. (Criminal Defendant)

247 P.3d 309 (Ore. 2011)

ADVANCES IN TECHNOLOGY BRING NEW TWISTS TO QUESTIONS OF "POSSESSION"

I'm happy to spill all my secrets-- even secrets I kept from my owner!

stus.com

■INSTANT FACTS Barger (D) was convicted of possessing or controlling child pornography based on evidence that incriminating images were in the temporary Internet file cache on his home computer, but he△ argued that such evidence did not support the conclusion that he "possessed" or "controlled" the pornographic images as required by the Oregon statute under which he was charged.

Stat. had 2 be rewritten

■BLACK LETTER RULE The requirement of "possession" or "control" of child pornography requires more than simply accessing and looking at such material on one's computer.

■ PROCEDURAL BASIS

State supreme court review of an intermediate appellate court decision affirming the circuit court's finding of guilt.

■ FACTS

When the police went to Barger's (D) home to investigate a report that Barger (D) had possibly sexually abused a child, his wife told an officer that there was "weird" material on the couple's home computer. She showed the officer the search history, which revealed some suspicious web addresses. A few weeks later, the police asked Barger's (D) wife if she would allow them to examine the computer, and she consented. An examination of the hard drive led to charging Barger (D) with eight counts of encouraging child sexual abuse by "possessing or controlling" a visual recording of sexually explicit conduct involving a child. The charges were based on digital images found in the computer's temporary Internet file cache. No child-pornography images were saved in Barger's (D) personal files. The investigator testified at trial that there was no way to tell whether the images had been accessed intentionally or were the result of pop-ups or redirects. After the state rested its case, Barger (D) moved for a judgment of acquittal, arguing that there was no evidence that the images resulted from an intentional or knowing act on his part, nor was there evidence that he knowingly "possessed or controlled" those images. The judge denied the motion and the jury returned guilty verdicts on all eight charges. Barger (D) appealed.

■ ISSUE

Can a person be found guilty of "possessing" or "controlling" digital images of sexually explicit conduct involving a child, as that phrase is used in Ore. Rev. Stat. § 163.686(1)(a), based on evidence showing only that the person searched for and found such images through the Internet on his or her computer?

■ **DECISION AND RATIONALE**

(Dyke, J.) No. The requirement of "possession" or "control" of child pornography requires more than simply accessing and looking at such material on one's computer. There is no evidence in the record suggesting that Barger (D) even knew about automatic caching or how to access material in the cache. Contrary to the state's argument, the mere *unexercised* ability to manipulate a thing cannot constitute constructive possession of it. If the mere ability to cause an item to appear on a computer screen is sufficient to constitute control or constructive possession of the item, then any person who uses the Internet, or who is in reach of some tangible item of child pornography, can be deemed guilty of violating the statute, at least so far as the element of possession and control is concerned. The state contends that a person who uses a computer to look at images of child pornography does more than just view the images that he brings to the screen; because computers have the capacity to save, print, post, and transmit those images with just a click or two of the mouse, web browsing is qualitatively different, the state insists, from the mere viewing of print copies, and falls within the intended meaning of "possesses or controls." We are not persuaded by the state's arguments and just do not see how or why, in the absence of some additional action by a computer user beyond that shown here, a user could be deemed to possess or control, in any recognizable sense, a digital image that he or she has called up on the screen. We are satisfied that the statute at issue embodies a legislative choice not to criminalize the mere obtaining or viewing of child pornography. In other words, the acts at issue here—navigating to a website and bringing the images that the site contains to a computer screen—are not acts that the legislature intended to criminalize. The defendant's motion for a judgment of acquittal should have been granted. Reversed.

Analysis:

The *Barger* decision was later distinguished in *State v. Urbina, 278 P.3d 33* (Ore. Ct. App. 2012). Whereas *Barger* involved the meaning of "possess" and "control," *Urbina* involved the meaning of the term "duplicate." The conduct at issue in *Barger* was limited to displaying digital images on a computer screen; to the extent that there were any copies made, it was an automatic "caching" function of the computer's web browser. In *Urbina*, by contrast, there was evidence that the defendant installed and used a file-sharing program that allowed him to save copies of the pornographic videos to his own computer, which he could then access whenever he wished. Urbina, unlike Barger (D), was found guilty of encouraging child sexual abuse.

■ **CASE VOCABULARY**

CONSTRUCTIVE POSSESSION: Control or dominion over a property without actual possession or custody of it.

POSSESSION: The fact of having or holding property in one's power; the exercise of dominion over property.

Lawrence v. Texas

(Homosexual Man) v. (Prosecuting Authority)

539 U.S. 558 (2003)

THE REGULATION OF SEXUAL EXPRESSION VIOLATES THE FUNDAMENTAL RIGHT OF PRIVACY

■**INSTANT FACTS** Lawrence (D) was convicted of deviate sexual intercourse with another man in violation of a state statute.

■**BLACK LETTER RULE** State laws criminalizing homosexual relations violate substantive due process.

■ **PROCEDURAL BASIS**

Certiorari to review a state court of appeals decision affirming the defendant's conviction.

■ **FACTS**

On a report of a weapons disturbance, Houston police officers entered Lawrence's (D) residence, where they discovered him having sexual relations with another man. The two men were arrested, charged, and convicted of violating a Texas statute prohibiting "deviate sexual intercourse with another individual of the same sex." The state court of appeals, following *Bowers v. Hardwick*, 478 U.S. 186 (1986), rejected Lawrence's (D) constitutional challenges and affirmed his conviction.

■ **ISSUE**

Does a statute prohibiting private sexual intercourse between consenting homosexual adults violate the Due Process Clause?

■ **DECISION AND RATIONALE**

(Kennedy, J.) Yes. State laws criminalizing homosexual relations violate substantive due process. The right of privacy includes the right to make decisions regarding the marital relationship. That right has been expanded beyond marital relations to include the right of unmarried individuals to decide whether to conceive a child. At its core, the right of privacy involves the right to be free from unwarranted government intrusion into fundamental personal decisions and liberty interests. Statutes prohibiting a certain type of sexual expression deprive individuals of more than a chosen sexual behavior. They infringe upon fundamental personal relationships in private homes between consenting adults. The Constitution protects individual choices to express personal relationships through intimate conduct.

Laws against homosexual behavior do not have "ancient roots" that make homosexual contact any less of a fundamental right than intimate conduct in general. Historical sodomy laws were not enforced against homosexuals in particular, but against society as a whole. Further, sodomy laws have not historically been enforced against consenting adults acting in private. Not until relatively recently in our country's history have states sought to specifically prohibit homosexual activity, and the more recent trend is toward abolishing such laws. Although, in *Bowers v. Hardwick*, the Court held that state laws prohibiting homosexual relations withstand constitutional scrutiny, the Court should have acknowledged this growing recognition of homosexual rights. In 1955, the Model Penal Code stated that "criminal penalties for consensual sexual relations conducted in private" were not recommended. Many states followed this guidance in their statutory schemes. Similarly, other nations had abandoned sodomy laws, indicating the growing tolerance of homosexual liberty interests throughout Western civilization. *Bowers* is overruled, and we hold that state laws criminalizing homosexual contact between consenting adults in private violate the Due Process Clause. Reversed and remanded.

Analysis:

The Court's decision has largely been criticized as results-oriented, without any logical resort to legal doctrine. In such an ideologically divisive topic as homosexual rights, it is easy to understand the Court's temptation to reach the desired outcome, using broad legal principles to justify its decision. Although the Justices are bound by oath to uphold the Constitution, personal beliefs undoubtedly form a solid basis for many Court decisions.

■ **CASE VOCABULARY**

SODOMY: Oral or anal copulation between humans, especially those of the same sex.

STARE DECISIS: The doctrine of precedent, under which it is necessary for a court to follow earlier judicial decisions when the same points arise again in litigation.

SUBSTANTIVE DUE PROCESS: The doctrine that the Due Process Clauses of the Fifth and Fourteenth Amendments require legislation to be fair and reasonable in content and to further a legitimate governmental objective.

People v. Newton

(Prosecuting Government) v. (Unruly Airplane Passenger)

72 Misc. 2d 646, 340 N.Y.S.2d 77 (1973)

ABSENT SOME VOLUNTARY ACT, THE DEFENDANT COMMITS NO CRIME

■INSTANT FACTS Due to an unscheduled landing, Newton (D), who had boarded a flight with a revolver and ammunition, was charged with violating a New York law prohibiting possession of an unregistered firearm.

■BLACK LETTER RULE An individual may not be charged with violating a law when he has done no voluntary act to commit it.

■ PROCEDURAL BASIS

Habeas corpus proceeding before the court.

■ FACTS

Newton (D), who was severely handicapped and able to walk only with the aid of prosthetics, boarded a flight from the Bahamas to Luxembourg, concealing a .38 revolver and ammunition. En route to Luxembourg, Newton (D) became unruly. The captain suspected Newton (D) had a concealed weapon and made an unscheduled landing at JFK International. The plane was met by Port Authority police. One of the officers boarded the plane and asked Newton (D) if he had a weapon. Newton (D) acknowledged that he did and allowed the officer to take it. He was then arrested for violation of the New York Penal Law making it a crime to possess a weapon without a license.

■ ISSUE

Could Newton (D) be found guilty of violating New York's law prohibiting the possession of an unregistered firearm when the plane he was on made an unscheduled landing in New York?

■ DECISION AND RATIONALE

(Weinstein, J.) No. Newton (D) did not voluntarily break the law he was accused of violating. Newton's (D) flight was not scheduled to take him inside the United States, so there was no way he could have anticipated needing to conform his conduct to the laws of the U.S. He could not foresee that he would need to register his gun with the New York authorities. The writ of habeas corpus must be sustained and Newton (D) should be released.

Analysis:

Newton (D) should have anticipated causing a stir. Even in 1973, boarding an international flight with a handgun and ammunition was not condoned. However, while Newton (D) took a chance that bringing a loaded weapon on his flight might be met with disdain by the

---

HIGH COURT CASE SUMMARIES

Luxembourg or Bahama police, he did not have the opportunity to conform his conduct to the New York law requiring a permit for his gun because it was not foreseeable it would be necessary.

■ **CASE VOCABULARY**

HABEAS CORPUS: A writ employed to bring a person before a court, most frequently to ensure that the party's imprisonment or detention is not illegal. In addition to being used to test the legality of an arrest or commitment, the writ may be used to obtain review of (1) the regularity of the extradition process, (2) the right to or amount of bail, or (3) the jurisdiction of a court that has imposed a criminal sentence.

Martin v. State

(Intoxicated Person) v. (State of Alabama)

17 So. 2d 427 (Ala. App. 1944)

VIOLATION OF A PUBLIC DRUNKENNESS ORDINANCE REQUIRES A VOLUNTARY APPEARANCE IN PUBLIC

■INSTANT FACTS   Martin (D) was arrested for a public display of drunkenness after the arresting officers transported Martin (D) to a highway, where he became loud and obnoxious.

■BLACK LETTER RULE   A statute prohibiting intoxicated persons from appearing in any public place is not violated when an intoxicated individual is involuntarily taken into public; a violation presumes that the public appearance was voluntary.

■ PROCEDURAL BASIS

On appeal following the defendant's conviction.

■ FACTS

Martin (D) was arrested at his home. While transporting him to jail, police officers brought Martin (D) onto the highway, where he exhibited his drunken condition, using loud and profane language. He was subsequently convicted of being drunk on a public highway.

■ ISSUE

Did the defendant violate the statute prohibiting an intoxicated person from appearing in any public place if the defendant's appearance in public was involuntary?

■ DECISION AND RATIONALE

(Simpson, J.) No. Martin (D) was charged with violating a law that prohibited an individual from being in public and engaging in "boisterous or indecent conduct" due to intoxication. The statute presumes that the appearance in public was voluntary. Proof of public drunkenness is be established when the evidence shows that the defendant was forcibly carried to the public place by the arresting officer. Reversed.

Analysis:

The involuntary aspect of Martin's (D) conduct was important here, not just because he was dragged from his home, where he was free to be as drunk as he wished, but also because the parties placing him in the position to be arrested were police officers. Compare the result in this case with *U.S. v. Coleman*, 475 F. Supp. 422 (E.D. Pa. 1979), in which the defendant had been drinking and was brought inside a post office, where he was detained while police were summoned. While inside, Coleman assaulted one of the workers and was charged with assault under a statute prohibiting assault "within the special maritime and territorial jurisdiction of the United States." Coleman argued that, like Martin (D) here, he was dragged into the post office against his will, but unlike the defendant here, who committed no voluntary act, in *Coleman* the assault itself fulfilled the voluntary act requirement and the conviction stood.

■ **CASE VOCABULARY**

INVOLUNTARY: Not resulting from a free and unrestrained choice; not subject to control by the will.

VOLUNTARY: Done by design or intention; unconstrained by interference; not impelled by outside influence.

(State of Illinois) v. *(Epileptic)*

46 Ill. App. 3d 125, 360 N.E.2d 809 (1977)

A CRIMINAL CONVICTION REQUIRES A VOLUNTARY ACT

■**INSTANT FACTS** Grant (D) ran through a crowd and hurled himself at the police, who were arresting another man, injuring one of the officers; following his arrest, Grant (D) was taken to the hospital and treated for several days for a grand mal seizure.

■**BLACK LETTER RULE** A conviction for battery and obstructing a police officer cannot be sustained when the defendant's allegedly criminal actions were involuntary.

■ **PROCEDURAL BASIS**

On appeal from the defendant's conviction for aggravated battery and obstructing a police officer.

■ **FACTS**

Grant (D) was at the *Watering Place*, a Lincoln bar, where he had four whiskey and colas in two and a half hours. Grant (D) witnessed a fight begin between the bar's owner and another patron. The police were summoned and they arrested the fighting patron, who resisted arrest. As the police left, a mob of forty people followed them, cheering the arrested patron. Without warning, and though he had not been involved in the earlier commotion, Grant (D) rushed through the crowd, vaulted off a parking meter, and struck one of the officers twice in the face. The other officer arrested Grant (D) and he was forcibly placed in the police car and taken to jail, where he was placed in a cell. About an hour later, Grant (D) was observed having a seizure and was taken to a local hospital for treatment. He remained in the hospital the next ten days. Grant (D) was diagnosed as having psychomotor epilepsy, which accounted for several past assaults, including one assaulted of a hospital employee in which Grant (D) was only subdued when a police officer shot him in the pelvis. Grant (D) insisted he remembered nothing of the incident outside the bar, but he acknowledged having epilepsy and taking medication to control it. At trial, the testimony of Dr. Ludin confirmed Grant's (D) epilepsy and that Grant (D) was having a seizure at the time he attacked the police officer. Nonetheless, Grant (D) was sentenced to three to nine years in prison after being found guilty of aggravated battery and obstructing a police officer.

■ **ISSUE**

May a conviction for battery and obstructing a police officer be sustained when the jury was not allowed to consider that the offense may have been involuntary, based on evidence that the defendant's actions may have been caused by an epileptic seizure?

■ DECISION AND RATIONALE

(Reardon, J.) No. A conviction for battery and obstructing a police officer cannot be sustained when the defendant's allegedly criminal actions were involuntary. At trial, the judge instructed the jury as to Grant's (D) sanity, but the instruction did not distinguish between the behavior of a person who lacks the ability to appreciate the criminal nature of his actions and one who may have the capacity but who lacks the ability to control his behavior. Automatism is not insanity; it manifests itself through the performance of involuntary acts. It is a component of many conditions, including epilepsy and organic brain disease. As the law provides that every offense must contain a voluntary act or omission, this instruction should have been read to the jury. If defects in a jury's instructions are substantial, the error is not waived by the failure to make timely objections. Accordingly, as the defendant's conviction rested on substantially defective instructions, the conviction must be set aside.

This case is distinguishable from *People v. Espenscheid*, 109 Ill. App. 2d 107, 249 N.E.2d 866 (1969), in which the instruction was denied based on a lack of evidence to prove the defendant's actions were not voluntary. Here, evidence established that Grant (D) was subject to moments in which he was unable to control his actions. The issue here was, then, whether the evidence of the grand mal seizure post-arrest was sufficient to establish the impact of the neurological condition on Grant's (D) behavior at the time just before that. If it can be shown at retrial that he was suffering from an involuntary episode at the time he assaulted the police officer, he cannot be convicted. Of course, on retrial, the jury may still find that although Grant (D) was acting involuntarily, he still had notice of his susceptibility to engage in involuntary, violent acts after drinking that would make him responsible for his actions, if he voluntarily started drinking. Reversed and remanded.

Analysis:

In the court's concluding comments, it tempered Grant's (D) "get out of jail free" pass by reminding him of his obligation to avoid situations that cause him to lose control. Grant (D) might not know what he is doing if he has a seizure, but he ought to know that once he starts drinking he could have a seizure, lose control, and hurt someone. In such cases, he could be responsible for risking another's safety by voluntarily consuming alcohol.

■ CASE VOCABULARY

AGGRAVATED BATTERY: A criminal battery accomplished by circumstances that make it more severe, such as the use of a deadly weapon or the fact that the battery resulted in serious bodily harm.

AUTOMATISM: Action or conduct occurring without will, purpose, or reasoned intention, such as sleepwalking; behavior carried out in a state of unconsciousness or mental dissociation without full awareness. Automatism may be asserted as a defense to negate the requisite mental state of voluntariness for commission of a crime.

Robinson v. California

(Drug Addict) v. (State)

370 U.S. 660, 82 S.Ct. 1417 (1962)

THE EIGHTH AMENDMENT PROHIBITS CRIMES BASED ON ILLNESS OR STATUS

■INSTANT FACTS Robinson (D) was convicted of violating a statute that made it illegal to be addicted to narcotics.

■BLACK LETTER RULE It is unconstitutional, as cruel and unusual punishment, to prosecute a defendant for a crime based not on any voluntary act, but on his or her status or illness.

■ PROCEDURAL BASIS

Not provided.

■ FACTS

Robinson (D) was convicted in a trial by jury on evidence that he used narcotics. The statute under which the conviction was obtained made it illegal to be addicted to narcotics. An offender could be prosecuted at any time before he or she was successfully treated.

■ ISSUE

Does the Constitution prohibit the enforcement of criminal laws that are based not on voluntary acts, but on illness?

■ DECISION AND RATIONALE

(Stewart, J.) Yes. The California law in question makes it an offense to be addicted to narcotics. A person may be guilty of the offense even though the person has never used or possessed narcotics in the state of California. The state would not consider making it illegal to have leprosy or some other affliction, since punishing individuals for those offenses would be contrary to the Eighth Amendment's prohibition of cruel and unusual punishment, but it has no problem here with punishing drug addiction. Addiction to narcotics is also a disease, whether it has been contracted voluntarily or involuntarily. Therefore, a law that seeks to incarcerate an individual afflicted with the illness, even when the punishment is slight, is too harsh. Reversed.

■ CONCURRENCE

(Harlan, J.) Based on current medical knowledge of how drugs affect human beings, a law of this type is not necessarily wrong, especially if it is connected with use or possession within the state. Here, the court's instruction that neither use nor possession within California was necessary to support a conviction was wrong. As applied, the statute punishes someone for having simply the desire to commit a criminal act—use illegal narcotics.

■ **DISSENT**

(White, J.) Robinson's (D) conviction was not a punishment for having an illness; instead, he is being punished for his habitual and repeated use of narcotics before his arrest. The majority bases its decision on the fact that the jury was not instructed it could avoid convicting Robinson (D) if it decided the use of narcotics was beyond his control. Holding that Robinson (D) should not be found guilty of a crime for his addiction is simply one step removed from refusing to find he should be punished for the conduct that transformed him into an addicted user.

Analysis:

In People v. Grant, 46 Ill. App. 3d 125, 360 N.E.2d 809 (1977), the court warned the defendant that if he continually put himself in a position where he created his own episodes, he could be held responsible for the consequences even if he had a medical excuse for his conduct. In this case, the court is telling Robinson (D) that because his use of drugs has passed from bad behavior into an illness, he is not responsible. While Justice White seems to find this case a departure from *Grant*, the cases actually are consistent. In *Grant*, the defendant would not be jailed simply for his epilepsy, but he was responsible for exposing himself to alcohol, since that would ignite his condition. Here, the prosecution is not telling Robinson (D) he will be permitted to steal money to buy drugs, simply that his desire to use drugs will not expose him to criminal sanctions.

■ **CASE VOCABULARY**

STATUS CRIME: A crime of which a person is guilty by being in a certain condition or of a specific character, such as vagrancy.

INGESTION OF DRUGS DURING PREGNANCY IS NOT DELIVERY OF CONTROLLED SUBSTANCES TO A MINOR CHILD

■**INSTANT FACTS** Johnson (D) gave birth and admitted to using illegal drugs prior to going into labor.

■**BLACK LETTER RULE** Delivering an illegal drug by way of the blood passing through the umbilical cord is not a violation of the statutory prohibition against delivery by an adult of a controlled substance to minor.

■ **PROCEDURAL BASIS**

Appeal by Johnson (D) from two convictions for delivering a controlled substance to her minor children.

■ **FACTS**

Johnson (D) delivered a baby boy with no complications, although she admitted to using cocaine the night before giving birth. Approximately ninety seconds elapsed between the time the baby was delivered and the cutting of the umbilical cord. Absent evidence to the contrary, it can be presumed that blood flow circulated between mother and child during those ninety seconds. A blood test performed on the infant showed traces of cocaine in his blood. While pregnant with her daughter, Johnson (D) suffered a crack overdose. She told paramedics she had ingested $200 worth of crack earlier in the evening and was concerned about its effect on her unborn child, so she was taken to the hospital for observation. The following month, Johnson went into labor and told her doctor she had used crack that morning. There were no complications from that birth. Again, between sixty and ninety seconds elapsed between the time the baby was delivered and when the cord was cut. The next day, the Department of Health followed up on the report of drug abuse and learned that Johnson (D) had smoked pot and crack multiple times each day nearly every other day during her two pregnancies. There was no medical testimony offered at trial to support a finding that the controlled substances were, in fact, "delivered" to the infants.

■ **ISSUE**

Does Florida law permit the criminal prosecution of a woman who ingested a controlled substance while pregnant under a law prohibiting the delivery of an illegal drug to a minor child?

■ **DECISION AND RATIONALE**

(Harding, J.) No. [The court adopted the text of the lower court's dissent.] Based on the state's theory of this case, Johnson (D) delivered cocaine to her two children through the blood flow in the umbilical cord after the children were delivered and prior to the cord being cut. No medical testimony was offered at trial to establish transfer actually occurred during birth, nor to establish that Johnson (D) timed her ingestion of cocaine to effect a transfer to her child. If labor had not occurred after taking the drug, there would have been no crime. Once labor began, the only way Johnson (D) could avoid committing a crime would have been to sever the umbilical cord before the delivery, which would have meant the likely death of the child and her. The object of the statute was to prevent abuse, neglect, and harm. Under the 1987 Act, harm was defined to include contributing to the dependency of a newborn on controlled drugs. Since some in the legislature feared the bill would allow prosecution of mothers for giving birth to drug-dependent children, the bill was amended to provide that no parent could be subject to criminal investigation *solely* by giving birth to a drug-dependent child. The statute was intended to provide an opening for intervention, not prosecution, to help keep these families together. To now permit the statute to be used to prosecute mothers who ingested drugs close to the delivery of their children would undermine those goals. Section 893.13(1)(c)1 did not envision "delivery" of a drug to include transmission via umbilical cord immediately following birth. There is no denying the fact that drug use during pregnancy can have grave consequences; however, prosecution of the mother for "delivering" drugs to her newly born child is not an effective response to the problem. The decision below is quashed. Reversed and remanded.

Analysis:

This case seems to go a step beyond *People v. Grant*, 46 Ill. App. 3d 125, 360 N.E.2d 809 (1977), and *Robinson v. California*, 370 U.S. 660 (1962). In *Grant*, the court drew the line between punishing conduct that could not be avoided because of a physical condition and holding a person responsible for unavoidable consequences from a chain reaction that he had set in motion. In *Robinson*, the court refused to punish the desire to use drugs as distinct from actual illegal drug use. Here, the court's opinion does not establish whether Johnson (D) claimed to be addicted, and it is likely it would not have made any difference. Whether or not the *Grant* or *Robinson* courts would have punished Johnson (D), this court felt compelled to withhold punishment based on its reading of the legislative intent behind the law.

■ **CASE VOCABULARY**

QUASH: To annul or make void; to terminate.

Keeler v. Superior Court
(Criminal Defendant) v. (Criminal Tribunal)

2 Cal. 3d 619, 87 Cal. Rptr. 481 (1971)

VIABIILITY DID NOT DETERMINE "HUMAN BEING" STATUS IN THE CALIFORNIA OF THE 1970S

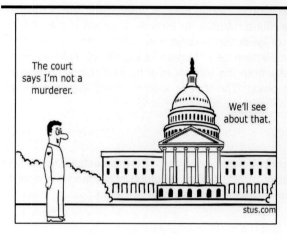

■**INSTANT FACTS** Keeler (D) assaulted his pregnant ex-wife so violently that the fetus died, and he was charged with murder; he appealed, arguing that "murder" can only relate to a live human being, not a fetus.

■**BLACK LETTER RULE** Under the California Penal Code, "murder" is the unlawful killing of a "human being," which means a person who has been born alive.

■ **PROCEDURAL BASIS**

State supreme court review of the defendant's murder conviction.

■ **FACTS**

Keeler (D) and his wife were recently divorced when he learned she was pregnant with another man's child. Coming upon her in her car, Keeler (D) announced to his ex-wife that he was going to stomp the baby out of her, and he proceeded to kick and punch her in the abdomen. The fetus died, and Keeler (D) was charged with murder. The doctor who removed the fetus testified that it was mature enough to be viable, and that had it been born it would have had as much as a 96% chance of survival. Keeler (D) appealed from his conviction.

■ **ISSUE**

Was Keeler (D) guilty of murder for killing the unborn fetus?

■ **DECISION AND RATIONALE**

(Mosk, J.) No. Under the California Penal Code, "murder" is the unlawful killing of a "human being," which means a person who has been born alive. The state argues that advances in obstetrics and pediatrics have increased the likelihood of the survival of fetuses born even as premature as at twenty-eight weeks' gestation. The moment of live birth, the state says, should not be the determinant of when a "human being" exists. Under the state's theory, because a viable fetus is fully capable of independent life, one should be subject to a murder prosecution for killing such a fetus. But we cannot side with the state in this case, for both jurisdictional and constitutional reasons. Jurisdictionally, it is up to the legislature to expand the scope of the statute by extending liability for murder to those who kill an unborn but viable fetus. Constitutionally, even if we did have the power to expand the statute, we could only do so prospectively, which would be of no avail to Keeler (D). The essence of due process is fair warning of the act that is made punishable as a crime. The judicial enlargement of the Penal

Code urged upon us by the state, if adopted in this case, would impermissibly deny the defendant of due process of law.

Analysis:

The Legislature reacted swiftly to this decision. Shortly after it was filed, the California legislature considered an amendment to the murder statute to include a provision that a fetus advanced to or beyond the twentieth week of gestation is a human being. Although an early version of the bill included a fetus in the definition of a human being, in its final form the statute treats the murder of a fetus separately from the murder of a human being, no attempt being made to classify a fetus as a human being. The statute also provides that it does not apply to acts that comply with statutes regulating lawful abortion.

■ **CASE VOCABULARY**

DUE PROCESS: The conduct of legal proceedings according to established rules and principles for the protection and enforcement of private rights, including notice and the right to a fair hearing before a tribunal with the power to decide the case.

THE CIRCUIT COURT OF THE UNITED STATES DOES NOT HAVE COMMON LAW JURISDICTION IN CRIMINAL CASES

■**INSTANT FACTS** A newspaper was indicted for libel based on an article it printed on the President's true motives for a treaty.

■**BLACK LETTER RULE** The courts of the United States have no common law jurisdiction in criminal cases absent a grant of authority in the U.S. Constitution or a grant under a specific congressional enactment.

■ **PROCEDURAL BASIS**

On appeal by writ of certiorari from a decision of the Circuit Court for the District of Connecticut following general demurrer to an indictment for a libel on the President and Congress.

■ **FACTS**

On May 7, 1806, the *Connecticut Currant* published an article stating that the President and Congress of the United States had secretly voted to give $2 million to Napoleon Bonaparte to make a treaty with Spain. The lower court remained divided on whether it had common law jurisdiction in the case of libel.

■ **ISSUE**

Does the Circuit Court of the United States have the right to exercise common law jurisdiction in criminal cases?

■ **DECISION AND RATIONALE**

(Johnson, J.) No. The existence of this right of jurisdiction has not been asserted for years, exhibiting an acquiescence that the right does not exist. The basis for this conclusion is simple. The government gets it power by concessions from the states. What is not given is retained by the states. This proposition applies to courts; only the Supreme Court derives its authority from the Constitution. The jurisdiction sought here has not been granted by any political body. The legislative authority of the Union must first designate an act as a crime and provide for its punishment. Then, it may declare which court would have jurisdiction over the offense. Implied powers are granted to federal courts, but jurisdiction to hear crimes against the state is not among them, nor is the authority to hear criminal cases brought under the common law.

Analysis:

Jurisdiction is a prerequisite to all legal cases, both civil and criminal. In the absence of a specific grant of authority to hear a matter, no jurisdiction may be implied. Compare the result in *Young v. U.S. ex rel. Vuitton et Fils S.A.*, 481 U.S. 787 (1987), in which the Court held that, while it could not take for itself the authority to decide cases without Constitutional or statutory mandate, "[t]o fine for contempt—imprison for contumacy—inforce the observance of order, etc. are powers which cannot be dispensed with in a Court, because they are necessary to the exercise of all others."

■ CASE VOCABULARY

COMMON LAW CRIME: A crime that is punishable under the common law, rather than by force of statute.

JURISDICTION: A court's power to decide a case or issue a decree.

Rogers v. Tennessee

(Murderer) v. (State)

532 U.S. 451, 121 S.Ct. 1693 (2001)

ABANDONING COMMON LAW PRECEDENT DOES NOT VIOLATE DUE PROCESS OR CONSTITUTE AN EX POST FACTO LAW

If he dies, we'll charge the stabber with murder.

stus.com

■**INSTANT FACTS** Rogers (D) stabbed Bowdery, causing injuries that led to cardiac arrest and brain damage and culminated in Bowdery's death fifteen months after Rogers' (D) attack; Rogers (D) was convicted of murder.

■**BLACK LETTER RULE** The constitutional prohibition of ex post facto laws is directed at legislative bodies, not courts, as the very nature of the common law permits a court to overrule or abandon existing precedent.

■ PROCEDURAL BASIS

On appeal to the U.S. Supreme Court from a decision by the Tennessee Supreme Court affirming the defendant's conviction for murder.

■ FACTS

Petitioner Rogers (D) stabbed Bowdery in the heart, which caused cardiac arrest that led to brain damage. Bowdery then slipped into a coma. As is common with coma patients, Bowdery developed a kidney infection fifteen months after the attack and died from the infection. Rogers (D) was convicted of second-degree murder under a statute that made no mention of the "year-and-a-day rule," which precluded a defendant from being convicted of murder when the victim died from injuries inflicted by the defendant beyond a year and a day of the attack. Criminal homicide was defined simply as the "unlawful killing of another." On appeal, Rogers (D) insisted that, despite the absence of the year-and-a-day rule in Tennessee statutes, the rule persisted as part of the state's common law. The Tennessee Supreme Court held that the reasons behind the rule no longer existed. The court disagreed that its refusal to apply the rule for Rogers (D) would violate the prohibition on ex post facto laws, as that rule refers only to legislative acts.

■ ISSUE

Did the state, by abolishing the defense of the year-and-a-day rule, deny the defendant due process under the Fourteenth Amendment?

■ DECISION AND RATIONALE

(O'Connor, J.) No. While the defendant contends that the state has violated due process in not allowing him to apply the year-and-a-day rule, his argument is based on the limits on *ex post facto* laws. The constitutional prohibition of ex post facto laws protects citizens against four types of laws: first, those laws that make an act committed prior to the enactment of the illegal; second, those laws that aggravate a crime, making it more serious than it once was;

third, those laws that provide for the infliction of greater punishment than was in effect when the crime was committed; and fourth, those laws that alter rules of evidence, changing the evidence that can be received to convict the offender. The constitutional clause applies to the legislature, however, and not to the courts. The courts have nonetheless recognized that limits on their use of ex post facto laws are inherent in the concept of due process. In *Bouie v. City of Columbia*, 378 U.S. 347 (1964), for instance, the Court held that earlier trespass cases had not given the defendants any reason to believe they could be prosecuted for trespass when they failed to leave once they had been told to leave. A statute cannot be construed by the courts as retroactively having a new meaning without violating due process, because a criminal statute must give fair warning that the conduct it proscribes is a crime.

Here, Rogers (D) argued that the ex post facto clause of the Constitution similarly prohibits the retroactive *abolition* of the year-and-a-day rule by the courts. When the legislature would not be permitted to act, he argues, due process requires courts to conform to the same conduct. But this argument misreads *Bouie*. In the common law process, doctrines are reevaluated frequently as new fact patterns are presented. Each case constitutes a part of the court's role in the making of common law. By its very nature, common law is often at odds with the concept of ex post facto laws, since it must change as the next fact pattern is presented. Here, the Tennessee courts abolished the year-and-a-day rule; the action is justifiable as it is frequently viewed as outdated. Rogers (D) has given no good reason for retaining the rule except that it would work to his benefit. The rule had its beginnings in the court's recognition that medical professionals were often unable to determine the cause of an individual's death when a great deal of time elapsed between the injury and the death. Medical advances have now rendered that rule unnecessary. Moreover, the rule never served as a basis for any decision involving the charge of murder in Tennessee, and so was never an entrenched part of Tennessee law. Affirmed.

■ DISSENT

(Scalia, J.) The decision here permits a man to be charged with murder even when he did not commit murder when he acted. The majority has allowed a court to do what a legislature cannot—retroactively make an act murder when the act, when taken, would not been perceived as such. Historically, courts have recognized that understanding of what the law is can change. However, courts are not pretending to make new law, but freely admit to correcting the old. In this case, though, making new law was exactly what the court did. If, as the majority said, due process is only violated when there has been no fair warning, that warning is not found here and the majority gives no indication of what that fair warning was. The majority seems to hold that the defendant should have predicted that the law would change, but even if it were predictable the law may change, it should not be deemed predictable it would change retroactively. The defendant received nothing that could be said to be fair warning that Tennessee would "retroactively eliminate one of the elements of the crime of murder."

Analysis:

In *Keeler v. Superior Court*, 87 Cal. Rptr. 481 (Cal. 1970), the defendant was charged with homicide in the killing of the unborn child his ex-wife was carrying. The court considered medical advances since earlier law in making its decision in that case, but while the *Rogers* court found advances in medical science to work against the defendant, in *Keeler* the ability of medicine to sustain a fetus delivered at eight months was unpersuasive. The key distinction between the cases was that the crime charged in *Keeler* was legislatively defined, whereas the defense in *Rogers* was court-made. Note, too, that Rogers (D) here is complaining about the fair notice of which he was deprived by the court's casting aside the year-and-a-day rule, but it is unlikely that Rogers was even aware of the rule when he engaged in the fight.

■ **CASE VOCABULARY**

DUE PROCESS: The conduct of legal proceedings according to established rules and principles for the protection and enforcement of private rights, including notice and the right to a fair hearing before a tribunal with the power to decide the case.

EX POST FACTO LAW: A law that applies retroactively, especially in a way that negatively affects a person's rights, as by criminalizing an action that was legal when it was committed.

JUS DARE: To give or make the law. This is the function and prerogative of the legislature.

JUS DICERE: To declare or decide the law. This is the function and prerogative of the judiciary.

SECOND–DEGREE MURDER: Murder that is not aggravated by any of the circumstances of first-degree murder.

YEAR–AND–A–DAY RULE: The common law principle that an act causing death is not homicide if the death occurs more than a year and a day after the act was committed.

Chicago v. Morales

(Chicago City Council) v. (Gang Member)

527 U.S. 41, 119 S.Ct. 1849 (1999)

AN ORDINANCE PROHIBITING BEING IN A PLACE FOR NO APPARENT PURPOSE IS VAGUE

■INSTANT FACTS A Chicago ordinance banned loitering in public places in an effort to discourage gang members from intimidating law-abiding people who seek to make use of public areas.

■BLACK LETTER RULE An ordinance that seeks to impose criminal penalties for conduct that is vaguely defined and for which violations are deemed to have been committed at the discretion of law enforcement officers will not be enforced as in contravention of due process.

■ **PROCEDURAL BASIS**

On appeal to the U.S. Supreme Court from a finding by the Illinois Supreme Court that the ordinance violated the due process considerations of definiteness and clarity.

■ **FACTS**

In 1992, Chicago passed the Gang Congregation Ordinance, banning "criminal street gang members" from "loitering" in public as part of an effort to correct the problems caused by the city's gang population and its loitering in public areas. Gang activity was blamed for an increase in drug-related and violent crime, including murder. The gang presence in many neighborhoods had the effect of driving law-abiding people from the areas. Because of the fear of gang members, the plaintiff concluded that it needed to take action to discourage gang members from public loitering, so the city enacted an ordinance making loitering a crime punishable by a fine of up to $500, six months in prison, and up to 120 hours of community service. The crime has four elements: (1) a "police officer must reasonably believe that at least one of the two or more persons present in a 'public place' is a 'criminal street gang membe[r]' "; (2) "the persons must be in the place for 'no apparent purpose' "; (3) the persons must be told by the police officer to leave; and (4) the persons must disobey. Any person who disobeys the police order to disperse is guilty of violating the ordinance. To help with the enforcement of the ordinance, the Chicago Police Department enacted guidelines for its officers. The police suggested that enforcement of the ordinance be confined to those known to be gang members and that it be enforced most aggressively in areas where gang presence was known to pose a serious problem. During the three years since the ordinance's enactment, 89,000 orders were issued and more than 42,000 people were arrested. The Illinois Supreme Court held the ordinance violated due process, as it was "impermissibly vague on its face and an arbitrary restriction on personal liberties."

■ **ISSUE**

Was the Illinois Supreme Court correct in holding that the gang-related loitering ordinance violated the Due Process Clause?

■ **DECISION AND RATIONALE**

(Stevens, J.) Yes. An ordinance may be void for vagueness for two reasons: (1) it may fail to provide adequate notice to a citizen as to what conduct the law finds criminal, and (2) it may lead to arbitrary enforcement. When a law is so vague as to provide inadequate notice of the conduct the law finds criminal, it violates the requirements of due process. While the word "loiter" may have a generally accepted meaning, the meaning adopted by the ordinance for "loiter" does not reflect that meaning. What determines whether persons are standing in a place with or without a purpose? Is talking to another person a purpose? How about waiting for a friend? The law makes no distinction between conduct that is innocent and conduct that threatens harm. The City (P) argues that there is no notice problem here since the offender cannot be arrested until he or she has failed to obey a police officer's order to leave the area, but this argument fails for two reasons. First, the purpose of fair notice is to allow ordinary citizens to comply with the law. While a loiterer may not be criminally responsible until he or she disobeys the order to leave, the ordinance is designed to prohibit loitering. If that conduct is innocent until the officer designates it as otherwise, then the law allows the police to issue an order proscribing innocent conduct. Second, once the order is issued, the appropriate response to the order is unclear—how far away from each other must the parties move and for how long? The Constitution prohibits passing an overly broad ordinance and leaving it to the courts to decide who was unintentionally caught in the net.

The ordinance also fails to provide minimal guidelines to assist police with the enforcement of the law. This ordinance provides law enforcement officers with almost unfettered discretion as to what constitutes a violation. Chicago raises three points that establish a restraint on the police's enforcement. First, no one who is moving along or has an apparent purpose can be issued an order. Second, individuals who obey the order to move cannot be arrested. Third, the officer can only issue a citation when he believes the loiterer to be a member of a gang. While the limitations sound appealing, the public has no reason to trust the law will only be enforced as intended. Further, a law-abiding person, simply by stopping to talk to a gang member, runs the risk of violating the law. Taken to the absurd, a group of gang members stopped to conduct a drug transaction would not fit within the ordinance's language, since the gang members clearly had a purpose. Based on the foregoing, it is apparent that the Illinois Supreme Court was correct in concluding that the ordinance did not meet with constitutional standards for definiteness and clarity. Affirmed.

Analysis:

The arguments raised in this case surfaced again in *Fuller v. Decatur Public School Board of Education*, 78 F. Supp. 2d 812 (C.D. Ill. 2000). In *Fuller*, students were expelled from school for participation in "gang-related" conduct. The school's ordinance was vaguely drafted, akin to that discussed in this case, but there the court declined to find the ordinance unconstitutional. In *Fuller*, the court determined that a school's disciplinary needs allow its rules to be less detailed than criminal ordinances in order to provide the schools with the flexibility they need to address a variety of disruptive conduct.

■ **CASE VOCABULARY**

FAIR WARNING: The requirement that a criminal statute define an offense with enough precision so that a reasonable person can know what conduct is prohibited and so that a reasonably skilled lawyer can predict what conduct falls within the statute's scope.

VOID FOR VAGUENESS: Establishing a requirement or punishment without specifying what is required or what conduct is punishable, and therefore void because violative of due process.

CHAPTER THREE

The Guilty Mind

People v. Dillard

Instant Facts: Dillard (D) retrieved his rifle from his father's house and headed home on his bike, not knowing the rifle still contained ammunition; he was charged with having a loaded weapon in public.

Black Letter Rule: While scienter is an element of nearly every crime, a regulatory offense is designed to protect the public welfare from a serious danger, and proof of a violation does not require proof of knowledge or intent.

United States v. Wulff

Instant Facts: Wulff (D) sold a necklace made of the talons of birds protected by the Migratory Bird Treaty Act (MBTA) and was indicted for a felony violation of the MBTA.

Black Letter Rule: When an offense does not require proof of scienter and is not known to the common law, it cannot be prosecuted as a felony.

Lambert v. California

Instant Facts: Lambert (D) was residing in Los Angeles when she was arrested for failing to register as a felon with the Los Angeles Police Department following her conviction for forgery.

Black Letter Rule: A law requiring registration of a felon contravenes due process when the person charged with violating the requirement had no reason to know of the registration requirement.

Regina v. Faulkner

Instant Facts: Faulkner (D), a seaman on board the ship Zemindar, accidentally lit the ship on fire as he was stealing rum from the cargo hold.

Black Letter Rule: Having the intent to commit a specific crime does not serve to establish the intent to commit a second crime that occurs by accident.

Regina v. Prince

Instant Facts: Prince (D) was charged with taking a girl under the age of sixteen from her parents; Prince (D) argued he lacked the intent to commit the crime because he believed the girl was much older.

Black Letter Rule: It is not a defense to the crime of taking an underage girl that the defendant thought the girl was not underage when the statute does not make knowledge of the girl's age an element of the crime.

People v. Ryan

Instant Facts: Ryan (D) was arrested for knowingly possessing 624 milligrams of a hallucinogen contained in a two-pound box of illegal mushrooms.

Black Letter Rule: If a criminal statute makes reference to a single mens rea, that mental state is presumed to apply to all elements of the offense absent a contrary legislative intent.

People v. Bray

Instant Facts: Bray (D) pleaded guilty to a crime in Kansas and received probation; it was unclear whether the crime was a felony or a misdemeanor.

Black Letter Rule: When knowledge is an essential element of a crime, a justifiable mistake or ignorance of fact may excuse the defendant from compliance with a criminal statute.

United States v. Baker

Instant Facts: Baker (D) was convicted of dealing in counterfeit Rolex watches.

Black Letter Rule: A statute that criminalizes intentional trafficking or attempting to traffic in goods or services and knowingly using counterfeit marks on or in connection with goods or services does not require that the defendant know the criminal nature of his conduct.

Cheek v. United States

Instant Facts: Cheek (D) failed to pay federal taxes or file tax returns for several years based on his claim that the U.S. tax statutes were unconstitutional

Black Letter Rule: A good-faith belief that the tax laws did not impose a duty on him to file returns or pay taxes did not have to be objectively reasonable in order to be considered as a defense by the jury.

Commonwealth v. Twitchell

Instant Facts: The Twitchells' (D) child developed a condition typically treatable by surgery, but they declined to have the surgery performed based on their beliefs as Christian Scientists.

Black Letter Rule: A statute insulating parents from prosecution for neglect under child welfare laws cannot be used to avoid prosecution for involuntary manslaughter; however, parents should be permitted to assert an affirmative defense that they reasonably relied on an Attorney General's opinion in deciding which actions to take.

Hendershott v. People

Instant Facts: Hendershott (D) physically attacked Styskal and defended against the charges by claiming he lacked the intent to commit the offense due to adult minimal brain dysfunction.

Black Letter Rule: Due process demands that a defendant be permitted to offer evidence establishing his impaired mental condition as an affirmative defense for a non-specific intent crime; to hold contrary renders the prosecution's evidence incontestable in violation of the constitutional presumption of innocence.

State v. Cameron

Instant Facts: Cameron (D) assaulted McKinney, resisted arrest, and argued she was not guilty of the crimes she was accused of committing since she was too drunk to appreciate her actions.

Black Letter Rule: By statute, intoxication may be a defense to crimes requiring either "purposeful" or "knowing" mental states, but the level of intoxication must be high enough to have caused "prostration of faculties."

Montana v. Egelhoff

Instant Facts: The defendant was convicted of "purposely or knowingly" causing death although he was intoxicated at the time.

Black Letter Rule: A state may prohibit a defendant from having a jury consider evidence of voluntary intoxication in deciding an accused's mental state without violating a "fundamental principle of justice."

CONVICTION OF A REGULATORY CRIME NEED NOT BE SUPPORTED BY PROOF OF KNOWLEDGE OR INTENT

■**INSTANT FACTS** Dillard (D) retrieved his rifle from his father's house and headed home on his bike, not knowing the rifle still contained ammunition; he was charged with having a loaded weapon in public.

■**BLACK LETTER RULE** While scienter is an element of nearly every crime, a regulatory offense is designed to protect the public welfare from a serious danger, and proof of a violation does not require proof of knowledge or intent.

■ **PROCEDURAL BASIS**

On appeal following the defendant's conviction.

■ **FACTS**

Dillard (D) was observed riding a bicycle and carrying a rifle case. Officer Torres asked Dillard (D) to stop and place the case on the hood of Torres' patrol car. Torres removed the rifle from its case and found that the 30.30 Winchester was nearly fully loaded and that several rounds of ammunition were in the case. Dillard (D) explained that he owned the rifle and had picked it up from his father's house a few hours earlier. He told the officer that he had not opened the case since taking it from there. Dillard (D) insisted he had lent the rifle to his father on many occasions to use for hunting; as Dillard's (D) father had never returned the rifle to him loaded with ammunition in the past, Dillard (D) contended he had no reason to check the rifle this time before taking it with him. The trial court refused to permit the introduction of evidence to establish that Dillard (D) did not know the rifle was loaded. Over Dillard's (D) objections, the jury was instructed that it need not find Dillard (D) knew the weapon was loaded in order to find him guilty of the misdemeanor.

■ **ISSUE**

In order to be held responsible for violating the law against carrying a loaded firearm in public, must a defendant know the firearm is loaded?

■ **DECISION AND RATIONALE**

(Panelli, J.) No. Dillard (D) argues that reading the offense as not requiring knowledge that the gun is loaded prohibits him from exercising his due process right to present a defense. Dillard (D) also argues that that failing to take into consideration his knowledge of whether the gun was loaded dispenses with the long-established requirement that, to commit a crime, there must be both a wrongful intent and an act. While Dillard's arguments have some merit, they do not absolve him from liability here. California law does provide that crimes are a union between an act and intent; however, the law has also recognized the existence of "regulatory offenses" designed to protect the health, welfare, and safety of the public, for which punishment may be imposed regardless of the proof of intent in the traditional sense. Because these offenses are not crimes in the strict sense of the word, intent is not required. Many of these offenses are committed by failing to take action or act with care by creating a danger or hazard. With or without intent, the harm or potential harm posed to society from the action is the same. When the law on carrying a loaded weapon was passed, it was part of a series of laws passed in response to the increasing numbers of people deciding to arm themselves and the inability of the existing laws to protect the public from this potential hazard. Carrying a loaded weapon in public is so potentially damaging to public order, and intent is often so difficult to prove, that in the interests of justice the need to establish intent has been eliminated. In a case such as this, where the weapon was so powerful, the likelihood of inflicting a fatal wound, even by discharging the weapon by accident, was extremely high. It is not unfair to impose a duty upon the person carrying a weapon to determine whether it is loaded before transporting it. Where one carries a loaded weapon thinking it is not loaded, as Dillard (D) did here, he poses a greater danger to the public than one who knows the gun he has is loaded. Constitutionally, a defendant only has a right to present a valid defense. Where knowledge is not an element of a crime, lack of knowledge is not a valid defense. Dillard's (D) rights were not infringed by this prosecution.

Analysis:

Two years later, in *People v. Arnold*, 179 Cal. App. 3d 175, 224 Cal. Rptr. 484 (1986), the defendant was convicted of involuntary manslaughter following a "road rage" incident in which he shot and killed the driver of a truck who cut him off. Involuntary manslaughter applied to conduct resulting in a death that occurred during "commission of a misdemeanor which is inherently dangerous to human life." In contrast with the result here, the *Arnold* court held that simply having a loaded weapon in public (that is not used or brandished) posed no danger to the public, and that a violation of the weapons law did not eliminate the need for proof of intent.

■ CASE VOCABULARY

PUBLIC–WELFARE OFFENSE: A minor offense that does not involve moral delinquency and is prohibited only to secure the effective regulation of conduct in the interest of the community. An example is driving a car with one brake light missing. Also termed REGULATORY OFFENSE.

United States v. Wulff

(Prosecuting Government) v. (Bird-part Salesman)

758 F.2d 1121 (6th Cir. 1985)

A FELONY CONVICTION REQUIRES PROOF OF INTENT

Are these real bird talons?

stus.com

■INSTANT FACTS Wulff (D) sold a necklace made of the talons of birds protected by the Migratory Bird Treaty Act (MBTA) and was indicted for a felony violation of the MBTA.

■BLACK LETTER RULE When an offense does not require proof of scienter and is not known to the common law, it cannot be prosecuted as a felony.

■ **PROCEDURAL BASIS**

On appeal by the government from a district court's holding that a violation of the MBTA, absent a finding of intent, would be punished as a misdemeanor.

■ **FACTS**

Wulff (D) was arrested when he sold a necklace made from the talons of red-tailed hawks and great-horned owls to a federal officer. Both the hawk and the owl are protected species under the MBTA. The federal grand jury indicted Wulff (D) on a single-count indictment for selling migratory bird parts in violation of the MBTA. The defendant filed a motion to dismiss the charges or to be sentenced for a misdemeanor violation, rather than a felony. Wulff (D) argued that the law, by not requiring proof of his knowledge, exposed him to a felony conviction in violation of due process. The district court agreed and the government now appeals.

■ **ISSUE**

Is a felony conviction for the sale of migratory bird parts in violation of the MBTA a deprivation of due process under the Fifth Amendment since it does not require proof of scienter?

■ **DECISION AND RATIONALE**

(Milburn, J.) Yes. When an offense does not require proof of scienter and is not known to the common law, it cannot be prosecuted as a felony. At trial, the defendant relied on the holding of *Holdridge v. United States*, 282 F.2d 302 (8th Cir. 1960), in which the court explained the circumstances under which minor infractions may be penalized without proving intent and without conflicting with due process. Distinguishing *Holdridge* from Wulff's (D) case, the trial court concluded that the penalties imposed under the MBTA were not minor and, due to the felony nature of the conviction and the stigma attached to it, the absence of the need to prove intent violated due process. Courts typically permit an absence of criminal intent on a showing of a relatively minor penalty and minimal effect of the defendant's reputation. Here, the MBTA provides for a penalty of a prison term of up to two years, a $2000 fine, or both. These

---

H I G H   C O U R T   C A S E   S U M M A R I E S

57

punishments are substantial. It is unfair to subject a person with an innocent state of mind to such a weighty penalty. In order to impose such a penalty for a violation of the MBTA, Congress must first require proof of scienter. Affirmed.

Analysis:

In a case with more severe results, *Stanley v. Turner*, 6 F.3d 399 (6th Cir. 1993), the defendant was charged with vehicular homicide. He argued that since the vehicular homicide law did not require the prosecution to prove intent before he could be sentenced for a felony, the law violated his due process rights. The *Stanley* court upheld the defendant's conviction on a finding that, unlike in this case, where Wulff was unaware of the proscriptions of the MBTA, Stanley was presumed to be familiar with the state's traffic laws and his obligation to uphold them.

■ **CASE VOCABULARY**

FELONY: A serious crime usually punishable by imprisonment for more than one year or by death. Examples include burglary, arson, rape, and murder.

MISDEMEANOR: A crime that is less serious than a felony and is usually punishable by fine, penalty, forfeiture, or confinement (usually for a brief term) in a place other than prison (such as a county jail).

SCIENTER: A degree of knowledge that makes a person legally responsible for the consequences of his or her act or omission; the fact of an act's having been done knowingly, especially as a ground for civil damages or criminal punishment.

Lambert v. California

(Unregistered Felon) v. (State of California)

355 U.S. 225, 78 S.Ct. 240 (1957)

VIOLATION OF A REGISTRATION REQUIREMENT IS NOT PUNISHABLE IN THE ABSENCE OF KNOWLEDGE OF THE DUTY TO REGISTER

■**INSTANT FACTS** Lambert (D) was residing in Los Angeles when she was arrested for failing to register as a felon with the Los Angeles Police Department following her conviction for forgery.

■**BLACK LETTER RULE** A law requiring registration of a felon contravenes due process when the person charged with violating the requirement had no reason to know of the registration requirement.

■ **PROCEDURAL BASIS**

On appeal to the U.S. Supreme Court from the defendant's conviction.

■ **FACTS**

Lambert (D), a resident of Los Angeles for seven years, had a forgery conviction. A Los Angeles ordinance made it a crime for a convicted felon to be in Los Angeles for more than five days without registering with the Chief of Police. The ordinance also made it a crime for a convicted felon to enter the city more than five times during a thirty-day period without registering. Each day the registration was not made constituted a separate offense. Lambert (D) was arrested on suspicion of having committed another crime, but was charged with failing to comply with the registration requirement. At the time of her arrest, she had not registered with the Chief of Police. At trial, Lambert (D) argued that the registration requirement constituted a violation of due process because she did not know about it; Lambert's (D) objection was denied.

■ **ISSUE**

Does a conviction for failing to register as a felon when having regular contact with the city of Los Angeles violate due process, when the violator had no knowledge of the duty to register?

■ **DECISION AND RATIONALE**

(Douglas, J.) Yes. Los Angeles' registration requirement applies to require the registration of an individual convicted of a felony in California, or convicted of an offense elsewhere that would have been considered a felony in California. The ordinance does not require that the failure to register be willful. It is assumed that Lambert (D) did not know that she must register. In some situations, conduct without intent will be sufficient to constitute a crime; however, this is a passive crime. While ignorance of the law is frequently no excuse, due process places some limits on this adage. Notice is must be effective before consequences may ensue. Notice is a prerequisite to disturbing property interests, imposing penalties, or

---

declaring a forfeiture, especially when a penalty may be imposed for the failure to act. Registration acts are common, but this act is not intuitive. Its primary purpose is to provide law enforcement officials with a list of convicted felons within the community. Lambert's (D) first exposure to the ordinance's requirements provided her no opportunity to comply. Actual knowledge of the duty to register must be shown in order to support a conviction for the failure to do so.

■ DISSENT

(Frankfurter, J.) Many laws exist that citizens may be charged with violating even absent the citizen's knowledge that the laws exist. All too frequently, when a law is broken and the consequences are severe, the courts look for an opportunity to find a mental element lacking to soften the impact. What the majority is trying to do here, however, is distinguish between laws that require positive action and those that simply forbid action. This decision will affect countless legislation on the books of many states and should not be followed in subsequent cases.

Analysis:

In *U.S. v. Meade*, 175 F.3d 215 (1st Cir. 1999), the defendant was arrested for possession of a firearm in contravention of the law pertaining to individuals subject to a domestic restraining order. Meade argued that the court should have informed him of the consequences that attached to the order, including the federal prohibition on having a gun. In the absence of such a requirement, he said, it would be unconstitutional to hold him responsible for violating a provision of the law of which he was unaware. In reaching a contrary conclusion, the court explained that gun ownership, like drug possession or child pornography, when coupled with the fact that the defendant was subject to a restraining order for domestic abuse, did not involve conduct and circumstances so presumptively innocent as to fall within the narrow confines of the *Lambert* exception.

ABSENT PROOF OF INTENT, A CONVICTION FOR A CONSEQUENTIAL CRIME WILL NOT STAND

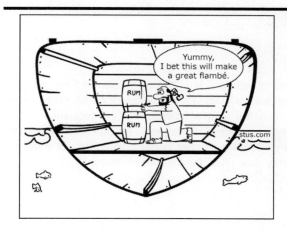

■**INSTANT FACTS** Faulkner (D), a seaman on board the ship Zemindar, accidentally lit the ship on fire as he was stealing rum from the cargo hold.

■**BLACK LETTER RULE** Having the intent to commit a specific crime does not serve to establish the intent to commit a second crime that occurs by accident.

■ PROCEDURAL BASIS

On appeal following conviction in a trial by jury.

■ FACTS

Faulkner (D) was a seaman on the Zemindar. He was alleged to have started a fire in the ship's cargo area and was charged with feloniously, unlawfully, and maliciously setting fire to a ship on the high seas. At trial, it was shown that the ship was on its voyage back to Ireland with a cargo of rum, sugar, and cotton. The fire started when Faulkner (D) went into the cargo area intending to steal rum. He took the liquor by drilling a hole in one of the casks, and after he had taken what he wanted, Faulkner (D) intended to cork the hole but did not. The alcohol that continued to leak from the cask was exposed to a lighted match in Faulkner's (D) hand, causing the fire. The ship was destroyed as a result. At the close of his case, Faulkner (D) requested an acquittal since the prosecution failed to establish his intent to start the fire. The prosecution argued that Faulkner (D) was committing a felony at the time the fire started, and that felony eliminated the need to prove intent. The judge acknowledged that Faulkner (D) did not appear to have intended to burn the ship; nonetheless, the judge told the jury the law did not require the jury to decide if the defendant knew the likely consequences of his actions. The jury was instructed that while it may find the prisoner did not intend to burn the ship, if he stole the rum and started the fire in the process, he should be found guilty of the arson as well. The jury then found Faulkner (D) guilty on both counts and he was sentenced to seven years confinement.

■ ISSUE

Did the trial judge commit an error in instructing the jury to disregard the intention of the defendant?

■ DECISION AND RATIONALE

(Dowse, B.) Yes. (No further opinion provided.)

■ CONCURRENCE

(Barry, J.) The prosecution has proposed that anyone committing a felony who accidentally commits another act that, if intentionally committed, would constitute a felony, is guilty of the second felony as well. While the law should not rush to limit the responsibility of those engaged in criminal conduct, neither should it agree to such a broad proposition. In the absence of authority to support this claim, it cannot stand.

■ CONCURRENCE

(Fitzgerald, J.) In order to establish the crime of setting a fire, it must be shown Faulkner (D) intended to commit that act or that the act was a necessary consequence of some other criminal activity in which he was involved. If a fire was a foreseeable consequence of his stealing the rum, that offense should have been presented to the jury. The prosecution insisted the defendant should be responsible for every effect he caused in the commission of a felony, whether it was foreseeable or not. No authority was cited for this broad-sweeping view of the law, so it must be rejected.

■ CONCURRENCE

(O'Brien, J.) It seemed as though the jury was instructed to disregard any unintended actions of Faulkner and that it was not asked to consider whether the defendant should have considered it a consequence of his theft. In *Reg v. Pembliton* (12 Cox C.C. 607), the case against the defendant was much stronger. There, the defendant broke a window when throwing a stone at someone in a crowd of people. He did not set out to break the window. On appeal, his conviction was overturned for lack of evidence that he intended to break the window. The prosecution here argues that the jury likely based its decision on the fact that the prisoner probably considered that a fire may result as a consequence of his stealing the rum and chose to act recklessly; however, no evidence to this effect was offered at trial. The defendant lit the match to be able to plug the cask after he stole the rum, not to burn the ship.

■ DISSENT

(Keogh, J.) This conviction should stand. The defendant was responsible for starting the fire while engaged in the felony of stealing the rum because he did, after all, start the fire. Without regard to whether his actions were reckless or foreseeable, he should be punished according to the conviction.

Analysis:

In this case, Faulkner (D) escaped liability for his role in burning the ship since he only intended to steal rum. Justice Keogh was the lone hold-out who believed that Faulkner (D) committed the act that caused the fire and should therefore be responsible for the consequences, whether he wanted to burn the ship or merely get drunk. The felony-murder rule is a doctrine similar to the one advanced by Justice Keogh and the prosecutor in this case. The felony-murder rule holds that "any death resulting from the commission or attempted commission of a dangerous felony is murder."

■ CASE VOCABULARY

RECKLESS: Characterized by the creation of a substantial and unjustifiable risk of harm to others and by a conscious (and sometimes deliberate) disregard for or indifference to that risk; heedless; rash.

Regina v. Prince

(Queen) v. (Criminal Defendant)

L.R. 2 Crim. Cas. Res. 154 (CCCR 1875)

A LAW PROHIBITING CONDUCT WITHOUT REFERENCE TO THE ACTOR'S STATE OF MIND PROVIDES THE ACTOR WITH NO EXCUSE FOR MISTAKE

■**INSTANT FACTS** Prince (D) was charged with taking a girl under the age of sixteen from her parents; Prince (D) argued he lacked the intent to commit the crime because he believed the girl was much older.

■**BLACK LETTER RULE** It is not a defense to the crime of taking an underage girl that the defendant thought the girl was not underage when the statute does not make knowledge of the girl's age an element of the crime.

■ **PROCEDURAL BASIS**

On appeal from a guilty verdict.

■ **FACTS**

Phillips, fourteen, told the defendant, Prince (D), that she was actually eighteen. Prince (D) believed her statement since she appeared to be at least eighteen years old. Prince (D) was charged with unlawfully taking out Phillips, a girl under the age of sixteen, without permission from her father. The jury found that Prince (D) reasonably believed her statement, but that he was nonetheless guilty of violating the law.

■ **ISSUE**

Is the fact that the defendant believed the girl was older a defense to the crime of taking a girl younger than sixteen years old from her parents?

■ **DECISION AND RATIONALE**

(Blackburn, J.) No. The argument in favor of the defendant must rest, if at all, on the fact that a guilty mind must exist to establish any crime. However, the statute does not provide that a person taking a girl under age sixteen must *know* she is under the age or believe she is not older. The defendant contends that any statute must read as though the word "knowingly" is understood as part of the statute even when the word does not appear; however, this is not the case. The legislature intended to punish the abduction of anyone under the age of sixteen. It would seem unfair to allow the punishment of a defendant to turn on the mind of the defendant, rather than on the facts. The intent of the legislature was to punish those who had abducted young girls who were too young to give their own consent. A man who takes up with a girl relying on her statement of age does so at his peril.

■ CONCURRENCE

(Bramwell, B.) The defendant here asks the court to imply additional language in the statute he is charged with violating that is not there, but the court may not add words to a statute. The commission of the forbidden act is wrong since the reason for taking the girl is generally for purposes of seduction. Regardless of whether the act is immoral, it is wrong. The legislature meant for the person taking the child to do so at the risk of the one doing the taking. Anyone taking a girl from someone else's care runs the risk that she is underage.

■ CONCURRENCE

(Denman, J.) Use of the word "unlawfully" in the statute clearly means "without lawful excuse." A legitimate excuse may be found by proving facts that support the defendant taking the girl to prevent harm from coming to her, such as where a child is being abused by her parents. Here, the defendant believed the girl was eighteen. Even an eighteen-year-old girl is deemed to still be within the lawful care of her father, who had a right to custody until she reached age twenty-one. So, had she been eighteen, that would provide the defendant with no excuse for taking her from her father. By taking an eighteen-year-old, he was assisting her with committing the illegal act of escaping the will of her guardian. Even if the facts were as the defendant claimed, he was "without lawful excuse" for his actions. He knowingly violated the rights of the girl's father and cannot seek to avoid punishment by arguing he committed a different wrong than the one he was charged with committing.

■ DISSENT

(Brett, J.) If the facts had been as the defendant assumed them to be, he would have been guilty of no crime. It is a part of the law that no act can be punished without a criminal mind.

Analysis:

In *Regina v. Faulkner*, 13 Cox C.C. 550 (Ir. CCC 1877), the seaman was able to avoid responsibility for burning the vessel from which he stole rum because the statute that concerned starting a fire required proof of an evil intent to commit the crime. In this case, the purpose of the law was to protect underage girls from unseemly advances. The need to protect the girls was due to their inability to make appropriate judgments for themselves. To permit the defendant here to evade punishment based on the statements of a girl in need of protection defeats the purpose of the statute.

■ CASE VOCABULARY

ASSIZES: A session of a court or council, or a law enacted by such a body, usually one setting the measure, weight, or price of a thing; the procedure provided for by such an enactment; the court that hears cases involving that procedure; a jury, a jury trial, or a jury's finding.

(State of New York) v. (Possessor of Mushrooms)

82 N.Y.2d 497, 626 N.E.2d 51, 605 N.Y.S.2d 235 (1993)

THE CRIMINAL POSSESSION OF A STATED WEIGHT OF A SUBSTANCE REQUIRES KNOWLEDGE OF THE WEIGHT

I had no idea how much the hallucinogen in my mushrooms weighed.

It's a stretch, but that just might win.

stus.com

■**INSTANT FACTS** Ryan (D) was arrested for knowingly possessing 624 milligrams of a hallucinogen contained in a two-pound box of illegal mushrooms.

■**BLACK LETTER RULE** If a criminal statute makes reference to a single mens rea, that mental state is presumed to apply to all elements of the offense absent a contrary legislative intent.

■ **PROCEDURAL BASIS**

On appeal from the appellate division's affirmance of the trial court's denial of the defendant's motion to dismiss.

■ **FACTS**

Defendant Ryan (D) asked a friend, Hopkins (D) to order hallucinogenic mushrooms for him. An investigator, posing as a deliveryman, delivered the package of mushrooms to the defendant. Hopkins (D) was arrested when he accepted the package. Hopkins (D) explained that the package was for Ryan (D) and agreed to deliver the mushrooms to Ryan (D) under police supervision. Hopkins (D) phoned Ryan (D) and told him the mushrooms had arrived and that he had two pounds of them; the two men agreed to meet. Ryan (D) was arrested moments after accepting delivery of the mushrooms. At trial, evidence of the transaction was offered and a police chemist testified that the mushrooms weighed approximately two pounds. Testimony was also offered that just a small sample of the mushrooms contained 796 milligrams of the hallucinogen—more than the statutory minimum. At the close of the state's case, Ryan (D) moved to dismiss, arguing the state failed to establish that he knew the level of hallucinogens in the mushrooms. On the defendant's first appeal, the court held that the word "knowingly" in the statute referred only to possession and did not require that the defendant know the quantity. This appeal followed.

■ **ISSUE**

When a statute prohibits the knowing possession of certain quantity of a substance, does use of the use of the word "knowingly" apply directly to the weight of the controlled substance?

■ **DECISION AND RATIONALE**

(Kaye, C.J.) Yes. A reading of the statute would appear to require "knowingly" to apply to the weight of the proscribed substance. Thus, a defendant must knowingly possess the hallucinogen and knowingly possess the quantity proscribed in the statute. To eliminate the knowing requirement from the quantity would defeat the purpose of the statute. Statutes are to be interpreted using two rules. First, unless the statute imposes strict liability, there must be an element of mens rea. By not requiring that the defendant know the weight of the hallucinogen he possesses, the court has made the offense a strict liability crime, which is an erroneous result without clear proof of that intent by the legislature. Second, New York penal law provides that when a word defining mental state is used only once in a statute, it is presumed to apply to each and every element of the offense unless clearly limited. In this statute, the word "knowingly" is used only once; so, it must apply to the entire statute.

The distinction between each of the six degrees of criminal possession of a controlled substance rests with the quantity possessed. To allow the legislature to impose increasingly severe penalties based on the weight without proof of knowledge would be inconsistent with notions of justice. It is not true that these convictions would be nearly impossible to obtain were it required that the defendant knew the exact weight of the substance he or she possessed. Frequently, the amount of the drug is part of the negotiations between the parties. The weight may also be surmised from the defendant's handling of the substance. If the legislature wishes to amend the laws to adopt measures more easily known to the parties, it may do so. At trial, there was evidence on which the jury could conclude the defendant knowingly possessed two pounds of the illegal mushrooms. The testimony was clear that the mushrooms contained the 650 milligrams of psilocybin prohibited by the statute. There was, however, no testimony offered that demonstrated how the weight of the mushrooms correlated to the amount of the hallucinogenic chemical it contained. Reversed.

Analysis:

Shortly after this case was decided, the New York legislature revised the general criminal statutes. N.Y. Penal Law § 15.20(4) (McKinney 1998) now provides that "knowledge by the defendant of the aggregate weight of such controlled substance . . . is not an element of any such offense." The court here was concerned with over-penalizing the defendant for a crime he had no way of knowing he had committed, since a casual user of hallucinogenic mushrooms is probably unfamiliar with the quantity of a specific chemical in each batch he buys. The legislature, on the other hand, was more concerned with limiting the amount of drugs a person possessed.

■ **CASE VOCABULARY**

KNOWING: Having or showing awareness or understanding; well informed; deliberate or conscious.

MENS REA: [Latin, "guilty mind."] The state of mind that the prosecution, to secure a conviction, must provide that a defendant had when committing a crime; criminal intent or recklessness.

People v. Bray

(State of California) v. (Weapons Law Violator)

52 Cal. App. 3d 494, 124 Cal. Rptr. 913 (1975)

A CONVICTION CANNOT REST ON A REASONABLE MISTAKE OF FACT

■**INSTANT FACTS** Bray (D) pleaded guilty to a crime in Kansas and received probation; it was unclear whether the crime was a felony or a misdemeanor.

■**BLACK LETTER RULE** When knowledge is an essential element of a crime, a justifiable mistake or ignorance of fact may excuse the defendant from compliance with a criminal statute.

■ PROCEDURAL BASIS

Appeal from the defendant's conviction.

■ FACTS

Bray (D) pleaded guilty in Kansas to being an accessory after the fact and was sentenced to probation since he had no previous record and appeared to have been an unwilling participant. He completed his probation and moved to California. In California, Bray (D) was gainfully employed. When Bray (D) wanted to register to vote, he discussed his earlier conviction with an official in the Registrar of Voters office. Based on his explanation of the circumstances of his conviction in Kansas, he was permitted to vote. Bray (D) then applied for work as a security guard. On his application, he admitted to having been arrested, but did not mention his felony conviction; he did, however, explain the arrest and probation. He then received notice that he had been registered as a guard. Bray (D) then purchased a .38 caliber revolver for use on those jobs that required an armed patrolman. On the application for the gun permit, he stated he had not been convicted of a felony or of a crime with a punishment in excess of a year. He received his gun after the five-day waiting period. On two other occasions, Bray (D) filled out employment applications requesting information on felony convictions. He did not answer affirmatively, but explained the circumstances of his arrest and probation. During a later search of Bray's (D) home and car by investigators from the district attorney's office, Bray (D) voluntarily showed the investigators his .38 and .22 caliber weapons. Bray (D) was then charged with two courts of possession of a firearm by a felon.

■ ISSUE

When evidence established the defendant's good faith belief that his earlier crime was not a felony, did his mistake or ignorance of fact affect whether he violated the law prohibiting convicted felons from owning guns?

■ **DECISION AND RATIONALE**

(Brown, Presiding J.) Yes. In order to convict Bray (D) of the crime here, the prosecutor must prove (1) a prior felony conviction, and (2) ownership of a firearm capable of being concealed. It was shown that Bray (D) possessed concealable weapons and it was unquestionable that Bray (D) had been convicted of the crime of accessory in Kansas. Bray argues that the prosecution must also be able to show he *knew* he was a felon. Alternatively, Bray argues he must be permitted to prove he was mistaken as to whether he was a felon, but the trial court precluded him from doing that. No precedent exists as to whether the statute in question requires knowledge of felony status. Courts tend to dislike criminal statutes that impose strict liability. While the prosecution agrees that the statute should not be read to impose strict liability, the prosecution insisted it was not required to prove the defendant's knowledge. What is important here is whether Bray (D) knew that he fell within the statute's prohibition on gun ownership. Knowledge of a felony conviction is important when there is doubt the individual is a felon. Experts from Kansas agreed that it was difficult to determine whether a crime was a felony simply by its sentence. When it is difficult to determine the level of a crime within the state of its prosecution, it is no easier for prosecutors in other states. Here, Bray (D) no doubt knew he had committed a crime, but he was not sure it was a felony. Without specific knowledge, he could not be aware of the facts that would bring his conduct within that prohibited by § 12021. Reversed.

Analysis:

Subsequent cases have characterized this case as "very unusual." In Bray's case, the state authorities both in Kansas and in California were confused by Bray's status. State agencies that were given the specifics of Bray's conviction were unable to determine with clarity that he was guilty of a felony. In *People v. Snyder*, 121 Cal. App. 3d 73, 175 Cal. Rptr. 153 (1981), the defendant relied on *Bray* to show that she was confused as to her felony status. In *Snyder*, though, the court found the defendant's confusion to be the product of statements from her own lawyer, who told her that her plea of guilty meant her conviction would be a misdemeanor, not a felony. No one else involved in Snyder's case held that mistaken belief.

■ **CASE VOCABULARY**

MISTAKE OF FACT: A mistake about the legal effect of a known fact or situation; the defense asserting that a defendant did not understand the criminal consequences of certain conduct.

United States v. Baker

(Prosecuting Government) v. (Black-Market Salesman)

807 F.2d 427 (5th Cir. 1986)

KNOWLEDGE OF THE CRIMINAL NATURE OF AN ACTIVITY IS NOT A PREREQUISITE TO GUILT

■INSTANT FACTS Baker (D) was convicted of dealing in counterfeit Rolex watches.

■BLACK LETTER RULE A statute that criminalizes intentional trafficking or attempting to traffic in goods or services and knowingly using counterfeit marks on or in connection with goods or services does not require that the defendant know the criminal nature of his conduct.

■ PROCEDURAL BASIS

Appeal by the defendant from a conviction for trafficking in counterfeit goods.

■ FACTS

Baker (D) was convicted of dealing in counterfeit Rolex watches under a statute that criminalized intentional trafficking or attempting to traffic in goods or services and knowingly using counterfeit marks on or in connection with goods or services. He argued that he did not know the criminal nature of his conduct.

■ ISSUE

Is the defendant's knowledge of the criminality of his conduct an element of the crime of trafficking in counterfeit goods?

■ DECISION AND RATIONALE

(Reavley, J.) No. The Trademark Counterfeiting Act of 1984 criminalizes the actions of anyone who intentionally buys or sells goods using a counterfeit mark in connection with the transaction. Baker (D) argues that while he knew he was selling counterfeit watches, he did not know that doing so was illegal. Baker (D) contends that he cannot be convicted of an act he did not know to be criminal. The statute requires that the defendant knowingly sell goods and knowingly use a counterfeit trademark in the process, but it does not require the defendant know that the act is illegal. Criminal law does not require knowledge that an act is illegal or blameworthy. A defendant cannot avoid responsibility for his actions simply by claiming "he had not brushed up on the law." Affirmed.

Analysis:

In *U.S. v. Hooker*, 997 F.2d 67 (5th Cir. 1993), the court was asked to rely on this case to find the defendant guilty of possessing guns with altered or removed serial numbers without

---

showing that the defendant had knowledge of the alteration or removal. The prosecution argued that while the defendant may not have known specifically that filing the serial numbers off weapons was illegal, he had to have known, as a drug dealer, that the serial numbers on his weapons had been removed. The court rejected the prosecution's argument since it focused not on the knowledge required by the statute, but on an assessment of the defendant's credibility, which is a completely distinct issue.

■ **CASE VOCABULARY**

LANHAM ACT: A federal trademark statute, enacted in 1946, that provides for a national system of trademark registration and protects the owner of a federally registered mark against the use of similar marks. The Lanham Act's scope is independent of and concurrent with state common law.

TRADEMARK: A word, phrase, logo, or other graphic symbol used by a manufacturer or seller to distinguish its product or products from those of others. The main purpose of a trademark is to guarantee a product's genuineness. In effect, the trademark is the commercial substitute for one's signature. To receive federal protection, a trademark must be (1) distinctive rather than merely descriptive, (2) affixed to a product that is actually sold in the marketplace, and (3) registered with the U.S. Patent and Trademark Office. In its broadest sense, the term *trademark* includes a servicemark.

TRAFFIC: To trade or deal in goods, especially illicit drugs or other contraband.

Cheek v. United States

(Tax Evader) v. (Prosecuting Government)

498 U.S. 192, 111 S.Ct. 604 (1991)

A GOOD—FAITH BELIEF IN A DEFENSE NEED NOT BE REASONABLE TO BE VALID

■INSTANT FACTS Cheek (D) failed to pay federal taxes or file tax returns for several years based on his claim that the U.S. tax statutes were unconstitutional.

■BLACK LETTER RULE A good-faith belief that the tax laws did not impose a duty on him to file returns or pay taxes did not have to be objectively reasonable in order to be considered as a defense by the jury.

■ **PROCEDURAL BASIS**

On appeal from a decision by the Seventh Circuit Court of Appeals affirming the conviction rendered by the District Court.

■ **FACTS**

Cheek (D) worked for American Airlines as a pilot but stopped filing federal income tax returns. He also increased the number of his withholding allowances, claiming he was exempt from the withholding of federal taxes. He was charged with ten violations of the federal tax law, including six counts of willfully failing to file a tax return in violation of federal law and three counts of willfully attempting to evade income tax. These offenses were all specific intent crimes requiring the defendant to have acted willfully. At trial, Cheek (D) provided evidence that showed he was involved in at least four civil cases challenging the federal tax system. Cheek (D) was told each time that his arguments were frivolous and they were repeatedly rejected by the courts. At trial on the criminal charges, Cheek (D) acted *pro se* and admitted not filing tax returns based on the belief that federal income tax is unconstitutional. He claimed he attended several seminars held by attorneys who gave their opinions on the invalidity of the U.S. tax system. Cheek (D) argued that, based on the information he had, the tax laws were unconstitutional. His actions were, he said, therefore lawful, so he lacked the mental capacity to commit the offenses he was charged with committing. The jury was instructed that a defense to "willfulness" could be established by showing a reasonable good-faith misunderstanding of the law, but not simply a disagreement with the law. The jury had difficulty determining whether Cheek (D) honestly and reasonably believed he was not obligated to pay taxes and asked for clarification. The trial court responded by telling the jury that a mere opinion that tax laws are unconstitutional, or a disagreement with tax policies, is not a good-faith misunderstanding of the law. The jury was still unable to reach a decision. The next instruction explained that an "unreasonable belief" is not a defense to an obligation to pay taxes. "Persistent refusal to acknowledge the law" cannot serve as evidence of a good faith misunderstanding, the court said. The jury then returned two hours later with a guilty verdict. Cheek (D) argued that the trial court erred by instructing the jury to use an objective standard in determining willfulness. The Court of Appeals for the Seventh Circuit rejected his argument and affirmed his conviction.

■ ISSUE

Must a defendant's good-faith belief that he was acting lawfully be objectively reasonable in order for it to defeat the "willful" requirement of a criminal law violation?

■ DECISION AND RATIONALE

(White, J.) No. The harsh result of the adage "ignorance of the law is no excuse" has been softened by Congressional efforts to include specific intent an element of many offenses, including criminal tax crimes. In the tax context, this was done to ensure that no taxpayer with a reasonable misunderstanding as to his tax liability would become a criminal by his failure. The court in *United States v. Murdock*, 290 U.S. 389 (1933), stated that a defendant was entitled to an instruction that took into account a good-faith belief, as prior cases held that willfulness implied bad faith or an evil motive. Here, the government was required to make a three-part showing. First, the prosecution must show the law imposed a duty on the defendant. Second, the defendant must have known of the duty. Third, the prosecution must show that the defendant voluntarily and intentionally violated the duty. The important question here is whether the defendant knew of the duty imposed by the statute. If Cheek (D) had contended he really believed the IRS could not treat wages as income and the jury believed him, the government would not have proven willfulness, even if Cheek's (D) beliefs had been unreasonable. However, arguing that the provisions of the tax code are unconstitutional demonstrates not an innocent mistake due to the complex nature of the tax code. Instead, it shows a thorough understanding of the Code. Cheek (D) had remedies available to him to challenge the Code and he failed to use them. A defendant's views about the validity of the statute he is charged with violating are irrelevant to the issue of willfulness. Therefore, his requests for an instruction about his belief that the statutes are unconstitutional were properly disregarded. Cheek's (D) beliefs that wages were not income and that he was not a taxpayer under the Code were, however, relevant and should have been considered by the jury. Remanded.

Analysis:

The tax statutes were designed to punish willful conduct, and when a defendant believes in good faith that he does not have an obligation to file returns or pay taxes, he cannot be said to be acting willfully. This is true even if the defendant's belief was not objectively reasonable, so long as he held the belief in good faith. In an effort to limit this type of defense to the smallest number of cases, the courts have shown a preference for its application in cases with complex issues, such as those involving the tax code. The court declined to extend the same considerations to the defendant in *United States v. Atkinson*, 232 F.3d 897 (9th Cir. 2000), which involved violations of FAA regulations requiring medical evaluations that the court found "simple" in comparison.

■ CASE VOCABULARY

WILLFULNESS: The fact or quality of acting purposely or by design; deliberateness; intention; the voluntary, intentional violation or disregard of a known legal duty. Willfulness does not necessarily imply malice, but it involves more than just knowledge.

Commonwealth v. Twitchell

(State of Massachusetts) v. (Parents of Infant)

416 Mass. 114, 617 N.E.2d 609 (1993)

A CRIMINAL DEFENSE MUST DERIVE FROM THE CRIMINAL LAW

■INSTANT FACTS The Twitchells' (D) child developed a condition typically treatable by surgery, but they declined to have the surgery performed based on their beliefs as Christian Scientists.

■BLACK LETTER RULE A statute insulating parents from prosecution for neglect under child welfare laws cannot be used to avoid prosecution for involuntary manslaughter; however, parents should be permitted to assert an affirmative defense that they reasonably relied on an Attorney General's opinion in deciding which actions to take.

■ PROCEDURAL BASIS

On appeal from the trial court's conviction of the parents for involuntary manslaughter.

■ FACTS

The Twitchells (D) were practicing Christian Scientists who believed in healing through spiritual treatment. Their two-and-a-half-year-old son, Robyn, developed peritonitis due to a perforation in his bowel. The condition is easily treatable through surgery considered almost routine. Instead of pursuing surgery, the Twitchells (D) consulted with a Christian Science practitioner for their son's treatment. The parents (D) also conferred with another member of the church concerning the obligations of a Christian Scientist for the care of their children under Massachusetts law. They were allowed to read a pamphlet that explained that a child would not be deemed neglected or lacking in proper care when the parent provided the child with care under the tenets of a recognized religious denomination. Based on their understanding of their right to treat their son in accordance with the Christian Scientist beliefs, the boy did not have surgery and he died. The Twitchells (D) were charged with involuntary manslaughter.

■ ISSUE

Can a statute that purports to insulate parents from prosecution for neglect based on religious teachings be relied upon to avoid prosecution for involuntary manslaughter?

■ DECISION AND RATIONALE

(Wilkins, J.) No. The Commonwealth argued that the parents were guilty of involuntary manslaughter because their failure to seek medical treatment posed such a likely probability of harm as to constitute wanton or reckless behavior. At common law, a parent has a duty to provide medical treatment for a child and the failure to do so may form the basis for a conviction for involuntary manslaughter. The defendants insist that the spiritual treatment they sought for Robyn discharged them from their responsibility for seeking medical treatment;

---

however, that is not the case. Massachusetts law does not provide a complete shield for a parent who fails to seek appropriate medical care for his or her child; it simply alleviates a finding of neglect. But child protection laws are not on a par with manslaughter. Since manslaughter does not require proof of willful conduct, spiritual treatment is not a defense.

The Twitchells (D) argue that they did not have fair warning of the impact of their actions since they based their conduct on the opinion of the Attorney General as to whether parents would be liable for the failure to seek medical treatment for their children based on religious grounds. However, the opinion concludes that a child may receive treatment notwithstanding the inability to prosecute the parents. The Twitchells (D) did not read the Attorney General's opinion for themselves, but learned of the opinion from a Christian Scientist publication. To hold parents responsible for the death of their child where they sought and received legal advice that told them they could treat their child in accordance with their religious doctrines constitutes entrapment by estoppel. In this case, the Twitchells (D) were entitled to present a defense based on that fact. Whether the Twitchells (D) were reasonable in relying on the information they received from their church presents a question of fact. Judgments reversed, verdicts set aside and cause remanded for a new trial, if necessary.

Analysis:

While courts have appeared willing to shield parents from prosecution when their religious beliefs affect a child's treatment, the majority of the jurisdictions prohibit a parent from relying on religious beliefs to treat a child when the illness or condition has become life threatening. In such instances, the state takes a *parens patriae* role; that is, it stands in the shoes of the parent, and medical treatment is administered by court order, against the wishes of the parent.

■ CASE VOCABULARY

PARENS PATRIAE: [Latin, "parent of his or her country."] The state regarded as a sovereign; the state in its capacity as provider of protection to those unable to care for themselves; a doctrine by which a government has standing to prosecute a lawsuit on behalf of a citizen, especially on behalf of someone who is under a legal disability to prosecute the suit.

Hendershott v. People

(Criminal Defendant) v. (State of Colorado)

653 P.2d 385 (Colo. 1982)

MENTAL IMPAIRMENT IS AN AFFIRMATIVE DEFENSE TO A GENERAL INTENT CRIME

What are you doing here?

stus.com

■**INSTANT FACTS** Hendershott (D) physically attacked Styskal and defended against the charges by claiming he lacked the intent to commit the offense due to adult minimal brain dysfunction.

■**BLACK LETTER RULE** Due process demands that a defendant be permitted to offer evidence establishing his impaired mental condition as an affirmative defense for a non-specific intent crime; to hold contrary renders the prosecution's evidence incontestable in violation of the constitutional presumption of innocence.

■ **PROCEDURAL BASIS**

On appeal to the state supreme court on petition for certiorari following the district court's affirming of the trial court's conviction.

■ **FACTS**

Hendershott (D) was living in a rooming house owned by Styskal. Hendershott (D) and Styskal had dated on and off for three years. Hendershott (D) developed a drinking problem and was told to move out. One evening Styskal returned home to find Hendershott (D) waiting for her. He accused her of being out with another man and proceeded to beat her. She fled the house and phoned police from a neighbor's house. The police found Hendershott (D) unconscious in Styskal's room; he was immediately arrested and charged with third-degree assault. As part of discovery, the defense gave notice of its intention to offer evidence to establish that the defendant suffered from adult minimal brain dysfunction and was unable to act knowingly or recklessly, both of which were elements of the assault charge. The prosecution sought to exclude that evidence, arguing that third-degree assault was not a specific-intent crime. The trial court excluded the evidence and the jury returned a verdict of guilty. On appeal, the district court affirmed the conviction.

■ **ISSUE**

Where the crimes charged require a showing of recklessness or a knowing commission of the act, must the defendant be allowed to offer evidence establishing an impaired mental condition as an affirmative defense?

■ **DECISION AND RATIONALE**

(Quinn, J.) Yes. It is the responsibility of the legislature to define the elements of a crime. However, once an individual has been charged, it is up to the courts to ensure that constitutional considerations are respected, including the due process requirement that every element of an offense be proven beyond a reasonable doubt. It is also up to the legislature to designate justifications and defenses to crimes, so long as the rights of the accused are unimpaired. Evidence of an affirmative defense, however, is distinguishable from evidence that tends to cast doubt on the prosecution's case. Due process demands that a defendant be permitted to introduce evidence to contest the mental state the prosecution seeks to establish beyond a reasonable doubt. To find otherwise would be to render the prosecution's evidence incontestable. Here the trial court refused to allow the defendant to offer proof of the mental impairment affecting his ability to form intent based on a statute providing that evidence of mental capacity that is not insanity may be offered in a case when intent is a part of the crime. The trial court concluded that, under the statute, mental impairment evidence was inadmissible in cases in which specific intent was not an element. This conclusion is incorrect. In addition to a presumption of innocence, a defendant is entitled to have the prosecution prove mens rea beyond a reasonable doubt. Unless the defendant is permitted to introduce evidence of his limited mental capabilities, the state's evidence as to mens rea becomes incontrovertible. The prosecution argued that allowing a defendant to introduce mental-impairment evidence in general intent cases does away with a need for an insanity defense for general intent crimes, but legal sanity is not the same as mens rea. Reversed and remanded.

Analysis:

The court in this case pointed out the critical distinction between mens rea and sanity/insanity. In *People v. Vanrees*, 80 P.3d 840 (Colo. Ct. App. 2003), the court also distinguished between a defense such as the one raised here, and one in which the defendant pleads insanity. In the former case, the formal requirements are fewer, and the defendant is not required to enter a plea of not guilty by reason of insanity prior to introducing evidence as to his cognitive abilities.

■ CASE VOCABULARY

AFFIRMATIVE DEFENSE: A defendant's assertion raising new facts and arguments that, if true, will defeat the plaintiff's or prosecution's claim, even if all allegations in the complaint are true. Examples of affirmative defenses include duress and contributory negligence (in a civil case) and insanity and self-defense (in a criminal case).

GENERAL INTENT: The intent to perform an act even though the actor does not desire the consequences that result. This is the state of mind required for the commission of certain common law crimes not requiring a specific intent or not imposing strict liability. General intent usually takes the form of recklessness (involving actual awareness of a risk and the culpable taking of that risk) or negligence (involving blameworthy inadvertence).

GENERAL INTENT CRIME: A crime that involves performing a particular act without intending a further act or a further result.

INSANITY: Any mental disorder severe enough that it prevents a person from having legal capacity and excuses the person from criminal or civil responsibility. Insanity is a legal, not a medical, standard.

JUSTIFICATION: A lawful or sufficient reason for one's acts or omissions.

SPECIFIC INTENT: The intent to accomplish the precise criminal act that one is later charged with.

State v. Cameron

(New Jersey) v. (Intoxicated Female Fighter)

104 N.J. 42, 514 A.2d 1302 (1986)

INTOXICATION MAY BE A DEFENSE TO KNOWING OR PURPOSEFUL BEHAVIOR

■**INSTANT FACTS** Cameron (D) assaulted McKinney, resisted arrest, and argued she was not guilty of the crimes she was accused of committing since she was too drunk to appreciate her actions.

■**BLACK LETTER RULE** By statute, intoxication may be a defense to crimes requiring either "purposeful" or "knowing" mental states, but the level of intoxication must be high enough to have caused "prostration of faculties."

■ **PROCEDURAL BASIS**

On appeal to the New Jersey Supreme Court from a reversal of the trial court's decision by the court of appeals.

■ **FACTS**

Defendant Cameron (D) approached five men playing cards in a vacant lot. Cameron (D) disrupted their card game, so the men moved their table. Cameron (D) followed them and turned over their table. The men set the table back up and resumed play. Cameron (D) then attacked one of the men, McKinney, with a broken bottle. McKinney received a permanent injury to his hand that required thirty-six stitches. When the police arrived, Cameron (D) continued to act violently and had to be restrained. Cameron (D) was indicted for second-degree aggravated assault, possession of a weapon (a broken bottle), and resisting arrest. She was convicted of all charges. On appeal, the appeals court found that Cameron's (D) voluntary intoxication negated an essential element of the crimes she was charged with—that of purposeful conduct—and reversed her conviction.

■ **ISSUE**

Can the element of purposeful conduct be negated by a finding of voluntary intoxication?

■ **DECISION AND RATIONALE**

(Clifford, J.) Yes. Each crime Cameron (D) was charged with required the element of purposeful conduct. The common law did not recognize intoxication as a defense to criminal conduct, although it did recognize that intoxication could be used to show an absence of specific intent. Problems arose when disputes arose over the distinctions between specific and general intent crimes. When New Jersey codified its criminal law, it provided that intoxication would *not* be a defense to a crime unless (1) it negated an element of the offense; (2) the actor was so intoxicated as to not be able to appreciate the reckless nature of his conduct; or (3) the intoxication was involuntary and existed to such a degree as to prevent the defendant (a) from appreciating the wrongfulness of his conduct, or (b) from conforming his conduct to

---

the law. The statute disregarded the distinction between specific and general intent crimes and concentrated on the four states of mind: negligence, recklessness, knowing, and purposeful. Negligence and recklessness approximate the common law standard applicable to general intent crimes. Knowing and purposeful approximate the standard relevant to specific intent crimes. Intoxication can only be a defense when it causes the actor to be unable to form the correlating state of mind.

The crimes that Cameron (D) is charged with committing in this case all require purposeful or knowing conduct. The question, then, is what level of intoxication must be shown before the defense of intoxication may be submitted to a jury. It must be noted that not everyone who has a few drinks will be able to avail himself or herself of this defense. The requisite state of intoxication will likely exist in only a few cases. Here, Cameron (D) apparently had a pint of wine that she was drinking, not alone, but with several others. Notwithstanding the defendant's violent conduct, there was no evidence that she was so drunk that she did not know what she was doing. Cameron (D) argued that her conduct was the result of an attack by McKinney and others, and that she did what she did in order to ward off their advances. This argument shows an appreciation for the circumstances that is inconsistent with a finding that Cameron (D) was too drunk to be capable of knowing or purposeful conduct. Reversed.

Analysis:

The court here endeavored to raise the bar on a defense of intoxication. While intoxication would be permitted to establish the defendant could not have formed the mental intent to commit the crime charged, the court is saying that the level of intoxication must be substantial, especially for general intent crimes. In *State v. Bauman*, 689 A.2d 173 (N.J. Super. Ct. App. Div. 1997), the court discussed the possible ways a defendant could establish the extent of his or her intoxication. While the court found the most common way to establish intoxication is by proof of a description of how much alcohol or drugs the defendant had consumed, courts have also accepted testimony of witnesses that establish the behavior of the defendant as "intoxicated" or "under the influence."

■ CASE VOCABULARY

INTOXICATION: A diminished ability to act with full mental and physical capabilities because of alcohol or drug consumption; drunkenness.

PURPOSEFUL: Done with a specific purpose in mind; deliberate.

Montana v. Egelhoff
(Prosecuting State) v. (Convicted Murder)

518 U.S. 37, 116 S.Ct. 2013 (1996)

EXCLUDING EVIDENCE OF VOLUNTARY INTOXICATION DOES NOT VIOLATE DUE PROCESS

This looks bad, hiccup, which is enough to convict in Montana.

stus.com

■**INSTANT FACTS** The defendant was convicted of "purposely or knowingly" causing death although he was intoxicated at the time.

■**BLACK LETTER RULE** A state may prohibit a defendant from having a jury consider evidence of voluntary intoxication in deciding an accused's mental state without violating a "fundamental principle of justice."

■ **PROCEDURAL BASIS**

On review to the U.S. Supreme Court following reversal of the defendant's conviction by the state supreme court.

■ **FACTS**

Egelhoff (D) was convicted of "purposely or knowingly" causing the death of another. Egelhoff (D) insisted that he was intoxicated at the time of the crime and could not have achieved the mental state required to commit the offense he was charged with. Following his conviction, Egelhoff (D) appealed to the Montana Supreme Court, where his conviction was overturned. The Montana Supreme Court held that Egelhoff's (D) intoxication was relevant to the offense and found that Egelhoff's (D) inability to present evidence to that effect violated his right to due process. The Montana court thereafter struck down the Montana law prohibiting Egelhoff (D) from introducing evidence of voluntary intoxication as unconstitutional. The prosecution appealed.

■ **ISSUE**

Does the exclusion of evidence establishing a mental element of an offense violate due process by applying a presumption of culpability rather than innocence?

■ **DECISION AND RATIONALE**

(Scalia, J.) No. A state has the right to exclude exculpatory evidence relative to a defendant's mental state. Reversed.

■ **CONCURRENCE**

(Ginsburg, J.) Montana's legislature has disallowed the defense of voluntary intoxication when determining a defendant's mental state when the mental state is an element of the crime charged. The dissent argues that any law designed to prevent the introduction of exculpatory

---

evidence offends due process. Of course, a state is free to redefine an offense and exclude whatever evidence it chooses to make irrelevant it to the crime. The real question here is not, however, whether the law prohibits rebuttal of evidence or redefines the mens rea of the crime. The issue is whether a state may choose to punish two actors who commit the same crime to the same extent when one commits the act sober and the other has voluntarily lost his self-control due to intoxication. The rule prohibiting the introduction of this evidence is not an evidentiary rule. The statute is included within the general rules of criminal liability. Its effect is to remove consideration of voluntary intoxication from a determination of mens rea. Under this structure, Montana need not prove a defendant caused the death of his victim "purposely or knowingly"; the prosecution need only show that the death resulted under circumstances where a person would have "purposely or knowingly" caused the death, but for the intoxication. Defining a crime's mens rea without regard to intoxication does not offend a "fundamental principle of justice." There is nothing constitutionally infirm about Montana's statute.

Analysis:

In *State v. Brown*, 931 P.2d 69 (N.M.1996), the defendant was on trial for committing depraved murder, defined as "the killing of one human being . . . by any act greatly dangerous to the lives of others, *indicating a depraved mind regardless of human life.*" At trial, Brown was prevented from presenting evidence of intoxication and its effect on his mental state. The New Mexico court determined that this offense required a state of mind somewhere between a specific and a general intent. The court concluded that, unlike the state of Montana in *Egelhoff*, the state of New Mexico did not have a statute precluding the use of evidence of intoxication as a defense to certain murder accusations. It was not free to cast aside evidence as to the defendant's mental state without similar clear instruction from the legislature.

■ CASE VOCABULARY

VOLUNTARY INTOXICATION: A willing ingestion of alcohol or drugs to the point of impairment done with the knowledge that one's physical and mental capabilities would be impaired. Voluntary intoxication is not a defense, but may be admitted to refute the existence of a particular state of mind.

CHAPTER FOUR

Causation

Regina v. Martin Dyos

Instant Facts: Martin Dyos (M.D.), a minor, and his friends started taunting R.M. at a youth dance and a fight broke out; as a result of a blow to the head delivered by M.D., R.M. died.

Black Letter Rule: Unless an injury can be linked with certainty to the actions of the defendant and the injury can be said with certainty to have caused the victim's death, the defendant cannot be held responsible for the death of the victim.

R. v. Benge

Instant Facts: A crew working to repair broken train track did not complete the repair in time for the arrival of the next train and, due to the negligence of the crew's flagman, an approaching train was not given enough warning to stop ahead of the crew, many of whom were killed.

Black Letter Rule: One with substantial culpability for an act cannot find an excuse for his negligence in others whose conduct, while perhaps negligent as well, was not material.

Hubbard v. Commonwealth

Instant Facts: Hubbard (D) was convicted of voluntary manslaughter following a scuffle between Hubbard (D) and the sheriff that caused the sheriff to suffer a fatal heart attack.

Black Letter Rule: When death or serious bodily harm was not a probable and natural consequence of the defendant's actions and other, more serious factors intervened to cause the victim's death, the defendant cannot be responsible for the death.

Commonwealth v. Rhoades

Instant Facts: Rhoades (D) was charged with setting fire to an apartment and with second-degree murder for the resulting death.

Black Letter Rule: For an arsonist to be held liable for a death resulting from his fire, the fire must have been the proximate cause of the victim's death, meaning that the fire was part of a natural and continuous sequence from which the death resulted and without which the death would not have occurred.

Commonwealth v. Root

Instant Facts: Two men engaged in a drag race on a stretch of highway; one racer tried to pass the other—Root (D)—in a no-passing zone and was struck head-on by a truck and killed.

Black Letter Rule: Tort law concepts of proximate cause are insufficient to impose criminal liability for death and serious injury; a more direct, causal connection between the illegal activity and the crime must be demonstrated.

United States v. Hamilton

Instant Facts: Hamilton (D) and the decedent began fighting and Hamilton (D) kicked the decedent in the head; at the hospital later that night, the decedent removed the tubes that were helping him breathe and died.

Black Letter Rule: One who engages in a fight with another and strikes a blow that may not be fatal, but that nonetheless starts a chain of events that leads to death, is guilty of homicide even if victim contributes to his own death or hastens it by failing to take proper treatment.

Stephenson v. State

Instant Facts: Stephenson (D) abducted Oberholtzer, who obtained poison and drank it in an effort to end her ordeal; Stephenson (D) was charged with second-degree murder.

Black Letter Rule: When a victim commits suicide during the course of a kidnapping, the defendant may not avoid responsibility for her death by establishing that the victim took poison voluntarily and caused her own death.

People v. Kevorkian

Instant Facts: Dr. Kevorkian (D) assisted two women who wanted to commit suicide and was charged with their murders.

Black Letter Rule: When a defendant's involvement in another's death is limited to the events leading up to the death, such as providing the means to commit suicide, the proper charge is assisting in a suicide, which may be prosecuted as a common-law felony in the absence of a statute that specifically prohibits assisting in a suicide.

Commonwealth v. Levesque

Instant Facts: When the defendants were unable to extinguish a fire they caused by knocking over a candle in the abandoned warehouse where they lived, they left the building but failed to report the fire; six fire fighters responding to a later emergency call lost their lives in the blaze, and the grand jury returned six involuntary manslaughter indictments against the defendants.

Black Letter Rule: An omission may form the basis for manslaughter where the defendant has a duty to act but fails to do so.

Regina v. Martin Dyos

(Prosecution) v. (Assailant)

Crim. L. Rev. 660–62 (1979)

WHEN MULTIPLE POTENTIAL CAUSES OF DEATH EXIST, THE DEFENDANT RESPONSIBLE FOR ONE OF THEM IS NOT CRIMINALLY LIABLE

■**INSTANT FACTS** Martin Dyos (M.D.), a minor, and his friends started taunting R.M. at a youth dance and a fight broke out; as a result of a blow to the head delivered by M.D., R.M. died.

■**BLACK LETTER RULE** Unless an injury can be linked with certainty to the actions of the defendant and the injury can be said with certainty to have caused the victim's death, the defendant cannot be held responsible for the death of the victim.

■ **PROCEDURAL BASIS**

On appeal from a trial court's determination that sufficient evidence had not been presented tending to establish M.D.'s responsibility for R.M.'s death.

■ **FACTS**

Several teenagers attended a community center dance. Two from one group of teens, R.M. and S.K., started acting cocky and showing off. These actions angered one of the boys in another group, B.T. B.T. and four of his friends started making insults and threats aimed at R.M., S.K. and the other five teenagers in their group. R.M. and S.K.'s group left the dance in search of a cab, with B.T. and his four friends following behind them, continuing to make threats. One of the B.T.'s group, M.D., as well as others, were seen picking up rocks, tossing them at R.M. and S.K.'s group. One of the rocks hit P.S. in the head. P.S. turned around and hit B.T.; a short fight ensued. R.M. and G.M., twin brothers, were left lying in the street bleeding from severe head injuries. The boys from B.T.'s group fled. One of R.M.'s injuries was caused when he was struck by M.D. with a brick. M.D. admitted hitting R.M. with the brick. Nine days after the fight, R.M. died. All the members of B.T.'s group were indicted and pleaded guilty to unlawful assembly. M.D. was also charged with murder. The autopsy concluded that R.M.'s injuries were slight, except for the two blows to the head, only one of which was admittedly delivered by M.D. Either blow could have been fatal; however, there was no way to determine which blow was first. At the close of the evidence, the defense argued that the jury should not be left to decide whether M.D. delivered the fatal blow or whether the blow was delivered by someone or something else. The trial court agreed.

■ **ISSUE**

Where two possible injuries could have been the cause of the victim's death and only one can be shown to be the act of the defendant, may the defendant be held responsible for the victim's death?

■ **DECISION AND RATIONALE**

(Cantley, J.) No. When the victim's death would have likely occurred without the actions of the defendant, the defendant cannot be held responsible for the death. Before submitting the case to a jury, the prosecution must show that the victim's death was *not* caused by some other injury or by the actions of some other actor. Here, the evidence established there was another injury that could have been the actual cause of death and that injury cannot be ascribed to the defendant. Affirmed.

Analysis:

In this case, the defense conceded that if the defendant's actions had led to the fatal act—such as M.D. chasing the decedent into the path of an oncoming car that struck and killed him—M.D. would be responsible for R.M.'s death. While this argument did not work against M.D., the argument might have been successful against B.T. B.T. encouraged his friends to go with him to pursue the first group of teenagers. It was B.T.'s encouragement that caused R.M. to be hit in the head and suffer the injuries, any one of which could have been the cause of R.M.'s death.

■ **CASE VOCABULARY**

BUT—FOR CAUSE: The cause without which the event could not have occurred.

R. v. Benge

(Prosecutor) v. (Foreman of Railroad Crew)

44 F. & F. 504 (Maidstone Crown Court 1865)

ONE WHOSE CONDUCT MATERIALLY CONTRIBUTES TO A DEATH IS NOT EXCUSED BY EVIDENCE OF THE NEGLIGENCE OF OTHERS

■**INSTANT FACTS** A crew working to repair broken train track did not complete the repair in time for the arrival of the next train and, due to the negligence of the crew's flagman, an approaching train was not given enough warning to stop ahead of the crew, many of whom were killed.

■**BLACK LETTER RULE** One with substantial culpability for an act cannot find an excuse for his negligence in others whose conduct, while perhaps negligent as well, was not material.

■ PROCEDURAL BASIS

Before the trial court to determine responsibility for the train derailment.

■ FACTS

Benge (D) was the foreman of a crew engaged to fix a portion of train track, including the line leading to Staplehurst. Benge (D) had a train schedule and a work manual and was free to decide when the work should be done. The arrival of the train at Staplehurst varied with the tide. On the day of the accident, the trains were due at Staplehurst at 3:15 p.m. Benge (D) misread the schedule and determined the train's arrival time based on the next day's schedule. Thinking he had more time to complete the work than he did, he started a crew working on the job. While it was customary for a crew removing track to send a flagman a distance up the track to signal an oncoming train to stop with sufficient distance, the flagman on this crew was not sent far enough down the track. Moreover, the train's engineer was not keeping a sharp lookout and did not notice the flagman until it was too late. At the time the train reached the spot where the track was missing, it was traveling at fifty miles per hour. The train derailed and many workers were killed. At trial, Benge (D) argued that, as foreman, he had done nothing criminal, and that had the members of his crew adequately done their jobs and warned the approaching train, the accident would have been avoided.

■ ISSUE

Does the minor negligence of others contributing to an accident excuse the primary actor from liability for his or her own negligent behavior?

■ DECISION AND RATIONALE

(Pigott, J.) No. If the defendant materially contributed to the accident, it is irrelevant that others were also negligent and contributed to the accident's occurrence. If the defendant's actions were primarily responsible for the deaths of the crewmembers, criminal liability will be imposed. To hold otherwise would be to allow the incident to go unpunished because of the interaction of more than one actor. In this case, the absence of the tracks was the primary cause of the accident. The tracks had been removed because of the defendant's miscalculation of the train's arrival. While other safeguards should have been in place to avoid an accident, they did not serve to alleviate the defendant's responsibility for the job and the resulting accident. The crew foreman is guilty.

Analysis:

Compare the result in this case with the result in *Regina v. Martin Dyos*, Crim. L. Rev. 660–62 (1979). In *Dyos*, the defendant was not held responsible for the victim's death because the prosecution could not show with reasonable certainty that the injury inflicted by M.D. was the injury that caused the death of R.M. Here, while the foreman was certainly not the only negligent person at the worksite, the court chose to find him the "most negligent," and thus criminally responsible for the deaths of the workers. While the result in *Dyos* seems inconsistent with the result here, the individual defendants in *Dyos* were only responsible for their individual actions, whereas the foreman here was responsible for the entire job. Consequently, it was not improper to hold him responsible for the deaths of those on his crew.

Hubbard v. Commonwealth

(Unruly Drunk) v. (State of Kentucky)

304 Ky. 818, 202 S.W.2d 634 (1947)

WHEN INTERVENING ACTIONS CAUSE A VICTIM'S DEATH, THE DEFENDANT IS
ABSOLVED FROM RESPONSIBILITY

■INSTANT FACTS Hubbard (D) was convicted of voluntary manslaughter following a scuffle between Hubbard (D) and the sheriff that caused the sheriff to suffer a fatal heart attack.

■BLACK LETTER RULE When death or serious bodily harm was not a probable and natural consequence of the defendant's actions and other, more serious factors intervened to cause the victim's death, the defendant cannot be responsible for the death.

■ **PROCEDURAL BASIS**

Appeal from the circuit court's conviction of Hubbard (D) for voluntary manslaughter.

■ **FACTS**

When Hubbard (D) was home on leave from the Army, he was arrested for public drunkenness and ordered to jail to sober up and then stand trial. Dyche, a jailer, and Newman, his deputy, attempted to get Hubbard (D) to jail, but he resisted. After considerable effort, Dyche backed away and asked for help. When Hubbard (D) was finally restrained, though still belligerent, Dyche followed the group as they attempted to transport Hubbard (D) to jail. Dyche followed them out of the courthouse but then sat down with his hand over his heart. He fell to the ground and died of a heart attack within thirty minutes. Dyche had complained of a heart condition for some time and had told a friend several hours before the incident that he was not feeling well. The doctors determined that Dyche died of acute dilatation of the heart, accelerated by physical exercise and excitement. Hubbard (D) was found guilty of voluntary manslaughter and sentenced to two years in prison.

■ **ISSUE**

When an intervening cause not attributable to the defendant's acts is responsible for a victim's death, may the defendant nonetheless be held criminally responsible?

■ **DECISION AND RATIONALE**

(Stanley, Comm'r.) No. Hubbard (D) was charged with the commission of a misdemeanor that resulted in Dyche's death, and the misdemeanor was not the kind generally considered to result in death. On appeal, the attorney general conceded that the defendant should have received an instruction on involuntary manslaughter, since he doubts he was guilty of culpable homicide. Courts have held individuals responsible for causing death through fright or shock, but such responsibility is distinguishable from a situation in which an intervening cause leads to death and the initial actor is blameless. In a previous case, a woman died following the premature birth of her infant, which was caused by hearing a gun discharge. In that case, there was no liability on the part of the shooter because death was not the probable consequence of hearing a gunshot. In *Letner v. State*, by contrast, the defendant fired a gun near a boat to scare the passengers. Out of fear, one of the occupants jumped into the river, overturning the boat and drowning the other occupants. The court found the shooter responsible for causing their deaths since he had set in motion a chain of events, ultimately causing death of another. Based on these and other cases, when there is no physical contact or hostile act toward the victim, there can be no criminal liability unless the death or injury is a "probable and natural consequence" of the actions of the defendant. Here, the defendant's actions are remote. Dyche's death resulted from heart disease; Dyche continued to perform tasks he should have known to avoid. Once he felt the pain in his chest, he continued to writhe around, rather than lying still to allow the pain to subside. The actions of the defendant are not sufficiently proximate to support criminal liability. Reversed.

Analysis:

This case can be contrasted with *Adcock v. Commonwealth*, 702 S.W.2d 440 (Ky. 1986), in which the defendant broke in to the home of an elderly woman, intending to burglarize it. Finding the eighty-year old victim at home, the defendant also raped and beat her. She died twenty-nine days later. In that case, the court found the defendant guilty of her murder, holding that infliction of injury is a direct cause of death to the extent that injury hastens death and causes it to occur sooner rather than later, even though the person suffers from serious maladies from which he or she will eventually die. In such cases, the hastening of death that would not otherwise have occurred at the time is the cause of death.

■ CASE VOCABULARY

INTERVENING CAUSE: An event that comes between the initial event in a sequence and the end result, thereby altering the natural course of events that might have connected a wrongful act to an injury. If the intervening cause is strong enough to relieve the wrongdoer of any liability, it becomes a *superseding cause*. A *dependent intervening cause* is one that is not an act and is never a superseding cause. An *independent intervening cause* is one that operates on a condition produced by an antecedent cause but in no way resulted from that cause.

PROXIMATE CAUSE: A cause that is legally sufficient to result in liability; a cause that directly produces an event and without which the event would not have occurred.

VOLUNTARY MANSLAUGHTER: An act of murder reduced to manslaughter because of extenuating circumstances, such as adequate provocation (arousing the "heat of passion") or diminished capacity.

Commonwealth v. Rhoades
(State of Massachusetts) v. (Arsonist)

401 N.E.2d 342 (Mass. 1980)

THE DEFENDANT'S ACTIONS MUST BE THE PROXIMATE CAUSE OF THE VICTIM'S DEATH

■**INSTANT FACTS** Rhoades (D) was charged with setting fire to an apartment and with second-degree murder for the resulting death.

■**BLACK LETTER RULE** For an arsonist to be held liable for a death resulting from his fire, the fire must have been the proximate cause of the victim's death, meaning that the fire was part of a natural and continuous sequence from which the death resulted and without which the death would not have occurred.

■ **PROCEDURAL BASIS**

On appeal following a conviction for second-degree murder.

■ **FACTS**

The fire department responded to a three-alarm blaze and Captain Trainor, wearing standard gear, entered the burning building in an attempt to rescue anyone trapped inside. In the process of the rescue, Trainor encountered heavy smoke and intense heat and had difficulty getting air through his mask. Trainor collapsed on the roof of the building and was taken to a local hospital where he was pronounced dead. Medical testimony established his death was due to coronary thrombosis caused by a combination of smoke inhalation, cold weather, and stress. Fire investigators determined the fire was due to arson. Rhoades (D) was charged with the arson and with second-degree murder for Trainor's death. The trial judge instructed the jury that if they found that Trainor died "as a result" of Rhoades's (D) act or that his act played a part in causing Trainor's death, Rhoades (D) should be found guilty.

■ **ISSUE**

May a jury be instructed that, regardless of how remote the link, any evidence of the defendant's involvement in the chain of events leading to the victim's death is sufficient to support a conviction?

■ **DECISION AND RATIONALE**

(Abrams, J.) No. The upshot of the jury's instruction was that, should the jury find Rhoades (D) even remotely responsible for Trainor's death, he should be found guilty. This is a misstatement of the law and the misimpression it created was not corrected by the other instructions given. The jury should have been instructed that the proximate cause of the fire captain's death needed to be attributed to the defendant's act of starting the fire. While the judge emphasized that the fire need not be the sole cause of the captain's death, the judge's failure to clearly instruct the jury that the defendant's conduct must be the proximate cause—

---

the cause that necessarily sets in operation the factors which caused the death—was error. The judgment is reversed, the verdict set aside, and the case remanded.

Analysis:

In *Commonwealth. v. Osachuk*, 681 N.E.2d 292, 294 (Mass. App. Ct. 1997), another Massachusetts court addressed the effect of two potential causes of injury. The court decided there that, "[w]hen the conduct of two or more persons contributes concurrently to the death, the conduct of each is the proximate cause, regardless of the extent to which each contributes." On retrial of the present case, the likelihood is that Rhoades's (D) action of starting the fire will be deemed the proximate cause of the captain's death unless evidence is presented of the firefighter's poor physical condition or a malfunction of his breathing equipment.

■ **CASE VOCABULARY**

ARSON: Under modern statutes, the intentional and wrongful burning of someone else's property (as to destroy a building) or one's own property (as to fraudulently collect insurance).

Commonwealth v. Root

(State of Pennsylvania) v. (Illegal Car Racer)

403 Pa. 571, 170 A.2d 310 (1961)

CRIMINAL AND TORT PROXIMATE CAUSE ARE DIFFERENT STANDARDS

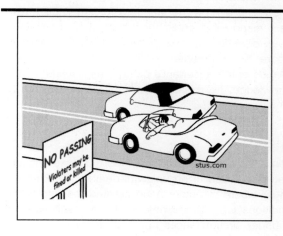

■INSTANT FACTS Two men engaged in a drag race on a stretch of highway; one racer tried to pass the other—Root (D)—in a no-passing zone and was struck head-on by a truck and killed.

■BLACK LETTER RULE Tort law concepts of proximate cause are insufficient to impose criminal liability for death and serious injury; a more direct, causal connection between the illegal activity and the crime must be demonstrated.

■ PROCEDURAL BASIS

On appeal from the sentencing entered on the jury's verdict.

■ FACTS

Root (D) was challenged by the deceased to an auto race. The two men drove on a rural three-lane highway with a speed limit of fifty miles per hour, but the racing drivers were traveling at speeds between seventy and ninety miles per hour. Just before the accident, Root (D) was in the lead, traveling in the right lane. The deceased attempted to pass Root (D) in a no-passing zone as they approached a bridge where the highway narrowed. As the deceased tried to pass, a truck appeared in the oncoming lane of traffic; the deceased crossed the yellow line, struck the truck, and was killed. Root (D) was tried and found guilty of involuntary manslaughter for another's death in the course of an auto race.

■ ISSUE

Is it appropriate to hold a defendant responsible for the victim's death when the victim's own reckless conduct led to his death?

■ DECISION AND RATIONALE

(Jones, C. J.) No. The record was full of evidence sufficient to support a conviction for speeding, reckless driving, and other vehicle code violations. However, reckless conduct is only one element of a charge of involuntary manslaughter. Another element requires that the reckless conduct be the *direct* cause of the victim's death. This element is clearly lacking. No previous cases have been found where involuntary manslaughter charges were pursued on similar facts. The closest case factually is *Commonwealth v. Levin*, where the conviction for involuntary manslaughter was sustained. In *Levin*, in contrast with this case, Levin made the driving maneuvers that led to the crash. Here, the decedent himself recklessly swerved his own car in an attempt to pass Root (D) and drove into the path of an oncoming car. The decedent's actions, and his alone, led to his death.

Tort law concepts of liability cannot be used in determining causation in a criminal matter. Proximate cause in tort law is a much looser standard that, if applied in the criminal arena, would serve to impose criminal liability for actions that are generally not considered likely to cause death. To allow the same concepts that would impose liability in a tort matter to serve as a predicate for criminal liability is too harsh. But even if the standard for tort liability were used here, the defendant would not be held responsible given the effect of a supervening cause—the decedent's own negligence. It was error for the trial judge to refuse to allow the jury to consider the decedent's lack of care as a defense to Root's (D) liability. The defendant's conduct was not the proximate cause of the decedent's death. The decedent knew his actions were dangerous; despite that knowledge, he passed Root's (D) car, causing the head-on collision that led to his death. Reversed.

■ DISSENT

(Eagen, J.) The majority admits that at the time the accident occurred, Root (D) was engaged in reckless conduct. There may be more than one cause of an unlawful death. Had Root (D) not engaged in an illegal car race, the danger would not have been created that led to the accident. The victim's response to the conditions was foreseeable and the result was not harsh. If the accident would have occurred under circumstances not likely to result in death, the majority's result would be correct. However, the result of car racing is too often injury to passengers and other motorists on the road. The decedent was clearly foolhardy in his actions, but he is not solely to blame.

Analysis:

This case is similar to *Hubbard v. Commonwealth*, 304 Ky. 818 (1947), 202 S.W.2d 634, in which the court noted that the sheriff had apparently known of his heart condition and chose to engage in the scuffle with Hubbard nonetheless; further, once the sheriff began feeling pain, he took no action to protect himself. Here, certainly the two racers both broke the law by racing, but the decedent understood the rules of the road and the dangers posed by driving into on-coming traffic.

■ CASE VOCABULARY

ALLOCATUR: It is allowed. This word formerly indicated that a writ, bill, or other pleading was allowed. It is still used today in Pennsylvania to denote permission to appeal.

DIRECT [PROXIMATE] CAUSE: A cause that is legally sufficient to result in liability; an act or omission that is considered in law to result in a consequence, so that liability can be imposed on the actor; a cause that directly produces an event and without which the event would not have occurred.

SUPERVENING [INTERVENING] CAUSE: An event that comes between the initial event in a sequence and the end result, thereby altering the natural course of events that might have connected a wrongful act to an injury. If the intervening cause is strong enough to relieve the wrongdoer of any liability, it becomes a *superseding cause*. A *dependent intervening cause* is one that is not an act and is never a superseding cause. An *independent intervening cause* is one that operates on a condition produced by an antecedent cause but in no way resulted from that cause.

United States v. Hamilton

(Prosecuting Government) v. (Poolroom Brawler)

182 F. Supp. 548 (D.D.C. 1960)

STRIKING A BLOW THAT LEADS TO A CHAIN OF EVENTS ENDING IN DEATH IS HOMICIDE

■**INSTANT FACTS** Hamilton (D) and the decedent began fighting and Hamilton (D) kicked the decedent in the head; at the hospital later that night, the decedent removed the tubes that were helping him breathe and died.

■**BLACK LETTER RULE** One who engages in a fight with another and strikes a blow that may not be fatal, but that nonetheless starts a chain of events that leads to death, is guilty of homicide even if victim contributes to his own death or hastens it by failing to take proper treatment.

■ **PROCEDURAL BASIS**

Trial for manslaughter.

■ **FACTS**

A number of men were gathered in a poolroom. The decedent and the defendant were both part of that group. One of their conversations developed into an intense argument between Hamilton (D) and the decedent, and both men were asked to leave. Outside, the two started fighting. The decedent was knocked to the ground and Hamilton (D) began kicking him in the face. The decedent was taken to a hospital where he was in shock. He was looked after by the chief neurological resident, and was given a transfusion and breathing assistance; he was also restrained to keep him from injuring himself. During the night, the decedent's bed became soiled with blood and had to be changed, which made it necessary to remove the patient's restraints. Since the patient was resting calmly, the staff decided the patient did not need to be restrained again. Early in the morning, the patient had a convulsion and, in the process, pulled out the breathing tubes. He died an hour later from asphyxia due to bleeding into his airways—a condition the breathing tubes were meant to avoid. Hamilton (D) argued that the decedent caused his own death when he pulled his breathing tubes out.

■ **ISSUE**

Is a defendant guilty of homicide when he injures the victim and sets in motion a chain of events that includes actions by the decedent that lead to his own death?

■ **DECISION AND RATIONALE**

(Holtzoff, J.) Yes. It is well established that one who sets in motion a chain of events leading to death is guilty of homicide. There is no exception to this rule for the situation in which the victim fails to receive adequate care or treatment. The defendant argues that the decedent here did not simply fail to seek medical assistance, but actively caused his own death by pulling out the breathing tubes. It is unclear whether the actions of the decedent were

---

deliberate, conscious acts, or whether they were involuntary reflexes. Whether or not the decedent would have lived had he not removed the breathing tubes is, however, irrelevant. In *People v. Lewis*, the decedent had been shot; rather than wait to die, the decedent slit his own throat, hastening death. The defendant there was still responsible for the decedent's death, as the decedent merely brought about his own death sooner rather than later. Similarly, in *Stephenson v. State*, the decedent was raped; because of her trauma, she drank poison and died. The court found the defendant responsible for her death since her despondency was a likely result of the abuse by the defendant. Since Hamilton (D) here inflicted the injuries upon the decedent that caused his death, he should be held responsible for that death, rather than just for the initial assault.

Analysis:

This case may appear to conflict with *Hubbard v. Commonwealth*, 304 Ky. 818, 202 S.W.2d 634 (1947), but in *Hubbard* the court noted that the decedent was well aware of his heart problems. The *Hubbard* decedent arguably could have had a heart attack at any time. Here, however, the decedent died from injuries he could only have received from the blows delivered by the defendant.

■ CASE VOCABULARY

MANSLAUGHTER: The unlawful killing of a human being without malice aforethought.

A KIDNAPPER IS CRIMINALLY REPONSIBLE FOR THE VICTIM'S SUICIDE

You kidnapped, assaulted, bit, and attempted to rape her. Then, you refused to take her to the hospital when she tried to commit suicide to stop her suffering. Now, you're trying to avoid responsibility for her death.

stus.com

Wow, when you put it that way, it sounds bad.

■**INSTANT FACTS** Stephenson (D) abducted Oberholtzer, who obtained poison and drank it in an effort to end her ordeal; Stephenson (D) was charged with second-degree murder.

■**BLACK LETTER RULE** When a victim commits suicide during the course of a kidnapping, the defendant may not avoid responsibility for her death by establishing that the victim took poison voluntarily and caused her own death.

■ **PROCEDURAL BASIS**

On appeal from a conviction for second-degree murder.

■ **FACTS**

Stephenson (D), with the help of several accomplices, abducted Oberholtzer. For days, Stephenson (D) assaulted, bit, and attempted to rape her. Unbeknownst to Stephenson (D), Oberholtzer found and ingested bicholoride of mercury. She became violently ill and Stephenson (D) refused to take her to the hospital. Instead, Stephenson (D) decided to take her back home. During a long car ride, Oberholtzer screamed in pain, but Stephenson (D) did nothing to help her. On returning home, Oberholtzer received medical attention; however, it was too late and she died. The death resulted from a combination of lack of food and sleep, the effect of the poison, lack of early treatment, and the ills Oberholtzer suffered at Stephenson's (D) hands.

■ **ISSUE**

Can a defendant avoid criminal responsibility for a death occurring during the course of a kidnapping, where the kidnapping victim took poison because of the mental stress caused by the treatment she received at the hands of the defendant?

■ **DECISION AND RATIONALE**

(Per curiam.) No. Stephenson (D) argues that the day he brought Oberholtzer to the hotel, she was able to leave and voluntarily returned after making purchases, including the poison. When Oberholtzer drank the poison, he was in a separate room. As a result, Oberholtzer's own actions broke the chain of events that would have made him responsible for her death, he claims. Many previous cases have established the fact that when a defendant causes physical and mental injuries and suicide follows, the defendant is responsible for the suicide as though it were murder. Here, while Stephenson (D) did not accompany Oberholtzer on her shopping trip, she was accompanied by one of Stephenson's (D) associates, who would not likely have allowed her to avoid returning to the hotel. At no time could Oberholtzer feel that she was able to walk away from Stephenson (D) and avoid further harm. To say there was no connection between the actions of Stephenson (D) and the death of Oberholtzer would be a miscarriage of justice. The conduct of the defendant was such that it was sufficient to render the deceased distracted and mentally incompetent. The result should have been expected and so, appellant is appropriately found guilty of second-degree murder. Affirmed.

Analysis:

This case is consistent with the decision rendered in United States v. Hamilton, 182 F. Supp. 548 (D.C. D.C. 1960), in which the decedent was hospitalized following a fight with the defendant. He died after he pulled out his breathing tubes during a convulsion. Just as the court in *Hamilton* had no problem finding the defendant responsible for placing the decedent in the position where he suffered the convulsion that caused him to be a threat to his own mortality, similarly Oberholtzer's kidnapper could not complain that she took her own life. Had Stephenson (D) not kidnapped Oberholtzer, the thought of suicide may never have crossed her mind.

■ **CASE VOCABULARY**

PER CURIAM: By the court as a whole.

KIDNAP: To seize and take away (a person) by force or fraud, often with a demand for ransom.

People v. Kevorkian

(State of Michigan) v. (Suicide–Assisting Doctor)

527 N.W.2d 714 (Mich. 1994)

ASSISTING WITH A SUICIDE IS NOT MURDER

■**INSTANT FACTS** Dr. Kevorkian (D) assisted two women who wanted to commit suicide and was charged with their murders.

■**BLACK LETTER RULE** When a defendant's involvement in another's death is limited to the events leading up to the death, such as providing the means to commit suicide, the proper charge is assisting in a suicide, which may be prosecuted as a common-law felony in the absence of a statute that specifically prohibits assisting in a suicide.

■ **PROCEDURAL BASIS**

Appeal from the grant of the defendant's motion to dismiss the murder charges concerning assisted suicides.

■ **FACTS**

Before Michigan enacted its statute regarding assisted suicide, Dr. Kevorkian (D) assisted Miller and Wantz in committing suicide. Each woman was suffering from a painful condition and sought out Kevorkian (D) for help. The defendant met both women at a cabin. Kevorkian brought a device to the cabin to assist with the suicides. The patients' arms were strapped to a board and an IV needle was placed into their arms. Controls were designed to allow the patient to begin dispensing chemicals into their blood that would help them fall asleep; the patients were then administered a dose of potassium chloride sufficient to cause death. The defendant could not get the IV started for Miller, so he left the cabin and returned with a cylinder of carbon monoxide and explained the mechanism to her. Kevorkian (D) successfully started the IV for Wantz and connected her to his "machine." The device was activated and Wantz died. He then placed a mask on Miller's face and handed her a screwdriver to activate the flow of gas. Miller's cause of death was determined to be carbon monoxide poisoning. Kevorkian (D) was indicted on two counts of murder. Following his preliminary examination, Kevorkian (D) moved to dismiss the charges; the court granted his motion. On appeal, the court reversed.

■ **ISSUE**

Was the information charging the defendant with murder for physician-assisted suicide appropriately quashed under Michigan law?

■ **DECISION AND RATIONALE**

(Cavanagh, C.J.) Yes. The decision from the court of appeals was based on People v. Roberts, 178 N.W. 690 (1920). In *Roberts*, the defendant's wife was suffering from advanced multiple sclerosis and asked him to provide her with poison. He presented her with a glass of poison that she then drank and died. Roberts was charged with murder and pleaded guilty. On appeal, the court found that by proffering the poison within the reach of his wife, the husband was guilty. Her request was of no legal effect, since without his assistance Roberts' wife would have had no other means to end her life.

Legally defined, murder is committed by performing an act that results in death. The death must be the natural and direct result of the act performed. Few jurisdictions hold to the precedent that assisting in a suicide is the equivalent of murder; most treat assisting a suicide as a separate crime. Those jurisdictions that do prosecute assisting a suicide as murder usually do so only when the actions surpass assisting with the preparations, such as in *People v. Cleaves*, where the defendant strangled his friend. The distinction between murder and assisting in a suicide lies in the degree of participation in the death. In the California case of *In re Joseph G.*, the court explained that a murder conviction is appropriate if the defendant participates in the final act leading to death—e.g., firing a gun or administering poison. Passive participation qualifies as aiding a suicide; active participation qualifies as murder. Michigan courts have tailored the common law in order to tie responsibility with the act, which also needs to be done here. Accordingly, *Roberts* is overruled. When a defendant merely participates in the provision of the means to commit suicide, the proper charge is assisting a suicide, not murder. Reversed (reinstating trial court decision).

■ DISSENT

(Boyle, J.) The majority has redefined the statutory offense of murder so that it no longer includes participation in the events leading to death. Consent still remains unavailable as a defense to murder. The acts performed by the defendant here did cause death as *a natural and direct result*, so the majority was incorrect in quashing the information. One who participates in causing the death of another should be charged with murder, regardless of the deceased's consent. At the time the defendant committed these offenses, the legislature had given no indication that assisted suicide should be treated any differently than murder. The majority's decision makes this change for the legislature. The plaintiff's actions "were both the cause in fact and the proximate or foreseeable cause of the decedents' deaths." The majority has now created a special rule for assisted suicides and has taken away from the jury and the legislature those considerations that should be addressed by them. Victims of these types of acts should get at least the same protection as is afforded their defendants. By reducing criminal liability for those who assist suicides, protection of the vulnerable is sacrificed.

Analysis:

In this case, Dr. Kevorkian enjoyed a victory to the extent that the court overruled People v. Roberts, 211 Mich. 187 (1920), 178 N.W. 690. However, his streak of "successes" ended shortly after this case, when he was held guilty of the crime of delivering a controlled substance without a license. Physician-assisted suicide continues to be a hotly debated social issue.

■ CASE VOCABULARY

ASSISTED SUICIDE: The intentional act of providing a person with the medical means or the medical knowledge to commit suicide. Also termed (when a doctor provides the means) PHYSICIAN–ASSISTED SUICIDE.

Commonwealth v. Levesque
(Prosecuting Authority) v. (Criminal Defendant)

436 Mass. 443 (Mass. 2002)

A PERSON'S FAILURE TO ALLEVIATE A RISK HE OR SHE CREATED CAN LEAD TO CRIMINAL LIABILITY

Should we call 9-1-1?

Nah, we might get in trouble.

stus.com

■**INSTANT FACTS** When the defendants were unable to extinguish a fire they caused by knocking over a candle in the abandoned warehouse where they lived, they left the building but failed to report the fire; six fire fighters responding to a later emergency call lost their lives in the blaze, and the grand jury returned six involuntary manslaughter indictments against the defendants.

■**BLACK LETTER RULE** An omission may form the basis for manslaughter where the defendant has a duty to act but fails to do so.

■ PROCEDURAL BASIS

State appellate court review of the lower court's dismissal of the indictments against the defendants.

■ FACTS

Levesque (D) and Barnes (D) lived together in a room on the second floor of an abandoned five-story warehouse. They had no electricity, and the windows were boarded up, so they used candles for light. One day, the defendants got into a physical altercation that resulted in their knocking over a lit candle. A fire started and the defendants were unable to put it out. The fire spread rapidly. The defendants left the warehouse, but did not report the fire to authorities, even though they passed several open businesses with phones. The fire was not reported until a couple hours later by an emergency caller. When they arrived on the scene, the fire fighters were informed there could be homeless persons inside, so they entered the flaming warehouse. During their efforts to locate possible inhabitants and combat the fire, six fire fighters lost their lives. Levesque (D) and Barnes (D) were charged with involuntary manslaughter, but moved to dismiss the indictments. The judge allowed the dismissals, ruling that the defendants had no legal duty to report the fire. The commonwealth appealed.

■ ISSUE

Was the evidence sufficient to support the degree of wanton and reckless conduct necessary for a manslaughter prosecution?

■ DECISION AND RATIONALE

(Cowin, J.) Yes. An omission may form the basis for manslaughter where the defendant has a duty to act but fails to do so. A duty to prevent harm to others arises when one creates a dangerous situation, whether the situation was intentionally or negligently created. According to the Restatement (Second) of Torts, if one does an act and then realizes, or should realize, that the act created an unreasonable risk of causing physical harm to another, he has a duty to use reasonable care to prevent the risk from taking effect. When one's actions create a life-threatening risk to another, there is a duty to take reasonable steps to alleviate the risk. And when a defendant's failure to exercise reasonable care to prevent the risk he created is reckless and results in death, the defendant can be convicted of involuntary manslaughter.

Here the defendants started the fire and then increased the risk of harm by allowing the fire to burn, without taking steps to control or report it. It is for the jury to decide whether the defendants' failure to take additional steps was reasonable, and if so, whether the omission was wanton or reckless.We have previously held that an arsonist can be charged with the murder of a fire fighter who responds to the resulting fire if the defendant's conduct was the cause that necessarily set in operation the factors that caused the death. The commonwealth presented sufficient evidence here that the delay permitted the fire to smolder and spread within the building, increasing the severity of the risk. Even a layperson knows that a fire spreads and becomes more dangerous the longer it is left unattended. The order allowing the motions to dismiss is reversed and the case is remanded.

Analysis:

Sometimes, when formulatingduties in the criminal context, the courts have drawn on well-established duties imposed by civil tort law. This is generally done only when several critical factors are present, particularly an unreasonable risk of harm to others (as in this case). The factors considered in determining whether tort-law application is appropriate include whether (1) civil law creates a specific duty applicable to the criminal situation at hand; (2) other jurisdictions have recognized this particular civil principle as a basis for criminal liability; (3) the courts of the forum state have previously expressed agreement with the underlying civil principle in a similar situation, even if they did not explicitly adopt it; and (4) public policy requires the application of the civil principle to the criminal context in order to deter conduct creating an unreasonable risk of danger to others.

■ CASE VOCABULARY

ARSON: Under modern statutes, the intentional and wrongful burning of someone else's property (as to destroy a building) or one's own property (as to fraudulently collect insurance).

CHAPTER FIVE

Intentional Homicide

Francis v. Franklin

Instant Facts: Raymond Lee Franklin (D) escaped from prison during a trip to the dentist and, in the course of his escape, shot and killed a man and was tried for murder.

Black Letter Rule: Shifting the burden of proof on an essential element of a criminal case back to the defendant violates the Due Process Clause.

United States v. Watson

Instant Facts: Watson (D) shot and killed an officer pursuing him on suspicion of car theft.

Black Letter Rule: A finding of premeditation and deliberation does not require evidence of the passage of days or hours, but simply a showing of any opportunity during which the defendant had the time to consider his actions.

People v. Walker

Instant Facts: Walker (D) was sitting on a porch with several others when they were approached by Stenneth, who demanded they gamble with him; when they refused, Stenneth became violent and Walker (D) killed him.

Black Letter Rule: When a defendant kills his victim after provocation and without a "cooling off" period, the defendant is guilty of manslaughter rather than murder.

Ex Parte Fraley

Instant Facts: Dan Parker was talking with some other gentlemen when Fraley (D) shot him, nine or ten months after Parker had shot and killed Fraley's (D) son.

Black Letter Rule: Provocation that occurred nine or ten months before a killing will not reduce the charges to manslaughter, since a deliberate killing in revenge is murder.

Rowland v. State

Instant Facts: When Rowland (D) discovered his estranged wife in bed with another man, he fired a shot at his wife's lover, but killed his wife instead.

Black Letter Rule: Finding one's spouse in the act of adultery provides sufficient provocation to reduce a charge of murder to manslaughter.

People v. Berry

Instant Facts: Shortly after being married, Berry's (D) wife began taunting him about leaving the marriage for another man; after one such episode, Berry (D) strangled her.

Black Letter Rule: A jury should be instructed on the "heat of passion" defense where evidence is offered that supports a continuous pattern of emotional torture that could accumulate into sufficient provocation.

People v. Wu

Instant Facts: Helen Wu (D) killed her young son and tried to commit suicide rather than bring him back to her native land, where she felt they would be mistreated.

Black Letter Rule: The jury may be instructed to consider evidence of the defendant's cultural background in determining the mental state of the defendant at the time of a killing.

Francis v. Franklin

(Warden) v. (Prisoner—Escapee)

471 U.S. 307, 105 S.Ct. 1965 (1985)

THE PROSECUTION BEARS THE BURDEN OF PROOF IN CRIMINAL CASES

■**INSTANT FACTS** Raymond Lee Franklin (D) escaped from prison during a trip to the dentist and, in the course of his escape, shot and killed a man and was tried for murder.

■**BLACK LETTER RULE** Shifting the burden of proof on an essential element of a criminal case back to the defendant violates the Due Process Clause.

■ **PROCEDURAL BASIS**

On appeal from grant of certiorari following issuance of a writ of habeas corpus by the Eleventh Circuit.

■ **FACTS**

Raymond Lee Franklin (D) devised a plan to escape from prison while he and three other inmates were taken from the prison to the dentist. To receive treatment, Franklin (D) was released from his shackles. The guard made the mistake of releasing the next prisoner for treatment before securing Franklin (D). Franklin (D) grabbed a weapon from one of the guards and escaped, using the dental assistant as a hostage. Unable to steal the dentist's car, Franklin (D) and the hygienist fled on foot. Franklin (D) tried stealing a different car but was again unsuccessful. He went to the home of Collie, a seventy-two-year-old retiree, and demanded his car. When Collie slammed the door on him, Franklin's (D) gun discharged and the bullet went through the door, killing Collie. The noise summoned Collie's wife. In the confusion, the hygienist fled the scene. Collie's wife refused to give Franklin (D) the car keys, as did Collie's daughter, who happened on the scene. Franklin (D) then just left the house. When Franklin (D) was captured, he gave a statement in which he admitted to shooting Collie. He insisted the shooting was not intentional and that his lack of desire to hurt anyone was supported by the absence of any further injuries. Franklin (D) was tried for kidnapping and malice murder.

The jury received the following instruction at trial: "The acts of a person of sound mind and discretion are presumed to be the product of the person's will, but the presumption may be rebutted. A person of sound mind and discretion is presumed to intend the natural and probable consequences of his acts but the presumption may be rebutted. A person will not be presumed to act with criminal intention but the trier of facts, that is, the Jury, may find criminal intention upon a consideration of the words, conduct, demeanor, motive and all other circumstances connected with the act for which the accused is prosecuted." An hour after the jury was instructed on the case, the jurors requested further instruction on "intent" and "accident." The jury deliberated ten more minutes and returned a verdict of guilty.

■ ISSUE

May a judge instruct a jury in such a way as to create the impression that, on proof of a minimum of facts, a mandatory presumption must be made, shifting the burden of persuasion to the defendant on the element of intent?

■ DECISION AND RATIONALE

(Brennan, J.) No. The instruction here appears to be a command; the jury was not told it had a choice in its decision, but rather was told the law presumed a certain conclusion. The instruction directs the jury to presume an essential element of the crime charged—intent—simply from proof that someone died. This serves to undermine the jury's responsibility to find the facts beyond a reasonable doubt. The jury was told the presumptions could be rebutted; however, the addition of that phrase does not cure the infirmity of the instruction. Even if the jury considered the instructions as creating a mandatory *rebuttable* presumption, the instructions are still improper. A mandatory rebuttable presumption has the effect of relieving the State of its burden of proof once it has established a minimum of facts. The defendant then has the burden of persuading the jury that such a finding is improper. Shifting the burden of proof of an essential element of the crime charged violates due process considerations. By instructing the jury that a presumption *may be rebutted*, the court in effect tells the jury that the defendant had the burden of persuasion. The result is that proof of the element of intent has been unconstitutionally shifted away from the prosecution.

The State argues that even if the instructions were improper, they were corrected by the many other instructions given to the jury, explaining the presumption of innocence, the presumption that a person does not act with criminal intent, and the state's burden of proof. This is unavailing. The differing instructions could have led the jury to conclude that while ordinarily intent must be proven beyond a reasonable doubt, proving that Franklin (D) fired the gun constituted proof of intent beyond a reasonable doubt, unless Franklin (D) offered sufficient evidence to the contrary. Due process prohibits a state from using jury instructions that have the effect of relieving the prosecution from carrying its burden of proof on a critical element of the crime. Affirmed.

Analysis:

In contrast with the mandatory instructions given here, *permissive* instructions were provided to the jury in *Heard v. State*, 334 S.E.2d 374 (Ga. Ct. App. 1985). On appeal, the court found *Heard's* instructions allowable because the instructions did not usurp the jury's discretion. The court in *Heard* took every reasonable precaution when instructing the jury, charging them as follows: "I charge you that every person *may be* presumed to be of sound mind and discretion, but this presumption may be rebutted. *You may infer, if you wish to do so,* that the acts of a person of sound mind and discretion are the product of his will and that a person of sound mind and discretion intends the natural and probable consequences of his act. Whether or not you make any such inference or inferences is a matter solely within your discretion as a jury."

■ CASE VOCABULARY

INFERENCE: A conclusion reached by considering other facts and deducing a logical consequence from them.

INTENT: The state of mind accompanying an act, especially a forbidden act. While motive is the inducement to do some act, intent is the mental resolution or determination to do it. When the intent to do an act that violates the law exists, motive becomes immaterial.

REASONABLE DOUBT: The doubt that prevents one from being firmly convinced of a defendant's guilt, or the belief that there is a real possibility that a defendant is not guilty. "Beyond a reasonable doubt" is the standard used by a jury to determine whether a criminal defendant is guilty. In deciding whether guilt has been proved beyond a reasonable doubt, the jury must begin with the presumption that the defendant is innocent.

REBUTTABLE PRESUMPTION: An inference drawn from certain facts that establish a prima facie case, which may be overcome by the introduction of contrary evidence.

United States v. Watson

(Prosecuting Government) v. (Convicted Murderer)

501 A.2d 791 (1985)

TIME TO THINK THINGS THROUGH SHOWS PREMEDITATION AND DELIBERATION

■INSTANT FACTS Watson (D) shot and killed an officer pursuing him on suspicion of car theft.

■BLACK LETTER RULE A finding of premeditation and deliberation does not require evidence of the passage of days or hours, but simply a showing of any opportunity during which the defendant had the time to consider his actions.

■ **PROCEDURAL BASIS**

On appeal from a conviction for first-degree murder.

■ **FACTS**

Two police officers saw a car reported to be stolen pull into a parking lot. The officers identified themselves as the police and ordered the driver to stop. The driver, Watson (D), jumped from the car and ran toward an apartment complex, and one officer pursued him. Watson (D) dashed into a nearby apartment building and into a unit where three girls were sitting at a table doing homework. Watson (D) asked to use the phone, then sat down at the table with the girls. The officer appeared at the door and told the defendant he was under arrest, but the defendant refused to surrender. Watson (D) stood up and, in an effort to avoid being handcuffed, put the officer in a bear hug. As the men struggled, the officer's gun fell to the floor. Eventually, Watson (D) had the officer immobilized. With the officer on his back, the defendant reached for the loose gun. The girls recalled hearing the officer tell the defendant "it isn't worth it." One of the girls ran to the back of the apartment and heard a shot. Another of the girls fled the apartment. She also heard the shot and then saw Watson (D) running from the building holding the officer's gun. Medical testimony established that the officer had been shot at close range. Though he had been shot, the officer chased after Watson (D), but fell to the ground. Watson (D) ran inside another unit and asked to use the phone. When the defendant was finally apprehended, he was uninjured. At trial, testimony was offered by the woman whose phone the defendant used to place his second call. She testified that Watson (D) told someone on the phone that he had just shot a policeman and needed to be picked up. The woman's sister corroborated this testimony and said that Watson (D) offered her money to hide the drugs he was carrying.

■ **ISSUE**

Was sufficient evidence presented from which a reasonable juror could conclude beyond a reasonable doubt that the defendant had an opportunity to consider the consequences of his action before shooting the police officer?

■ **DECISION AND RATIONALE**

(Rogers, Assoc. J.) Yes. Premeditation and deliberation does not require evidence of the passage of days or hours, but simply a showing of any opportunity during which the defendant had the time to consider his actions. First-degree murder is distinguishable from second-degree murder on the basis of being calculated and planned; second-degree murder is unplanned or impulsive. Thus, in charging first-degree murder, the government must prove that the defendant acted deliberately with premeditation; that is, the government must show the defendant made the decision to kill, which requires showing the accused gave thought to the idea, gave it a second thought, and then followed through. The time to consider the deed need not be measurable in days, hours, or minutes. Premeditation can be inferred from the facts and circumstances surrounding the murder.

Here, as the defendant sat at the table with the three girls, it was likely he was considering his course of action once the police found him. The defendant would have known any officer would have a gun and he would need to disarm him in order to escape. A jury could further assume that when the officer was telling Watson (D) it "wasn't worth it," he was suggesting to the defendant that stealing a car was not worth committing murder. Watson (D) had time to reconsider his decision to kill the officer. Once Watson (D) had the officer's gun, he could have fled the apartment, but rather than leave, Watson (D) made the decision to kill the officer. The defendant insists that the absence of eyewitness testimony to the actual firing of the gun leaves the jury to speculate on the impact of the officer's statements on Watson's (D) actions. However, eyewitness testimony is not required. Circumstantial evidence is sufficient. Watson (D) also argues that his actions were motivated by fear, panic, and concern that the officer would kill him. But based on the evidence presented at trial, a jury could reasonably conclude that Watson's (D) actions were not motivated by panic, but by deliberation, after having decided to kill the officer to ensure his escape. Affirmed.

Analysis:

Deliberation and premeditation are incapable of direct proof. In most cases involving elements of deliberation and premeditation, the mental state of the defendant is proven by external evidence. In *Commonwealth v. Karenbauer*, 715 A.2d 1086 (Pa. 1998), the court found an intent to kill from the fact that the defendant chose to attack vital organs, rather than less critical ones. In Tennessee, courts have compiled a list of factors that tend to show premeditation including such things as the use of a deadly weapon, the cruelty of the killing, the defendant's own statements, and preparations before the killing. *See State v. Bland*, 958 S.W.2d 651 (Tenn. 1997).

■ **CASE VOCABULARY**

DELIBERATION: The act of carefully considering issues and options before making a decision or taking some action.

PREMEDITATION: Conscious consideration and planning that precedes some act (such as committing a crime).

People v. Walker

(State of Illinois) v. (Murderer)

204 N.E.2d 594 (1965)

MANSLAUGHTER, RATHER THAN MURDER, OCCURS WHEN THE DEFENDANT HAS INSUFFICIENT TIME TO "COOL DOWN"

■**INSTANT FACTS** Walker (D) was sitting on a porch with several others when they were approached by Stenneth, who demanded they gamble with him; when they refused, Stenneth became violent and Walker (D) killed him.

■**BLACK LETTER RULE** When a defendant kills his victim after provocation and without a "cooling off" period, the defendant is guilty of manslaughter rather than murder.

■ **PROCEDURAL BASIS**

Appeal by the defendant from his murder conviction following a bench trial.

■ **FACTS**

Walker (D), Jenkins, Brown and McClinton were drinking together on a porch. Stenneth, approached them and demanded they gamble with him. When they declined, he came at them with a knife. McClinton threatened to hit Stenneth with a bottle if he came near them. Walker and Jenkins tried to convince McClinton to return to the porch, but every time McClinton started to retreat, Stenneth advanced toward him again. Walker (D) and Jenkins tried to guide McClinton back to the porch, but as they walked with him, Stenneth continued stabbing at each of them with his knife. McClinton did not, however, see either man get cut. Walker (D) then threw a brick at Stenneth that knocked him down; Walker (D) and the others then went over to Stenneth. Walker (D) suggested that he should cut Stenneth's throat with Stenneth's own knife; he did just that and was convicted of murder.

■ **ISSUE**

Should the defendant's conviction have been limited to manslaughter given that an emotional exchange had just occurred between the parties?

■ **DECISION AND RATIONALE**

(Drucker, J.) Yes. The defendant argues that the killing took place as part of the fight. He had not had time to cool off when he killed Stenneth, so he at most committed voluntary manslaughter. Walker (D) relies on *People v. Bissett*, 92 N.E. 949 (Ill. 1910), which discusses a killing occurring during the heat of passion when one has been provoked. In that case, there was no pause in the action that offered the assailant time to consider the consequences of his actions, and the court concluded the assailant could be guilty of no more than manslaughter. The *Bissett* court required a showing of a "serious and highly provoking

---

injury" that created an "irresistible passion," or a showing that the victim threatened to commit serious personal injury.

In the present case, the decedent was aggressive. He kept taunting the men with his knife. Walker (D) did not exchange words with the decedent, but when he went to the aid of McClinton, Walker (D) was himself cut by the deceased. The cutting led Walker (D) to strike the deceased with a brick. Walker (D) had no knife of his own; instead, he grabbed the deceased's knife and stabbed him with it. According to McClinton, the entire incident occurred quickly. Based on the evidence presented, it is clear that the defendant was guilty only of voluntary manslaughter. Cause remanded.

Analysis:

In *People v. Akins*, 351 N.E.2d 366 (Ill. App. Ct. 1976), the court explained that " '[w]hat constitutes a sufficient 'cooling-off period' depends upon the extent to which the passions have been aroused and the nature of the act which caused the provocation, and, for that reason no yardstick of time can be used by the court to measure a reasonable period of passion but it must vary as do the facts of every case. Humans react violently to the infliction of a serious injury, and the degree of pain which results therefrom not only governs the passion itself but also influences the duration of the cooling period.' "

■ **CASE VOCABULARY**

HEAT OF PASSION: Rage, terror, or furious hatred suddenly aroused by some immediate provocation, usually another person's words or actions. At common law, the heat of passion could serve as a mitigating circumstance that would reduce a murder charge to manslaughter.

PROVOCATION: The act of inciting another to do something, especially to commit a crime; something (such as words or actions) that affects a person's reason and self-control, especially causing the person to commit a crime impulsively.

VOLUNTARY MANSLAUGHTER: An act of murder reduced to manslaughter because of extenuating circumstances such as adequate provocation (arousing the "heat of passion") or diminished capacity.

WHEN SUBSTANTIAL TIME ELAPSES AFTER PROVOCATION, THE DEFENDANT IS PRESUMED TO HAVE COOLED DOWN

■**INSTANT FACTS** Dan Parker was talking with some other gentlemen when Fraley (D) shot him, nine or ten months after Parker had shot and killed Fraley's (D) son.

■**BLACK LETTER RULE** Provocation that occurred nine or ten months before a killing will not reduce the charges to manslaughter, since a deliberate killing in revenge is murder.

■ **PROCEDURAL BASIS**

On application for a writ of habeas corpus seeking bail pending the final hearing.

■ **FACTS**

Dan Parker was leaning against a railing in front of a drug store, engaged in conversation with other gentlemen, when Fraley (D) came around the corner, walked up to Parker, said hello, and shot him. Fraley (D) then walked over to Parker and fired four more shots. Testimony established that Fraley (D) then shouted at Parker that he had been warned that Fraley (D) would kill him since Parker killed Fraley's (D) son. Some nine or ten months prior to the incident, Parker had been accused of shooting and killing Fraley's (D) son, but was acquitted. After he was shot, it was noted that Parker had a gun; however, he did not draw it in response to Fraley's (D) actions.

■ **ISSUE**

Was there sufficient evidence supporting Fraley's (D) guilt on the capital charge such that bail should be denied?

■ **DECISION AND RATIONALE**

(Richardson, J.) Yes. Fraley (D) argues that on seeing Parker, he became impassioned thinking about Parker's murder of his son. Fraley (D) contended that he killed Parker in the heat of passion and without premeditation. In a previous case, though, this court held that a span of just four hours between the provocation and the killing posed a sufficient cooling-off period. In cases like this, the question is not whether the defendant has cooled down, but whether a reasonable man would have had sufficient time to cool down. If, after the passage of the time a reasonable man would have cooled down, even though the defendant has stayed enraged, his charge cannot be reduced from murder to manslaughter. A killing committed on provocation that arose several months earlier cannot be reduced from murder to manslaughter. Deliberately killing another as revenge is murder. Habeas corpus denied.

Analysis:

In contrast with the cases of *People v. Walker*, 204 N.E.2d 594 (1965), and *People v. Bissett*, 92 N.E. 949 (Ill. 1910), the killing here occurred nearly a year following the event that upset this defendant. While the death of the defendant's son may have caused him such grief that nearly a year later he was still incensed, the court notes that whether or not a particular defendant has cooled down is unimportant. Time to cool off will be determined objectively. Compare the concerns in this case with the factors discussed in *State v. Bland*, 958 S.W.2d 651 (Tenn. 1997), in support of a finding of premeditation. While the presence or absence of those factors tends to establish premeditation or the lack of it, in some cases, the presence of similar factors would tend to provide evidence that an actor had sufficient time to "cool down."

■ **CASE VOCABULARY**

EX PARTE: [Latin, "from the part."] On or from one party only, usually without notice to or argument from the adverse party.

HABEAS CORPUS: A writ employed to bring a person before a court, most frequently to ensure that the party's imprisonment or detention is not illegal.

Rowland v. State

(Killer of Adulterous Wife) v. (State of Mississippi)

35 So. 826 (Miss. 1904)

KILLING A SPOUSE CAUGHT IN THE ACT OF ADULTERY IS MANSLAUGHTER

■**INSTANT FACTS** When Rowland (D) discovered his estranged wife in bed with another man, he fired a shot at his wife's lover, but killed his wife instead.

■**BLACK LETTER RULE** Finding one's spouse in the act of adultery provides sufficient provocation to reduce a charge of murder to manslaughter.

■ **PROCEDURAL BASIS**

On appeal from a conviction for murder.

■ **FACTS**

Rowland (D) and his wife were separated but on good terms. He visited her frequently. One night Rowland (D) came to visit and noticed a horse belonging to a man named Thorn hitched to the fence. Upon entering the house, he caught his wife and Thorn in the act of adultery. The couple jumped from bed and ran past Rowland (D). Rowland (D) fired at Thorn and missed; the bullet struck and killed his wife. At trial, the jury was instructed on Oklahoma's murder laws and told that murder occurs when someone kills another without the authority of law, intending to cause the death of the other. If the jury could find that Rowland (D) killed his wife, he was guilty of murder.

■ **ISSUE**

Does a killing that immediately results from finding one's spouse in the act of adultery constitute murder?

■ **DECISION AND RATIONALE**

(Truly, J.) No. In *Reed v. State*, the court noted that if the defendant had killed his victim upon catching him in the act of adultery with his wife, the crime would have been decreased to manslaughter, based on the rule at common law that finding one's wife in the act of adultery was deemed sufficient to cause a man to take leave of all reason. There is no basis for a different finding whether the husband shoots his wife or her lover. In either event, the crime that results is manslaughter. Applying the law to the case here, finding Rowland (D) guilty of murder is not justified. According to the facts adduced at trial, his wife and Thorn were, in fact, in the midst of adultery. No evidence was offered to support a finding that Rowland (D) acted deliberately to kill either his wife or Thorn. Without deliberation, and based on the facts here, the crime of was not committed.

Analysis:

The issue of adultery as a reason to reduce a murder charge to manslaughter was also discussed in *Denham v. State*, 67 So. 2d 445 (Miss. 1953). In *Denham*, the court noted that previous cases, including this one, allowed adultery to serve as a mitigating factor. In *Denham*, however, the defendant had suspected his wife of infidelity and, according to evidence at trial, was looking for evidence he could use in a divorce proceeding. When Denham knew where his wife and her lover could be found, he went there and killed them both. Even though the defendant was found guilty of the lesser charge of manslaughter, he appealed. Finding the defendant had caught a break from the jury, the court noted that most cases involving the killing of an adulterous spouse arose from situations in which infidelity was not suspected. The jury could have found that Denham killed with premeditation but did not.

■ CASE VOCABULARY

PROVOCATION: The act of inciting another to do something, especially to commit a crime; something (such as words or actions) that affects a person's reason and self-control, especially causing the person to commit a crime impulsively.

REPEATED ACTS MAY CUMULATIVELY SUPPORT A FINDING OF PROVOCATION

My wife tormented me for weeks with mixed signals, lies, and outright intentional provocation until I finally snapped.

The same thing happens to me with a lot of lawyers.

stus.com

■ **INSTANT FACTS** Shortly after being married, Berry's (D) wife began taunting him about leaving the marriage for another man; after one such episode, Berry (D) strangled her.

■ **BLACK LETTER RULE** A jury should be instructed on the "heat of passion" defense where evidence is offered that supports a continuous pattern of emotional torture that could accumulate into sufficient provocation.

■ **PROCEDURAL BASIS**

On appeal from the defendant's conviction for first-degree murder.

■ **FACTS**

Berry (D) married Rachel Pessah (Rachel). Three days after the wedding, Rachel went to her native Israel for nearly two months. On returning from Israel, Rachel told Berry (D) that she had met a man and fallen in love, that the two of them had engaged in sexual relations, that this man would be coming to claim her, and that she wanted a divorce. Over the next two weeks, Rachel alternatively taunted Berry (D) that she wanted a divorce and that she wanted to remain with him. She humiliated Berry (D), telling him she thought she was pregnant with this other man's child and showing him photos of the two of them together. She would demand that Berry (D) have sex with her and then affirm her desire for the other man. Rachel would also make sexual advances and then pull back, saying she wanted to save herself for the new man. On one of the final occasions, Rachel had been tormenting Berry (D) again and Berry (D) got out of bed, deciding he should leave. Rachel continued screaming at him and he choked her. Berry (D) put Rachel in a cab and sent her to the hospital. He then took his things from the apartment and went to stay with a friend. The next day, he returned to the apartment to talk to Rachel and found she was not there, so he spent the night there. When she returned the next morning, she asked if he had come to kill her. He said he had, then denied it, then said he had. Finally, he told her he had come to talk, but she started screaming. He grabbed her to stop her from screaming, but she did not relent. He finally strangled her with a telephone cord. At trial, Dr. Blinder, a psychiatrist, testified on Berry's (D) behalf that Rachel was depressed and inclined toward suicide. Her mental condition caused her to taunt the defendant in an unconscious desire to have him kill her to fulfill her suicidal thoughts. It was Rachel's repeated taunting of her husband with stories of another man, intermingled with sexual advances, that led Berry (D) to choke and ultimately kill her. At trial, the jury found Berry (D) guilty of murder and he was sentenced to prison.

■ ISSUE

Was it error not to instruct the jury on the offense of manslaughter where the repeated acts of taunting, which were individually insufficient to reduce the charge to manslaughter, had accumulated and amounted to provocation?

■ DECISION AND RATIONALE

(Sullivan, J.) Yes. The defendant contends that the record contains sufficient evidence to show the homicide here was committed in an uncontrollable rage after being provoked. Based on this evidence, Berry (D) insists that he was entitled to have the jury instructed on the crime of voluntary manslaughter. The law provides that it is up to the jury to determine whether the defendant committed his crime in the heat of passion. The jury is required to make this decision based not on the actual mental state of the defendant, but on the mental state that would be aroused in the "ordinarily reasonable man." No specific type of provocation must be established; it simply must be shown to be violent or fraught with strong emotion. Taunting a defendant with statements of infidelity is sufficient to support a finding of provocation. Berry (D) was forced to endure two weeks of Rachel's taunting. Despite the Attorney General's contention that Berry (D) had hours to cool down before he murdered Rachel, the long course of provocation reached the breaking point when Rachel would not stop screaming. Reversed.

Analysis:

In *People v. Cole*, 17 Cal. Rptr. 3d 532 (Cal. 2004), the defendant was convicted of murder after he set fire his wife and she died. Before the murder, the two had a long history of violent fights and abuse. The court distinguished Cole's actions from Berry's (D) violence against Rachel in this case, saying that the couple in *Cole* had such a history of violence between them that the night Cole burned his wife was "nothing out of the ordinary." In other words, there was no heat of passion warranting a manslaughter charge.

■ CASE VOCABULARY

REASONABLE [ORDINARILY REASONABLE] PERSON: A hypothetical person used as a legal standard, especially to determine whether someone acted with negligence; specifically, a person who exercises the degree of attention, knowledge, intelligence, and judgment that society requires of its members for the protection of their own and of others' interests. The reasonable person acts sensibly, does things without serious delay, and takes proper but not excessive precautions.

THE JURY MAY CONSIDER CULTURAL DIFFERENCES IN DETERMINING THE
DEFENDANT'S MENTAL STATE

■**INSTANT FACTS** Helen Wu (D) killed her young son and tried to commit suicide rather than bring him back to her native land, where she felt they would be mistreated.

■**BLACK LETTER RULE** The jury may be instructed to consider evidence of the defendant's cultural background in determining the mental state of the defendant at the time of a killing.

■ **PROCEDURAL BASIS**

On appeal following a conviction for second-degree murder.

■ **FACTS**

Helen Wu (Helen) (D) was born in Saigon. She married at age nineteen and had a daughter. The following year, she met Henry Wu (Wu), who later married another woman and moved to the United States. After eight years of marriage, Helen got divorced. While engaged to be remarried, Helen's fiancé died. Helen (D) was then contacted by Wu, who had heard she had a daughter and was divorced. Wu complained to Helen (D) about his unsatisfactory marriage to a woman who could not have children. Wu told Helen (D) he planned to seek a divorce. Wu asked Helen (D) to come to the U.S. to have a child with him. Based on the belief that Wu would marry Helen (D) after he divorced his wife, Helen took $20,000 from Wu to apply for a visa and came to the U.S. Wu greeted Helen's (D) arrival warmly and promised to marry her when his divorce was final. He arranged for Helen (D) to stay with his mother, though Helen (D) was led to believe the mother was a family friend. Wu finally obtained a divorce but kept the decree a secret from Helen (D). Helen (D) became pregnant by Wu and went to live in her own apartment. After their son, Sidney, was born, Helen (D) became upset that Wu was not asking to marry her, so she threatened to return to Macau. Wu did not try to change her mind, so Helen (D) returned to Macau. She left Sidney with Wu, fearing they would be ostracized if she returned with an illegitimate child. Over the next few years, Helen (D) tried to encourage Wu to bring Sidney to see her, but he refused. Wu instead asked Helen to visit them, but Helen resisted, stating she needed to marry Wu before she came to the U.S. again. At some point, Helen moved to Hong Kong and Wu brought Sidney there to see Helen (D), lured by Helen's (D) promise of money for his restaurant. While there, Wu proposed to Helen (D), but she turned him down, thinking his proposal was motivated by his belief she had money. At that time, Helen (D) tried to fling herself from a window, but was unsuccessful. Helen (D) then came to the U.S. with a friend, Chung, and learned that Wu's mother was terminally ill. Wu's mother told Helen (D) to take Sidney back to Hong Kong with her since it was unlikely that Wu would give him good care. While in the U.S., Wu persuaded Helen (D) to meet him in Las Vegas and the two were married. Helen (D) persisted in the belief that Wu

---

had married her only for money. When confronted, Wu told Helen (D) she had no rights in the marriage without her money.

Shortly after the wedding, Helen was playing with Sidney when Sidney told her that Wu had said Helen was "psychotic" and troubled. Sidney told Helen that Wu had a relationship with a woman, Rosemary, who owned the home in which they lived. Rosemary's children were treated better than Sidney was. Helen (D) began to realize that Sidney would have no one when Wu's mother died, and so she decided the two of them must die. She strangled Sidney with a rope she cut from a window blind. She then recalls waking up and thinking about how quickly Sidney had died. Helen (D) wrote a note to Wu, telling him she died with no regrets; but she did not own up to Sidney's death. Unsuccessful at strangling herself, she tried slashing her wrist. Wu came home, discovered Helen (D) and Sidney, and phoned for paramedics. Sidney was pronounced dead and Helen (D), though her vital signs were normal, appeared less than fully conscious. Helen (D) was charged with the second-degree murder of her son.

■ **ISSUE**

When a defendant's cultural background affects her decisions, should the jury be instructed to consider the defendant's different culture in deciding whether the defendant had the requisite state of mind to commit a crime?

■ **DECISION AND RATIONALE**

(Timlin, Acting, P.J.) Yes. At trial, the prosecution argued that Helen (D) killed her son out of revenge against her son's father. The defense insisted that Helen's (D) son, Sidney, who lived with his father (Wu) was poorly treated by everyone but Wu's mother, who was now dying of cancer. Since Helen (D) would be unable to bring Sidney to live with her for fear of cultural reprisals, she killed Sidney and then tried to commit suicide. Helen (D) deserved to have the jury instructed on her cultural background so they could understand her theory of the case.

Generally speaking, all relevant evidence is admissible, and the trier of fact may consider any admitted evidence. Culture is relevant to issues surrounding the defendant's mental state, and her state of mind is an element of the charged offense. Evidence affecting her state of mind is relevant to (1) premeditation and deliberation, and may offer an explanation for her conduct; (2) malice aforethought and heat of passion, effectively reducing a charge of intentional killing to voluntary manslaughter; and (3) the existence of passion as a defense. Passion is not an emotion limited to rage or anger, but can be shown by any strong emotion. The defendant had many experiences that could have created sufficient stress. Evidence of Helen's (D) culture would explain the source of the stresses she was feeling and how they could rise to the level of a heat of passion. At the time she strangled Sidney, Helen (D) was upset about there being no one to take care of her son. She thought the only way for her to take care of his needs would be after death, through a murder-suicide. At trial, three mental health experts explained the effect of these cultural stresses on her ability to think rationally. The jury should have been told they should consider that evidence and its effect on Helen's mental status.

Analysis:

In a case such as this, it may be easy to sympathize with Helen (D) based on the predicament she believed she was facing. However, cultural defenses are not always as openly received, and it can be hard to draw the line between adherence to American criminal justice standards and respect for cultural differences. Several years ago, Vietnamese men in Los Angeles were surprised when they realized that they could be arrested and prosecuted for battering their wives. After some defendants were prosecuted, word of the prosecutions spread through the Vietnamese community, and wife battering subsided.

■ **CASE VOCABULARY**

EMOTIONAL INSANITY: Insanity produced by a violent excitement of the emotions or passions, although reasoning faculties may remain unimpaired; a passion that for a period creates complete derangement of intellect. Emotional insanity is sometimes described as an irresistible impulse to do an act.

HEAT OF PASSION: Rage, terror, or furious hatred suddenly aroused by some immediate provocation, usually another person's words or actions. At common law, the heat of passion could serve as a mitigation circumstance that would reduce a murder charge to manslaughter.

TEMPORARY INSANITY: Insanity that exists only at the time of a criminal act.

CHAPTER SIX

Unintentional Homicide

Commonwealth v. Welansky

Instant Facts: Welansky (D) operated a nightclub, and several people were killed when the club caught fire.

Black Letter Rule: Wanton or reckless conduct is intentional conduct, which may be either an act of commission or omission when there is a duty to act, that involves a high likelihood that substantial harm will result to another.

State v. Williams

Instant Facts: Williams's (D) child died from an illness that could have been prevented if the child had received medical attention; Williams (D) was convicted of manslaughter and appealed.

Black Letter Rule: A conviction for statutory manslaughter requires a showing of negligence that causes the death of another.

Mayes v. The People

Instant Facts: Mayes (D) threw a glass that hit an oil lamp carried by his wife; the lamp burst, and Mayes's (D) wife died from the burns she suffered.

Black Letter Rule: Malice may be implied when a defendant's actions were done without regard for the consequences of his or her actions.

State v. Martin

Instant Facts: Martin (D) set a fire that burned an apartment building and killed a person in the building; he was convicted of felony murder and appealed.

Black Letter Rule: A defendant is guilty of murder for a death that occurs during the commission of a violent felony if that death is not too remote, accidental in its occurrence, or too dependent on the volitional act of another to have a just bearing on the culpability of the defendant.

People v. Hickman

Instant Facts: Hickman (D) was fleeing from police officers after a burglary, and one of the pursuing officers shot and killed another officer; Hickman (D) was charged with felony murder for the officer's death.

Black Letter Rule: A person who commits a felony that causes another to take defensive action that kills an innocent third person is guilty of felony murder.

People v. Gladman

Instant Facts: Gladman (D) robbed a delicatessen and shot and killed a police officer while trying to evade capture; he was convicted of felony murder and appealed.

Black Letter Rule: A defendant is guilty of felony murder for a death caused while in immediate flight from a felony; the question of immediate flight is a factual one, to be determined by the jury.

People v. Cavitt

Instant Facts: A homeowner died after being bound by the defendants during a burglary.

Black Letter Rule: The felony-murder rule requires both a causal relationship and a temporal relationship between the underlying felony and the act resulting in death.

State v. Shock

Instant Facts: Shock (D) beat a child to death and was charged with felony murder; he appealed his conviction.

Black Letter Rule: The felony that underlies a conviction for felony murder must be a felony other than a crime of violence against the victim, which merges with the homicide.

Commonwealth v. Welansky

(Government) v. (Night Club Owner)

316 Mass. 383, 55 N.E.2d 902 (1944)

INTENTIONAL CONDUCT THAT INVOLVES A LIKELIHOOD OF SUBSTANTIAL HARM TO ANOTHER IS WANTON OR RECKLESS

■**INSTANT FACTS** Welansky (D) operated a nightclub, and several people were killed when the club caught fire.

■**BLACK LETTER RULE** Wanton or reckless conduct is intentional conduct, which may be either an act of commission or omission when there is a duty to act, that involves a high likelihood that substantial harm will result to another.

■ **PROCEDURAL BASIS**

Appeal from a conviction on twelve counts of manslaughter.

■ **FACTS**

Welansky (D) operated a nightclub in Boston. On November 16, he fell ill and was taken to a hospital. While he was in the hospital, Welansky (D) did not concern himself with the running of the nightclub, but on November 28, everything at the club was within Welansky's (D) usual practice despite his continued hospitalization. The nightclub consisted of several rooms, including a room that was scheduled to be opened to the public the next day, and had five emergency exits. One of the exits was in the office, however, and was locked; checked coats blocked another exit; two were known only to employees; and one was behind hooked doors and blocked by tables. Exits that were supposed to be provided, according to construction plans approved by the city, were not in place. On November 28, the club was full of patrons, with estimates ranging from 980 to 1250 people. There was evidence that there had been even larger crowds on the premises, though the club was licensed to hold only 650 patrons. On the evening in question, a bartender told a bar boy to turn on a light that had been turned off. The bar boy lit a match in order to see the bulb, turned the light on, blew out the match, and left. The flame from the match lit an artificial palm tree on fire and the flames spread to the low cloth ceiling near it. The fire spread quickly and the crowd rushed to get out. Some of the doors could not be opened except by force or were blocked. Many did not manage to escape, and 492 patrons, along with some employees, died.

■ **ISSUE**

Was Welansky (D) guilty of involuntary manslaughter through wanton or reckless conduct?

■ **DECISION AND RATIONALE**

(Lummus, J.) Yes. Wanton or reckless conduct is intentional conduct, either a commission or omission where there is a duty to act, that involves a high likelihood that substantial harm will result to another. Wanton or reckless conduct surpasses mere negligence and gross negligence. The fire was not, in itself, wanton or reckless conduct. There is always a risk of fire in public places. But there was a duty of care for the safety of business visitors. Welansky (D) had an obligation to provide adequate and accessible exits for patrons and employees, and his failure to provide such exits, in disregard of the probable dangers posed, constituted wanton and reckless conduct. Knowing facts that would cause a reasonable person to appreciate the danger is the same as having actual knowledge of the danger. Affirmed.

Analysis:

There are many people in this case whose inaction or actions could be said to have caused the deaths. For example, although the city approved construction plans with fire exits, no steps were taken to determine that the exits were in place, even though a new area that required those exits was scheduled to open the day after the fire. Yet a firefighter testified at trial that he had inspected the premises a few days before the fire and found everything to be satisfactory. In light of the apparent indifference of the safety authorities, it seems that Welansky (D) could have made an argument that he did not know of the danger posed to patrons. Subsequent investigation exonerated the bar boy who lit the match, and the cause of the fire remained officially undetermined, but traces of accelerants—chemicals used to speed the spread of fire—were found in the building, which may have accounted for the rapid spread of the flames.

■ CASE VOCABULARY

INVOLUNTARY MANSLAUGHTER: Homicide in which there is no intention to kill or do grievous bodily harm, but that is committed with criminal negligence or during the commission of a crime not included within the felony-murder rule.

MANSLAUGHTER: The unlawful killing of a human being without malice aforethought.

RECKLESS: Characterized by the creation of a substantial and unjustifiable risk of harm to others and by a conscious (and sometimes deliberate) disregard for or indifference to that risk; heedless; rash.

WANTON: Unreasonably or maliciously risking harm while being utterly indifferent to the consequences. In criminal law, *wanton* usually connotes malice (in the criminal-law sense), while *reckless* does not.

WILLFUL: Voluntary and intentional, but not necessarily malicious.

(Government) v. (Parent)

484 P.2d 1167 (Wash. Ct. App. 1971)

STATUTORY MANSLAUGHTER REQUIRES A SHOWING OF ORDINARY NEGLIGENCE

■INSTANT FACTS Williams's (D) child died from an illness that could have been prevented if the child had received medical attention; Williams (D) was convicted of manslaughter and appealed.

■BLACK LETTER RULE A conviction for statutory manslaughter requires a showing of negligence that causes the death of another.

■ PROCEDURAL BASIS

Appeal from a conviction for manslaughter.

■ FACTS

Williams's (D) child became ill. Williams (D) thought it was nothing more than a toothache and did not take the child to a doctor, but simply gave him baby aspirin. The child died after being ill for two weeks. At trial, the medical examiner testified that the child had an abscessed tooth that turned gangrenous, which made it impossible for the child to eat. The child became malnourished; his immune system deteriorated; and he contracted pneumonia, which caused his death. The examiner testified that the odor from the gangrene would have been apparent ten days before the child's death, and that medical care would have been required no less than one week before death to save the child's life. Williams (D) could have brought the child to a doctor, but did not do so, both because they were waiting for the swelling to subside, and out of fear that the child would be taken away by the welfare department. Williams (D) did not understand the significance of the child's symptoms.

■ ISSUE

Was Williams (D) guilty of manslaughter?

■ DECISION AND RATIONALE

(Horowitz, C.J.) Yes. A conviction for statutory manslaughter requires a showing of negligence that causes the death of another. While the common law required a showing of more than ordinary or simple negligence, the statute uses a different standard and requires only a showing of negligence. Williams (D) did not exercise ordinary caution in failing to seek medical treatment for the child. Although the initial symptoms were that of an ordinary toothache, the child's failure to improve and the later symptoms put Williams (D) on sufficient notice that the child needed medical attention. The failure to seek that attention was ordinary or simple negligence, sufficient to support a conviction for manslaughter. Affirmed

Analysis:

Cultural and social factors seem to be at play in this case. The court is dismissive of the parents' claim that they were afraid that their child would be taken from them if they went to the doctor. The trial court found that Williams (D) "had no excuse for not taking the baby to a doctor." Assuming that the fear was a well-grounded one, the court apparently reasoned that the child's need to see a doctor outweighed the parents' concerns over losing custody.

■ CASE VOCABULARY

NEGLIGENCE: The failure to exercise the standard of care that a reasonably prudent person would have exercised in a similar situation; any conduct that falls below the legal standard established to protect others against unreasonable risk of harm, except for conduct that is intentionally, wantonly, or willfully disregardful of others' rights.

Mayes v. The People

(Husband) v. (Government)

106 Ill. 306, 46 Am. Rep. 698 (1883)

ACTIONS DONE WITH AN "ABANDONED AND MALIGNANT HEART" ARE MALICIOUS

■**INSTANT FACTS** Mayes (D) threw a glass that hit an oil lamp carried by his wife; the lamp burst, and Mayes's (D) wife died from the burns she suffered.

■**BLACK LETTER RULE** Malice may be implied when a defendant's actions were done without regard for the consequences of his or her actions.

■ **PROCEDURAL BASIS**

Appeal from a conviction for murder.

■ **FACTS**

Mayes (D) entered a room where his wife, daughter, and mother-in-law were working. He was intoxicated. His wife noticed that one side of his face was dirty and asked him if he had fallen down. Mayes (D) replied that it was none of her business. His daughter gave him water and he washed his face. Mayes (D) asked for a glass and was given one, which he filled with beer and gave to his wife. Mayes's (D) wife brought him his supper, but he refused to eat it, and tried to throw a loaf of bread at his wife. Mayes (D) sat quietly, and then asked for arsenic. No one replied to him and he began cursing, saying that he would either kill his wife or she should kill him. Mayes (D) picked up a tin quart measure and threw it at his daughter. His wife directed the daughter to go to bed and started walking toward the bedroom herself, carrying an oil lamp in her hand. Mayes (D) threw the beer glass at her and hit the lamp. The lamp broke and scattered burning oil on her clothes. Mayes (D) did not try to extinguish the flames, but caught hold of his wife by her arms. Mayes's (D) wife died as a result of her burns. Mayes (D) testified that he did not intend to hit his wife with the glass, and that striking the lamp was an accident. Mayes (D) said that he was trying to pitch the glass out of the door, but his daughter and mother-in-law testified that the door was closed. At trial, Mayes (D) requested a jury instruction to the effect that the jury should acquit him if the prosecution did not prove beyond a reasonable doubt that he had the intent to strike his wife or cause her severe bodily injury. The trial court gave that instruction, but added that the jury could find Mayes (D) guilty of murder if the circumstances showed that Mayes (D) acted with an "abandoned and malignant heart."

■ **ISSUE**

Did Mayes (D) act maliciously, so as to make him guilty of murder?

■ DECISION AND RATIONALE

(Scholfield, J.) Yes. Malice may be implied when a defendant's actions were done without regard for the consequences. It was immaterial whether Mayes (D) intended to strike his wife, or anyone else, when he threw the beer glass. An unlawful act done with intent to cause some kind of harm or general mischief will show malice and will provide the intent necessary for a murder conviction. He acted from a general malicious intent, without regard to the consequences of his actions. Mayes (D) was fatally bent on mischief when he threw the glass, and demonstrated that he had the abandoned and malignant heart from which malice could be implied. Affirmed.

Analysis:

The jury instructions proposed by Mayes (D) would have required proof beyond a reasonable doubt of intent to cause bodily harm before Mayes (D) could be convicted of murder. The requested instruction would not bar the jury from inferring intent from Mayes's (D) actions. The instruction that was given gave the jury an alternate way of convicting Mayes (D), but there seems to have been sufficient evidence of intent that Mayes (D) could have been convicted even if his proposed instruction had been given.

■ CASE VOCABULARY

MALICE: The intent, without justification or excuse, to commit a wrongful act; reckless disregard of the law or of a person's legal rights; ill will or wickedness of heart.

MISCHIEF: A condition in which a person suffers a wrong or is under some hardship, especially one that a statute seeks to remove or for which equity provides a remedy; injury or damage caused by a specific person or thing; the act causing such injury or damage.

MURDER: The killing of a human being with malice aforethought.

NATURAL LIFE: A person's physical life span.

PLAINTIFF IN ERROR: *Archaic.* Appellant; petitioner.

(Government) v. (Partygoer)

573 A.2d 1359 (N.J. 1990)

FELONY MURDER IS COMMITTED IF THE DEATH OF ANOTHER PERSON WAS THE PROBABLE CONSEQUENCE OF THE COMMISSION OF A VIOLENT FELONY

■**INSTANT FACTS** Martin (D) set a fire that burned an apartment building and killed a person in the building; he was convicted of felony murder and appealed.

■**BLACK LETTER RULE** A defendant is guilty of murder for a death that occurs during the commission of a violent felony if that death is not too remote, accidental in its occurrence, or too dependent on the volitional act of another to have a just bearing on the culpability of the defendant.

■ **PROCEDURAL BASIS**

Appeal from an order of the appellate division affirming Martin's (D) conviction for felony murder, arson, and aggravated arson.

■ **FACTS**

Martin (D) and four others attended a party in the apartment of Baker. Martin (D) had been smoking marijuana and drinking beer, and was intoxicated. After two altercations between one of Martin's (D) companions and other partygoers, Martin (D) and his companions were told to leave. Martin (D) testified that, on his way out of the apartment building, he found a paper bag full of trash that he lit on fire. Martin (D) testified that he thought that the fire would just make a mess, and that he did not think it would spread. The fire did spread and burned the entire building. One person did not make it out; she died of smoke inhalation and carbon monoxide poisoning. There was evidence that the fire was started by pouring kerosene on the floor. At trial, the jury was instructed that Martin (D) was guilty if he did some act that caused the death.

■ **ISSUE**

Was the jury properly instructed on the felony murder rule, when the court did not make clear that the death had to be a probable consequence of the defendant's actions?

■ **DECISION AND RATIONALE**

(Pollock, J.) No. A defendant will be guilty of murder for a death that occurs during the commission of a violent felony if that death is not too remote, accidental in its occurrence, or too dependent on the volitional act of another to have a just bearing on the culpability of the defendant. The rule in New Jersey has long been that the application of the felony murder rule depends upon a finding that the death was a "probable consequence" of the underlying felony. Probable consequence means something more than "but for" causation, and is closely related to the foreseeability of the consequence. Some deaths are too remotely related to the

---

underlying felony to justify finding the defendant guilty of murder as well as the underlying felony.

The common law held that a perpetrator was guilty of murder for a death that occurred during the commission of a felony. The theory was that the intent to commit the felony was transferred to the intent to cause the death. The theoretical basis changed from transfer of intent to strict or absolute liability, which is contrary to the usual rules of criminal law. The Model Penal Code rejected strict liability, and created a presumption of recklessness when a homicide occurred during the commission of certain felonies. The drafters of the New Jersey Code ultimately rejected the presumption of recklessness. The New Jersey Code creates an affirmative defense for accomplices, which provides that an accomplice who was not in possession of a deadly weapon, who did not commit the homicidal act, and who had no reason to believe another accomplice was armed or intended to engage in conduct likely to cause death or serious injury would not be guilty of felony murder. The statutory provision that relates to absolute liability offenses provides that causation of a particular result is not established unless the actual result is a probable cause of the defendant's conduct. In this case, the jury should have been instructed regarding the meaning of "probable consequence," and Martin's (D) conviction is therefore reversed.

Analysis:

The court does not hold explicitly that the felony murder rule creates absolute liability, subject to certain affirmative defenses, but argues for the "probable consequence" rule based on the statute that relates to absolute liability crimes. It seems fair to conclude that the felony murder rule does create absolute liability, subject to the defenses available only to accomplices in the commission of the underlying felony. At common law, a death that occurred during the commission of any felony made the defendant guilty of murder. This rule evolved in a time when all felonies were violent crimes, and there were no felonies that could be committed without violence. The modern day statutes on the felony murder rule either set out certain felonies to which the rule applies (as does the New Jersey statute discussed in this case), or explicitly limit the rule to violent felonies.

■ CASE VOCABULARY

AGGRAVATED: (Of a crime) made worse or more serious by circumstances such as violence, the presence of a deadly weapon, or the intent to commit another crime.

ARSON: At common law, the malicious burning of someone else's dwelling house or outhouse that is either appurtenant to the dwelling house or within the curtilage; under modern statutes, the intentional and wrongful burning of someone else's property (as to destroy a building) or one's own property (as to fraudulently collect insurance).

BUT—FOR TEST: The doctrine that causation exists only when the result would not have occurred without the party's conduct.

FELONY MURDER: Murder that occurs during the commission of a dangerous felony (often limited to rape, kidnapping, robbery, burglary, and arson).

FELONY MURDER RULE: The doctrine holding that any death resulting from the commission or attempted commission of a dangerous felony is murder.

People v. Hickman

(Government) v. (Burglar)

12 Ill. App. 3d 412, 297 N.E.2d 582 (1973)

THE FELONY MURDER RULE IMPOSES LIABILITY FOR THE DEATH OF AN INNOCENT PARTY CAUSED BY SOMEONE OTHER THAN THE DEFENDANT

Drop the gun now or I'll shoot.

stus.com

■**INSTANT FACTS** Hickman (D) was fleeing from police officers after a burglary, and one of the pursuing officers shot and killed another officer; Hickman (D) was charged with felony murder for the officer's death.

■**BLACK LETTER RULE** A person who commits a felony that causes another to take defensive action that kills an innocent third person is guilty of felony murder.

■ **PROCEDURAL BASIS**

Appeal from an order arresting judgment for murder.

■ **FACTS**

Hickman (D) and others were surprised during a burglary and ran from the police. One officer tried to pursue them, but lost sight. That officer then saw a person holding a gun going in the same direction as Hickman (D) and the others. The officer ordered the person to stop and, when he did not stop, fired a shotgun at him. The person turned out to be a police detective, who died as a result of being shot. Hickman (D) was arrested later; he was unarmed. Hickman (D) was convicted of felony murder for the death of the detective.

■ **ISSUE**

Is Hickman (D) guilty of felony murder, even though he did not shoot the detective?

■ **DECISION AND RATIONALE**

(Scott, J.) Yes. A person who commits a felony that causes another to take defensive action that kills an innocent third person is guilty of felony murder. Commentary to the statute that sets out the felony murder rule stated that it is immaterial who does the killing, even if it is a third person who tries to stop the commission of the offense. Case law cited by Hickman (D) is distinguishable, in that it absolved a defendant from liability under the felony murder rule for the killing of an accomplice by another. The decedent in the distinguishable case helped set in motion the chain of events that caused his death. Arrest of judgment reversed; conviction affirmed.

Analysis:

The language of the statute quoted is clear in its limitation of felony murder to those who kill, not those who "cause the death of," another person. Committee notes and similar interpretive documents generally are relied upon by a court in analyzing a statute only when the meaning of a statute is unclear. In situations in which the language of the statute does not contain any ambiguities or poorly defined terms, courts customarily rely on the plain language of the statute itself. Note also that the bracketed note appended to the excerpt in the casebook is incorrect: the convictions were affirmed, and it was the arrest of judgment against Hickman (D) that was reversed.

■ CASE VOCABULARY

ARREST OF JUDGMENT: The staying of a judgment after its entry, especially a court's refusal to render or enforce a judgment because of a defect apparent from the record.

People v. Gladman
(Government) v. (Robber)

41 N.Y.2d 123, 359 N.E.2d 420 (1976)

A DEATH CAUSED WHILE IN IMMEDIATE FLIGHT FROM A FELONY IS FELONY MURDER

■INSTANT FACTS Gladman (D) robbed a delicatessen and shot and killed a police officer while trying to evade capture; he was convicted of felony murder and appealed.

■BLACK LETTER RULE A defendant is guilty of felony murder for a death caused while in immediate flight from a felony; the question of immediate flight is a factual one, to be determined by the jury.

■ PROCEDURAL BASIS

Appeal from a conviction for murder.

■ FACTS

Gladman (D) robbed a delicatessen at gunpoint. He fled the scene and police officers began to look for him. When he saw a police car enter a parking lot at the same time as he did, Gladman (D) hid under a parked car. An officer walked over to Gladman (D), who got up from underneath the car. The officer ordered Gladman (D) to put his gun on the hood of the car, but Gladman (D) fired at the officer, who later died from his wounds. Gladman (D) commandeered a car and was arrested later. The shooting took place less than fifteen minutes after the robbery, and less than one-half mile from the delicatessen that was robbed. Gladman (D) was convicted of felony murder for shooting the officer while in "immediate flight" from the robbery.

■ ISSUE

Was Gladman (D) in immediate flight from the robbery?

■ DECISION AND RATIONALE

(Jasen, J.) Yes. A defendant is guilty of felony murder for a death caused while in immediate flight from a felony, and the question of immediate flight is a factual one, to be determined by the jury. The jury is to look at factors such as the distance, if any, between the scene of the underlying felony and the scene of the killing, the interval of time involved, whether the defendants were in possession of the fruits of the crime, whether the defendants were being closely pursued, and whether the defendants had reached a place of temporary safety. There may be other variables to consider, depending upon the specific factual situation involved. The jury could legitimately have inferred that Gladman (D) was in immediate flight from the robbery. It does not matter that there was no evidence as to why the officer pulled into the parking lot, or that the officer suspected Gladman (D) of the crime. It is sufficient that Gladman (D) hid from the officer, showing that he thought the officer suspected him or

---

intended to arrest him. The standard is not what the officer believed. The former rule in New York was that a killing was a part of the underlying felony if it was committed while the defendant or his or her accomplice was "engaged in securing the plunder or in doing something immediately connected with the underlying crime." Other jurisdictions have adopted a "res gestae" theory, which looks to whether the killing was committed in, about, or as a part of the underlying transaction. The New York statute applicable in this case applied the felony murder rule to killings committed in "immediate flight" and eliminated technical questions that involved abandonment or completion of an offense. Affirmed.

Analysis:

When a court decides a case in accordance with a list of factors that may be considered, rather than by enunciating a hard-and-fast rule applicable in all cases, it is easy to come up with hypothetical situations to test the boundaries of the rule. In this case, Gladman (D) was arrested less than fifteen minutes after the robbery, and less than one-half mile from the delicatessen, but would it still be "immediate flight" after twenty minutes, and if he were a mile away? Terms such as immediate flight are perhaps best defined intuitively: the jury knows what it means, even if a precise definition cannot be enunciated. A list of factors to be considered allows a court and a jury to tailor decisions to the particular facts of the cases involved, rather than to abstractions.

■ CASE VOCABULARY

RES GESTAE: [Latin, "things done."] The events at issue, or other events contemporaneous with them.

People v. Cavitt

(Prosecuting Authority) v. (Burglar)

33 Cal. 4th 187, 14 Cal. Rptr. 3d 281 (2004)

THE FELONY—MURDER RULE APPLIES TO A NON—KILLER WHOSE INVOLVMENT IN A DANGEROUS FELONY LEADS TO A DEATH

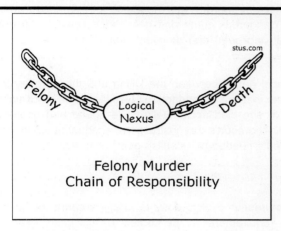

**Felony Murder
Chain of Responsibility**

■**INSTANT FACTS** A homeowner died after being bound by the defendants during a burglary.

■**BLACK LETTER RULE** The felony-murder rule requires both a causal relationship and a temporal relationship between the underlying felony and the act resulting in death.

■ PROCEDURAL BASIS

Appeal from the defendants' convictions.

■ FACTS

Cavitt (D) and Williams (D) plotted with Mianta McKnight to stage a break-in of Mianta's mother's home to steal her jewelry and other belongings. On the night of the theft, Cavitt (D) and Williams (D) entered the McKnight home, bound McKnight's mother with rope and duct tape, and placed a hood over her head. Before leaving, the two also tied up Mianta to relieve any suspicion of her involvement. By the time Mianta had freed herself and called her father to report the burglary, her mother had died of asphyxiation. Cavitt (D) and Williams (D) were charged with and convicted of felony murder. However, at trial, the defendants submitted evidence that after they left the house, Mianta deliberately suffocated her mother for reasons unrelated to the burglary. The trial court issued standard felony-murder jury instructions, but declined to explicitly instruct the jury that, if they found that the murder occurred after the commission of the burglary had been completed and for unrelated reasons, the felony-murder rule was inapplicable. The defendants appealed.

■ ISSUE

Does the felony-murder rule require both a causal and a temporal relationship between the felony and the resultant death?

■ DECISION AND RATIONALE

(Judge Undisclosed.) Yes. The felony-murder rule requires both a causal relationship and a temporal relationship between the underlying felony and the act resulting in death. This causal relationship is established when the evidence supports a logical nexus between the death-causing act and the underlying felony the criminal attempted or committed. The temporal relationship requires proof that the death and the felony were part of one continuous transaction. "The felony-murder rule does not apply to non-killers where the act resulting in death is completely unrelated to the underlying felony other than occurring in the same time and place." It is not essential, however, that the killing facilitated or aided in the commission of the felony. The felony-murder rule is designed to punish those who commit inherently dangerous crimes without the need to examine their particular intent with respect to the killing. A requirement that the act of killing aid the commission of the felony would necessitate such an evidentiary examination. Moreover, the felony-murder rule seeks to punish those who cause a death during the commission of a dangerous crime and deter such crimes to avoid negligent and unintentional deaths. These negligent and unintentional deaths will rarely facilitate or aid the commission of the intended felony.

Here, there is substantial evidence of a logical nexus between the killing and the burglary to support the conviction. The evidence suggests that the defendants either killed. Mrs. McKnight to eliminate the sole witness to their crime or she died accidentally while bound and beaten. Either theory supports the murder conviction. The court's jury instructions adequately informed the jury of the causal and temporal requirements needed to establish guilt. Affirmed.

Analysis:

Given the deterrent purpose of the felony-murder rule, it is easy to imagine courts going to great lengths to establish the logical nexus requirement. In the context of this case, even if Mianta had entirely separate reasons for killing her mother, she used the opportunity created by Cavitt (D) and Williams (D) to carry out her crime. The fact that the defendants left the victim bound after leaving the house arguably extends the temporal relationship between their felony and her death beyond the completion of the felony. By holding them responsible even for Mianta's actions, the policy of deterrence is fulfilled.

■ CASE VOCABULARY

FELONY—MURDER RULE: The doctrine holding that any death resulting from the commission or attempted commission of a dangerous felony is murder.

State v. Shock

(Government) v. (Child Beater)

68 Mo. 552 (1878)

THE UNDERLYING FELONY IN A FELONY MURDER CASE MAY NOT BE A CRIME OF VIOLENCE AGAINST THE VICTIM

■**INSTANT FACTS** Shock (D) beat a child to death and was charged with felony murder; he appealed his conviction.

■**BLACK LETTER RULE** The felony that underlies a conviction for felony murder must be a felony other than a crime of violence against the victim, which merges with the homicide.

■ **PROCEDURAL BASIS**

Appeal from a conviction for first-degree murder.

■ **FACTS**

Shock (D) was convicted of first-degree murder in the death of a young boy living in his home. The evidence showed that Shock (D) beat the boy with a piece of a fishing pole for several minutes. Shock (D) then got a piece of a grapevine and continued to beat the boy. The beating continued for approximately fifteen minutes. After several days, the boy died from the injuries he received from the beatings administered by Shock (D). Shock (D) was convicted of first-degree murder, pursuant to a jury instruction that provided that beating the child willfully or maliciously, or with the intent to cause great bodily harm, would support a conviction for first-degree murder.

■ **ISSUE**

Is Shock (D) guilty of felony murder?

■ **DECISION AND RATIONALE**

(Hough, J.) No. The felony that underlies a conviction for felony murder must be a felony other than a crime of violence on the victim, which merges with the homicide. The statute says that "any murder" committed in a particular manner, as well as a murder committed in the course of committing certain other listed felonies, shall be first-degree murder. The beating of the boy does not fall into one of the listed felonies, which all are crimes that could be committed without a homicide. The statute does not say "any homicide," but limits its application to crimes considered murder at common law. If the homicide was not murder at common law, it cannot be first-degree murder under the statute. At common law, a homicide committed as a result of the willful and malicious infliction of great bodily harm was murder, even though the defendant did not intend to cause death. It was murder because the infliction of bodily harm was *malum in se,* not because it was a felony. It is not murder in the first degree, since the crime did not involve premeditation, and it was not a death caused by the commission of one of the listed felonies. On the facts of this case, the jury could have been instructed on the law of first-degree murder as a willful, deliberate, and premeditated killing, but the jury was instructed only regarding felony murder. Conviction reversed and case remanded.

■ CONCURRING OPINION

(Henry, J.) The statute is not intended to enlarge the class of homicides that will be considered felony murders. The construction of the statute that would include as felony murder a death caused by the commission of *any* felony would nullify several sections of the criminal statutes, which specifically provide that a death caused by a violation of that statute will be some other degree of homicide.

■ DISSENTING OPINION

(Norton, J.) The felony of inflicting bodily harm on another does not merge into a homicide any more than a rape that causes death merges into a homicide. The felony murder statute lists rape and robbery as felonies that will underlie a conviction for felony murder, but neither of those crimes can be committed without a physical assault on the victim.

Analysis:

The jury could have received a charge on premeditated murder, and the court implies very strongly that such a conviction would be upheld. The distinction may seem moot: why overturn the conviction, when it is to be sent back for retrial and perhaps reach the same result? The jury was not, however, given the opportunity to determine the precise nature of the offense that Shock (D) committed. On the facts presented, the majority states that the jury could have found not only premeditated murder, but could alternatively have found fourth-degree manslaughter.

■ CASE VOCABULARY

FIRST—DEGREE MURDER: Murder that is willful, deliberate, or premeditated, or that is committed during the course of another dangerous felony.

HARMLESS ERROR: An error that does not affect a party's substantive rights or the case's outcome.

MALUM IN SE: [Latin, "evil in itself."] A crime or an act that is inherently immoral, such as murder, arson, or rape.

SECOND—DEGREE MURDER: Murder that is not aggravated by any of the circumstances of first-degree murder.

CHAPTER SEVEN

Capital Murder and the Death Penalty

Olsen v. State

Instant Facts: Olsen (D) robbed the Little Chief Bar and shot and killed three persons in the bar; he was tried under the Wyoming Capital Murder Statute and sentenced to death.

Black Letter Rule: A capital sentencing scheme must genuinely narrow the class of persons eligible for the death penalty and must reasonably justify the imposition of a more severe sentence for a particular defendant when compared to others found guilty of murder.

Tison v. Arizona

Instant Facts: Raymond Tison (D) and Ricky Tison (D) participated in a plan to break their father out of prison; in the process, their father and his former cellmate killed a family after stealing their car. Raymond (D) and Ricky (D) received death sentences for their participation under Arizona's felony murder rule.

Black Letter Rule: Reckless indifference to innocent life, shown by participating in the events leading up to and following a murder, makes the death sentence constitutionally permissible even when the defendant did not specifically intend to kill the victim and did not inflict the fatal wound.

McCleskey v. Kemp

Instant Facts: McCleskey (D), a black defendant, was sentenced to death following his conviction for the murder of a white police officer.

Black Letter Rule: A claim of racial bias in the imposition of the death penalty must be supported by evidence that sentencing was imposed with a discriminatory purpose.

Olsen v. State

(Murderer) v. (Wyoming)

67 P.3d 536 (2003)

A SENTENCING SCHEME MUST GENUINELY NARROW THOSE ELIGIBLE FOR THE DEATH PENALTY

■INSTANT FACTS Olsen (D) robbed the Little Chief Bar and shot and killed three persons in the bar; he was tried under the Wyoming Capital Murder Statute and sentenced to death.

■BLACK LETTER RULE A capital sentencing scheme must genuinely narrow the class of persons eligible for the death penalty and must reasonably justify the imposition of a more severe sentence for a particular defendant when compared to others found guilty of murder.

■ PROCEDURAL BASIS

On appeal from the defendant's conviction for capital murder and death sentence.

■ FACTS

Martin J. Olsen (D) went into the Little Chief Bar and instructed two patrons to lie down on the floor while he robbed the bar. He then instructed the bartender to lie down with the patrons and shot all three in the back of the head. Olsen (D) went from the bar to a gas station, bought gas, and chatted with the store clerk until the clerk asked if he knew what had brought the police to the area. He then went home and packed. Before Olsen (D) left home, he confessed the murders to his mother. His mother phoned the police and Olsen (D) was quickly apprehended. Olsen (D) confessed to the police and the confessions were taped. During one of the interviews, Olsen (D) told the officer he did not recall confessing to his mother, but he did not deny his responsibility for the killings. He said he had shot the victims because he was drunk and afraid of being caught. Evidence offered at trial supported the assertion that Olsen (D) was drunk when he committed the murders. Evidence also established that he had suffered from brain disorders including learning and behavioral problems. On the day of the murders, he had started taking a new drug to help control seizures. He was convicted of three counts of first-degree murder, three counts of felony murder, and one count of aggravated robbery. As required by Wyoming law, following the conviction for first-degree murder, the judge held a separate sentencing hearing to determine whether Olsen (D) should be sentenced to life in prison or to death. At that hearing, the jury heard, among other things, evidence as to mitigation or aggravation of the offense. The defendant was sentenced to death and appealed.

■ ISSUE

Was the defendant's death penalty sentence the result of careful consideration by the jury of all the appropriate mitigating and aggravating factors under the state law?

■ DECISION AND RATIONALE

(Golden, J.) No. Five aggravating factors were submitted to the jury and the jury found the facts established four of them. Olsen (D) argued that three of the aggravating factors found by the jury were improperly applied here. The prosecution advanced that (1) Olsen (D) created a great risk of death to two or more persons; (2) the murders were committed to avoid or prevent arrest; (3) the murders were especially atrocious or cruel, unnecessarily torturing the victims; (4) Olsen (D) posed a substantial threat of future danger and was likely to commit more acts of criminal violence; and (5) Olsen (D) killed another human being purposely and with premeditated malice in the commission of a robbery. First, as to the contention that the murders were especially atrocious or cruel, this factor has not been established. Evidence did not indicate that Olsen (D) tortured his victims. While all murders are detestable, nothing shows these murders were any more offensive than other murders. Second, though it may be said that Olsen (D) created a risk of death to two or more persons, this factor is generally established by evidence of the defendant's creation of a danger to individuals other than the targets of his criminal actions. It is not satisfied by a mere showing of multiple victims. The legislature could have extended the death penalty to multiple murders, but chose not to do so. No bystanders were placed at risk by Olsen's (D) activities. Third, the murders were not committed to avoid arrest. While nearly every felony-murder is committed to elude arrest by leaving no witnesses, the situation contemplated by this factor more often applies to those in which arrest is imminent. Fourth, while this was certainly a situation in which the felony murder rule applied, since the felony murder rule was used in this case to establish the existence of premeditation for first-degree murder, it cannot be used again to establish an aggravating factor.

When the jurors were instructed on mitigating circumstances, they were told that mitigating circumstances needed to be proven by a preponderance of the evidence. In the end, the jurors failed to find any mitigating circumstances simply because they could not all agree. But unanimity of opinion is not required for mitigating circumstances. Instead, the jurors should have been instructed that, as individuals, they were free to give weight to the mitigating factors as they saw fit and consider them in casting their vote for either life in prison or death. Finally, during deliberations, the jury questioned whether imposing three life terms would leave open the possibility of parole for Olsen (D) at some future date. The answer they received discussed the potential for pardons by the governor that could lead to a defendant being considered for parole. This instruction was improper, however, since it did not emphasize that, without a governor's pardon, the defendant would *not* be eligible for parole. Olsen's (D) sentence of death is set aside and the matter is remanded for a new sentencing hearing to be conducted by a new jury.

Analysis:

Here, the court stopped the prosecution from double-dipping with the felony-murder rule. The court refused to allow the prosecution to refer to the fact that the murders here were committed in the course of felony to serve as an aggravating factor. In *State v. Finch*, 46 P.3d 421 (Ariz. 2002), a defendant tried the reverse argument. Finch argued that the fact that he did not commit the murder should serve as a mitigating factor at sentencing. The court acknowledged that while there may be some merit to his argument, the fact that he took part in the planning and preparation of three serious felonies would tend to cancel out any "points" the jury would give him for not having pulled the trigger.

■ CASE VOCABULARY

AGGRAVATING CIRCUMSTANCE: A fact or situation that increases the degree of liability or culpability for a criminal act; a fact or situation that relates to a criminal offense or defendant and that is considered by the court in imposing punishment (especially a death sentence).

FELONY MURDER: Murder that occurs during the commission of a dangerous felony (often limited to rape, kidnapping, robbery, burglary, and arson).

MITIGATING CIRCUMSTANCE: A fact or situation that does not justify or excuse a wrongful act or offense but that reduces the degree of culpability and thus may reduce the damages (in a civil case) or the punishment (in a criminal case); a fact or situation that does not bear on the question of a defendant's guilt but that is considered by the court in imposing punishment and especially in lessening the severity of a sentence.

Tison v. Arizona

(Sons of Escapee) v. (State of Arizona)

481 U.S. 137, 107 S.Ct. 1676 (1987)

RECKLESS INDIFFERENCE TO HUMAN LIFE THROUGH PARTICIPATION IN A DANGEROUS FELONY SUPPORTS THE DEATH PENALTY

Dad! Why?!?

Sons, I was serving a life sentence for MURDER. This is what I do.

stus.com

■**INSTANT FACTS** Raymond Tison (D) and Ricky Tison (D) participated in a plan to break their father out of prison; in the process, their father and his former cellmate killed a family after stealing their car. Raymond (D) and Ricky (D) received death sentences for their participation under Arizona's felony murder rule.

■**BLACK LETTER RULE** Reckless indifference to innocent life, shown by participating in the events leading up to and following a murder, makes the death sentence constitutionally permissible even when the defendant did not specifically intend to kill the victim and did not inflict the fatal wound.

■ **PROCEDURAL BASIS**

On appeal to the Supreme Court from a decision by the Arizona Supreme Court upholding the imposition of the death penalties.

■ **FACTS**

Gary Tison was sentenced to life in prison because of a prison escape during which he killed a guard. After serving several years, his wife, three sons, brother and other relatives made plans to help Tison escape again. As part of the plan, weapons were obtained. Three of Tison's sons entered the prison carrying an ice chest filled with guns. They provided a weapon to their father and his cellmate, Greenawalt. The group locked several guards and other prison visitors in a closet and fled the grounds without firing a shot. They left the prison in a car they later abandoned in exchange for a white Lincoln. The Lincoln developed multiple flat tires. The group decided to flag down a passing motorist and steal their car. John Lyons and his wife, son, and niece stopped to assist them only to be forced inside the Lincoln. Raymond (D) and Donald Tison drove the Lincoln farther into the desert while the others followed in the Lyons' car. The prison group parked the car and told the Lyonses to stand in front of the Lincoln while they exchanged the contents of their respective cars. In the process, the family's belongings were picked over and the group found money and guns, which they kept. The Lincoln was then driven farther into the desert. The Lyonses started to beg for their lives. Gary Tison considered leaving the family in the desert but changed his mind. Greenawalt and Gary Tison shot and killed the members of the Lyons family; then the group got in the deceased family's Mazda and drove off. Over the course of a few days, Gary Tison's son Donald was killed in a police shootout, Greenawalt was recaptured, and Gary Tison died of exposure in the desert. Tison's two remaining sons, Raymond (D) and Ricky (D), were captured and tried for the many crimes associated with the prison break, including the Lyons family murders. The defendants were charged with capital murder based on the Arizona felony-murder rule.

■ **ISSUE**

Can a defendant's reckless indifference to innocent life, exhibited by his or her conduct both before and after a murder, make the death sentence constitutionally permissible, even though the defendant lacked the intent to kill the victim and did not inflict the fatal wound?

■ **DECISION AND RATIONALE**

(O'Connor, J.) Yes. Reckless indifference to innocent life, shown by participating in the events leading up to and following a murder, makes the death sentence constitutionally permissible even when the defendant did not specifically intend to kill the victim and did not inflict the fatal wound. But the circumstances of the case must justify such a result, and here it is unclear what the outcome should be. The Supreme Court reversed a defendant's death sentence in *Enmund v. Florida*, 458 U.S. 782 (1982), where the driver of the "getaway" car was charged under the felony-murder rule. In that Florida case, the victims were killed by Enmund's accomplices, and the Florida Supreme Court held that Enmund's willingness to assist his compatriots formed a sufficient basis to impose the death penalty. On appeal, the U.S. Supreme Court noted that Florida was one of only eight jurisdictions where the death penalty was authorized as punishment under the felony-murder rule. Eight other states require a finding of intent to kill as a prerequisite to imposing the death penalty, one state requires evidence of actual participation in the killing, and the remaining states have requirements somewhere in between. In *Enmunds*, the Court took note that of 739 inmates on death row, only three, including Enmunds, were not present at the actual killing and had lacked the intent to kill. The Court performed its own proportionality test and decided that the role Enmunds played in the crime was disproportionate to the sentence of death. The Court noted that the likelihood of a killing during a robbery is slim. If the odds were greater, it would make more sense that one participating in a robbery should share in the blame for any deaths. But the death penalty cannot serve as a deterrent where killing is infrequent. While noting that the death penalty also serves a societal need for retribution, the *Enmunds* court nonetheless concluded that where participation in the actual murder is attenuated, the death penalty imposes excessive retribution.

The *Enmunds* court examined felony murders in light of the Eighth Amendment and found Enmunds' personal involvement to be at one end of a continuum and his accomplices' actions at the other. Here, the involvement of Donald Tison's sons does not fall neatly at either end. No evidence was presented that showed Ricky (D) or Raymond (D) performed any action intending to cause death. The Arizona Supreme Court did not require a finding of "intent" in the traditional sense. The court was satisfied to find intent as a by-product of foreseeability. However, the foreseeability argument is the basis for the felony-murder rule; it is not evidence of intent. Under *Enmunds*, the defendants here do not fall within a category of killers who intended to bring about the deaths of their victims; however, the defendants are not merely minor players for whom the death penalty is obviously excessive. Raymond (D) brought an arsenal of weapons to the prison break that he shared with known felons. He flagged down the victims and robbed them. He guarded them at gunpoint and waited for instructions from his father. He also participated in a gunfight with the police. Ricky's (D) behavior is only slightly different. He also brought guns to the prison and knew from his father's violent tendencies that the possibility that innocent lives could be taken was real. Four states permit the imposition of the death penalty on defendants who, recklessly or with extreme indifference to human life, participate in a crime in which a death results. Under Arizona law, minor participation in the felony will serve as a mitigating factor. The more a defendant participates in the underlying crime, the stronger the evidence of his indifference to human life. In almost every state, however, prior to imposing a death sentence some aggravating factor must be shown, especially when the defendant's mental state fell short of the intent to kill. Focusing on whether the defendant intended to kill is a rather narrow focus for penalizing dangerous criminals. Many who kill do so accidentally or as a matter of self-defense or justification, or from provocation. Others kill with reckless indifference to the value of human life. Major participation in a felony, in combination with reckless indifference to human life, will satisfy the *Enmund's* requirement that the defendant have some culpability for the murder. The sentences here are vacated and the matter is remanded for a determination of whether major participation and reckless indifference were present here. Vacated and remanded.

Analysis:

The Court here did not reject the application of the death penalty to all accomplices who did not participate in the killings. Rather, the Court insisted that the prosecution must demonstrate that the condemned defendants appreciated that their acts were likely to result in the taking of innocent life. As a direct result of this case, in June 1990, the citizens of California adopted Proposition 115. The proposition amended the penal code to reflect the holding here.

■ **CASE VOCABULARY**

FELONY–MURDER RULE: The doctrine holding that any death resulting from the commission or attempted commission of a dangerous felony is murder.

RECKLESS: Characterized by the creation of a substantial and unjustifiable risk of harm to others and by a conscious (and sometimes deliberate) disregard for or indifference to that risk; heedless; rash. Reckless conduct is much more than mere negligence: it is a gross deviation from what a reasonable person would do.

SIMPLICITER: In a simple or summary manner; absolutely, unconditionally; per se.

McCleskey v. Kemp
(Convicted Murder) v. (Prosecutor)

481 U.S. 279, 107 S.Ct. 1756 (1987)

EVIDENCE OF DISCRIMINATORY PURPOSE IS REQUIRED TO ESTABLISH RACIAL BIAS IN THE IMPOSITION OF CAPITAL PUNISHMENT

■**INSTANT FACTS** McCleskey (D), a black defendant, was sentenced to death following his conviction for the murder of a white police officer.

■**BLACK LETTER RULE** A claim of racial bias in the imposition of the death penalty must be supported by evidence that sentencing was imposed with a discriminatory purpose.

■ **PROCEDURAL BASIS**

On certiorari to review the Eleventh Circuit Court of Appeals' affirmance of the trial court's imposition of the death sentence.

■ **FACTS**

McCleskey (D), a black defendant, was sentenced to death following his conviction for the murder of a white police officer. Following his conviction, McCleskey (D) filed a habeas corpus petition raising eighteen claims, including one alleging that Georgia's capital sentencing process is racially discriminatory in violation of the Eighth and Fourteenth Amendments. His claim of racial bias was supported by a statistical study by Professor Baldus based on 2000 murder cases in Georgia. The study suggested that when a murder victim is white, the defendant is more than ten times as likely to receive a death sentence than he or she is when the victim is non-white. The results also indicated that twice as many white defendants received the death penalty as non-whites. After adjusting for nonracial factors, Professor Baldus's study showed that black defendants charged with killing white victims were the most likely to receive death sentences. The district court declined to find any merit in the statistical study. On appeal to the Eleventh Circuit, the court presumed the study was valid, but concluded the statistics were insufficient to establish discrimination based on the Fourteenth Amendment. In fact, the court of appeals found the study supported the conclusion that the penalty was *not* being handed out discriminatorily.

■ **ISSUE**

Is the Eighth Amendment offended by inconsistencies based on the race of the defendants, when the penalty is imposed is based on objective circumstances of crime?

■ **DECISION AND RATIONALE**

(Powell, J.) No. McCleskey (D) argues that the Georgia death penalty process is racially tainted. He claims that both the killer of a white victim and a black murderer are more likely to

---

get a sentence of death than other murderers. However, absent a showing that the Georgia criminal justice system has operated arbitrarily and capriciously, there is no constitutional violation. As the Court held in *Gregg v. Georgia*, 428 U.S. 153 (1976), simply because discretion may be exercised as to extenuating or aggravating circumstances does not show an abuse of discretion. Since McCleskey's (D) sentence was imposed under a system that focused on the crime and the traits of the defendant, the sentence was likely not wantonly imposed.

McCleskey (D) also argues that while the system may look as though it is properly administered, it is actually applied arbitrarily and capriciously, and so the sentence here is excessive. McCleskey (D) contends that the Baldus statistics show an unacceptable risk of racial prejudice. However, while the Baldus statistics show that race may have been a factor, they do not establish that race was, in fact, the primary or only consideration. At most, they show that race may have received consideration in some cases. In addition to race, however, other factors likely influenced the outcome. Discretion is a necessary part of the justice system because it can provide benefits to the accused. Those benefits are frequently non-reviewable by a court and can been seen in ways that include charging a lesser offense or ensuring a life sentence over a death penalty. The Baldus study may show some statistical differences in sentences by race, but some statistical differences will always be seen. The most that can be expected, constitutionally, is that the sentence will be imposed under a system with the appropriate safeguards to minimize bias. Allowing a challenge like this would leave no limits on the use of statistics to find distortions in sentencing. If any challenge is to be made, it must be made to the legislature, whose right it is to determine the level of punishment for crimes. Affirmed.

Analysis:

Justice Blackmun, in his dissent in *Callins v. Collins*, 510 U.S. 1141 (1994), made note of twenty years of decisions since the Court held that the death penalty, if it is to be imposed, must "be imposed fairly, and with reasonable consistency, or not at all." He was appreciative of the many safeguards that states had adopted in two decades to help ensure the evenhanded administration of justice. He was also saddened. He concluded that it appeared that "no combination of procedural rules or substantive regulations ever can save the death penalty from its inherent constitutional deficiencies." It would appear Justice Blackmun does not agree with Justice Powell that inconsistencies in the system are evidence that reforms are working.

■ **CASE VOCABULARY**

HABEAS CORPUS: A writ employed to bring a person before a court, most frequently to ensure that the party's imprisonment or detention is not illegal. In addition to being used to test the legality of an arrest or commitment, the writ may be used to obtain review of (1) the regularity of the extradition process, (2) the right to or amount of bail, or (3) the jurisdiction of a court that has imposed a criminal sentence.

CHAPTER EIGHT

Defensive Force, Necessity, and Duress

People v. La Voie

Instant Facts: La Voie (D) shot and killed one member of a group who threatened and advanced on him in a menacing manner.

Black Letter Rule: When a person reasonably believes that the danger of being killed or of suffering severe bodily harm is imminent, he or she may use force to defend himself or herself, even to the extent of killing another, although it may turn out that there was no such imminent danger.

People v. Gleghorn

Instant Facts: Gleghorn (D) was shot in the back with an arrow, and he responded by attacking the shooter.

Black Letter Rule: A person who creates appearances that justify another person's use of deadly force may not use deadly force as a counterattack, unless he or she attempted to withdraw from combat and notified the other party of the withdrawal.

State v. Leidholm

Instant Facts: Leidholm (D) killed her husband and claimed she acted in self-defense, due to years of being abused by her husband.

Black Letter Rule: In cases involving a claim of self-defense, a defendant's conduct is evaluated according to what he or she reasonably, in good faith, honestly believed and had reasonable ground to believe was necessary to protect the defendant from apprehended death or great bodily injury.

People v. Goetz

Instant Facts: Goetz (D) shot four youths who asked him for money and claimed that he acted in self-defense because he thought they intended to rob him.

Black Letter Rule: The reasonableness of a belief in the need to use force is determined according to an objective standard of reasonableness, taking into account the circumstances or situation facing the defendant.

Tennessee v. Garner

Instant Facts: Garner (P) was shot by a police officer while fleeing from the scene of a break-in.

Black Letter Rule: The Fourth Amendment to the U.S. Constitution prohibits the use of deadly force against a fleeing suspect who is not believed to pose a threat of serious physical harm to others.

People v. Ceballos

Instant Facts: Ceballos (D) set up a trap with a gun to shoot intruders and was convicted of assault with a deadly weapon when the gunshot hit a person breaking in.

Black Letter Rule: Deadly force may be used to defend against a forcible and atrocious crime that causes human life or personal safety to be in great peril, or to be presumed to be in great peril.

The Queen v. Dudley & Stephens

Instant Facts: Dudley and Stephens (D) killed and ate a boy while on the verge of starvation.

Black Letter Rule: Necessity does not justify killing another person who poses no danger.

People v. Unger

Instant Facts: Unger (D) escaped from prison after his life was threatened.

Black Letter Rule: Necessity is a defense if the defendant did not cause or develop the situation and if the defendant reasonably believed his or her actions were necessary to avoid a greater injury than the injury that might reasonably result from the defendant's actions.

State v. Warshow

Instant Facts: Warshow (D) was arrested for trespass while protesting at a nuclear power plant and attempted to assert a defense of necessity.

Black Letter Rule: The defense of necessity requires a showing that the threatened harm is imminent or reasonably appears to be imminent.

State v. Crawford

Instant Facts: Crawford (D) was convicted of multiple crimes, and claimed that he was forced to commit them.

Black Letter Rule: The defense of compulsion requires a showing that the defendant acted out of a fear that he or she would suffer imminent bodily harm, not from some future threat of bodily harm.

State v. Hunter

Instant Facts: Hunter (D) was convicted of felony murder but claimed he was forced to participate in the criminal activity.

Black Letter Rule: Compulsion is not a defense to a homicide charge, unless the charge is felony murder.

(Prosecuting Government) v. (Pharmacist)

395 P.2d 1001 (Colo. 1964)

DEADLY FORCE MAY BE USED IN SELF—DEFENSE

■**INSTANT FACTS** La Voie (D) shot and killed one member of a group who threatened and advanced on him in a menacing manner.

■**BLACK LETTER RULE** When a person reasonably believes that the danger of being killed or of suffering severe bodily harm is imminent, he or she may use force to defend himself or herself, even to the extent of killing another, although it may turn out that there was no such imminent danger.

■ **PROCEDURAL BASIS**

Decision on a motion of the prosecution to disapprove a directed verdict.

■**FACTS**

As La Voie (D) was driving home from work at about 1:30 a.m., an automobile made contact with his rear bumper and began pushing La Voie's (D) automobile through a red light. La Voie (D) applied his brakes, but his car continued forward. When his car came to a stop, La Voie (D) got out and approached the other vehicle. He was armed with a revolver that he carried with a permit. The other car was occupied by four men, all of whom had been drinking, and who had agreed beforehand to ram La Voie's (D) car for "kicks." The four men also got out of their car and walked towards La Voie (D), threatening him, cursing at him, and saying that they would make La Voie (D) "eat" his gun. One of the men moved towards La Voie (D) in a threatening manner and La Voie (D) shot him. The trial court directed a verdict for La Voie (D).

■ **ISSUE**

Could La Voie (D) be prosecuted for homicide?

■ **DECISION AND RATIONALE**

(Moore, J.) No. When a person reasonably believes that the danger of being killed or of suffering severe bodily harm is imminent, he or she may use force to defend himself or herself, even to the extent of killing another, although it may turn out that there was no such imminent danger. La Voie (D) did not know any of the men in the other vehicle, and it was late at night. He was conducting himself peaceably when the other men accosted him. La Voie's (D) use of force was justified. Disapproval denied.

Analysis:

The nuances of self-defense vary widely from state to state. In many states, a person is not required to retreat before using deadly force. In this case, there is no suggestion that La Voie

---

(D) would have been unable to retreat. In fact, La Voie (D) got out of his car, carrying his gun, and walked towards the men in other car, rather than trying to avoid a confrontation, yet his actions were deemed justified.

■ **CASE VOCABULARY**

DEADLY FORCE: Violent action known to create a substantial risk of causing death or serious bodily harm.

DIRECTED VERDICT: A ruling by a trial judge taking a case from the jury because the evidence will permit only one reasonable verdict.

HOMICIDE: The killing of one person by another.

SELF—DEFENSE: The use of force to protect oneself, one's family, or one's property from a real or threatened attack. Generally, a person is justified in using a reasonable amount of force in self-defense if he or she believes that the danger of bodily harm is imminent and that force is necessary to avoid this danger.

(Prosecuting Government) v. (Housemate)

193 Cal. App. 3d 196, 238 Cal. Rptr. 82 (1987)

A PERSON WHO CREATES AN IMMINENT FEAR OF BODILY HARM MAY NOT USE SELF– DEFENSE AGAINST A COUNTERATTACK

Come on out, Fairall!

stus.com

■**INSTANT FACTS** Gleghorn (D) was shot in the back with an arrow, and he responded by attacking the shooter.

■**BLACK LETTER RULE** A person who creates appearances that justify another person's use of deadly force may not use deadly force as a counterattack, unless he or she attempted to withdraw from combat and notified the other party of the withdrawal.

■ PROCEDURAL BASIS

Appeal from convictions for assault and battery.

■ FACTS

Fairall rented a garage from Downes and let her have his stereo. Downes thought Fairall gave her the stereo as a part of his rent and sold it to another. Fairall said that he had only lent it to her and, in retaliation, vandalized Downes's house and car. Downes told Gleghorn (D) about the vandalism and, at approximately 3:00 a.m., Gleghorn (D) went to the garage where Fairall lived and told Fairall to come out so that Gleghorn (D) could kill him. Fairall declined to come out and Gleghorn (D) went into the garage. Gleghorn (D) beat a stick on the rafters of the garage where Fairall slept, and Fairall saw sparks where the board hit the rafters. Gleghorn (D) said that if Fairall did not come out, he would burn him out. Gleghorn (D) set some of Fairall's clothes on fire. Fairall took a bow and arrow that he had in the rafters and loosed an arrow, not seeing where it went. Gleghorn (D) had been struck by Fairall's arrow, which caused a gash in his back. Fairall swung down from the rafters and was hit from behind. Gleghorn (D) continued to beat Fairall. The jury found Gleghorn (D) guilty of simple assault for his actions prior to being shot by the arrow, and guilty of battery with the infliction of serious bodily injury for his actions after he was shot. Gleghorn (D) claimed that he should not have been convicted of the second count, since Fairall was not entitled to respond to simple assault with deadly force, and so Gleghorn (D) was entitled to respond to Fairall with deadly force.

■ ISSUE

Was Gleghorn (D) entitled to use deadly force in self-defense?

■ DECISION AND RATIONALE

(Stone, J.) No. A person who creates appearances that justify another person's use of deadly force may not use deadly force as a counterattack, unless he or she attempted to withdraw from combat and notified the other party of the withdrawal. If the victim of a simple assault responds with deadly force, the original aggressor may use deadly force in self-defense and is not required to withdraw. Fairall was justified in using deadly force. The right of self-defense is based on appearances at the time of the original attack; in other words, it is not based on the actual danger, but on the appearance of danger. Even if Fairall were not justified in using deadly force, Gleghorn (D) continued to beat him long after Fairall was disabled and could no longer attack. If a person's self-defense is so successful that the attacker cannot inflict injury, there is no further right to use force. Affirmed.

Analysis:

Self-defense should not be confused with a right to retaliate. Self-defense is to be used to prevent an attack, not to punish an attacker. Even if Gleghorn (D) had a legitimate claim to self-defense when he hit Fairall after he jumped down from the rafters, he clearly crossed the line between defense and retaliation when he continued to attack him. Note that Gleghorn's (D) concern for his own safety was not so great as to prevent him from beating Fairall while in a building that had a fire burning in it.

■ CASE VOCABULARY

ASSAULT: The threat or use of force on another that causes that person to have a reasonable apprehension of imminent harmful or offensive contact; the act of putting another person in reasonable fear or apprehension of an immediate battery by means of an act amounting to an attempt or threat to commit battery; an attempt to commit battery, requiring the specific intent to cause injury.

BATTERY: The use of force against another, resulting in harmful or offensive contact.

LESSER—INCLUDED OFFENSE: A crime that is composed of some, but not all, of the elements of a more serious crime and that is necessarily committed in carrying out the greater crime.

SIMPLE: (Of a crime) Not accompanied by aggravating circumstances.

THE REASONABLENESS OF A BELIEF IN THE NECESSITY OF DEADLY FORCE IS BASED ON THE SUBJECTIVE BELIEF OF THE ACTOR

■**INSTANT FACTS** Leidholm (D) killed her husband and claimed she acted in self-defense, due to years of being abused by her husband.

■**BLACK LETTER RULE** In cases involving a claim of self-defense, a defendant's conduct is evaluated according to what he or she reasonably, in good faith, honestly believed and had reasonable ground to believe was necessary to protect the defendant from apprehended death or great bodily injury.

■ **PROCEDURAL BASIS**

Appeal from a conviction for manslaughter.

■**FACTS**

Leidholm (D) was convicted of manslaughter for the killing of her husband. There was evidence that Leidholm (D) had been abused by her husband during the marriage. On the night of the killing, Leidholm (D) and her husband consumed a large amount of alcohol. They began to argue and continued arguing for some time. Leidholm (D) tried to call a deputy sheriff, but her husband shoved her and pushed her down, so she could not use the phone. Leidholm's (D) husband continued to push her down every time she stood up. After a time, Leidholm (D) and her husband went to bed. When her husband was asleep, Leidholm (D) got a knife and stabbed him. Leidholm (D) argued at trial that she stabbed her husband in self-defense and in reaction to the severe mistreatment she received from him. Expert evidence was introduced to show that Leidholm (D) suffered from "battered-woman syndrome," which is low self-esteem and "learned helplessness" caused by a regular pattern of spousal abuse. The trial court instructed the jury that Leidholm (D) was entitled to use deadly force if the circumstances were such as to "produce in the mind of reasonably prudent persons, regardless of their sex, similarly situated, the reasonable belief that the other person was then about to kill her or do serious bodily harm to her."

■ **ISSUE**

Was the jury correctly instructed on self-defense?

■ **DECISION AND RATIONALE**

(Vande Walle, J.) No. In cases involving a claim of self-defense, a defendant's conduct must be evaluated according to what he or she reasonably believed was necessary to protect himself or herself from apprehended death or great bodily injury. The standard of reasonableness is not an objective standard, but is a subjective one, taking into account the defendant's own viewpoint. Past decisions of the court, along with a belief that the subjective standard is more just and the fact that there is no statute compelling a contrary rule, all lead to a decision that the correct standard is a subjective one. The jury should be allowed to consider the unique physical and psychological aspects of the accused in order to judge the reasonableness of his or her actions. If a defendant's actual belief in the necessity of using deadly force is unreasonable, the defendant will be guilty of either negligent or reckless homicide. But an honest belief in the necessity of using deadly force will not support a murder conviction.

A special jury instruction on the effects of battered-woman syndrome is not necessary. Battered-woman syndrome is not a defense, but the jury must consider expert testimony regarding an accused's state of mind when evaluating the subjective reasonableness of his or her conduct. There is no merit to Leidholm's (D) argument that the statute that requires a person to retreat in his or her own dwelling before using deadly force against a cohabitant violates the Equal Protection Clause of the Fourteenth Amendment to the U.S. Constitution. If the circumstances are such that a person cannot retreat from a cohabitant assailant, the failure to retreat does not matter, and deadly force may be used. Reversed and remanded for a new trial.

Analysis:

Cases that involve battered spouses who claim self-defense often turn on the question of whether there is a threat of *imminent* harm. A sleeping victim, like Leidholm's (D) husband, does not present the same imminent threat that he did when he was awake, but the court found it adequate here. This case explains that the imminence of harm must be evaluated according to the physical and emotional state of the defendant.

■ CASE VOCABULARY

BATTERED–WOMAN SYNDROME: The medical and psychological condition of a woman who has suffered physical, sexual, or emotional abuse at the hands of a spouse or partner.

MANSLAUGHTER: The unlawful killing of a human being without malice aforethought.

(Prosecuting Government) v. (Shooter)

68 N.Y.2d 96, 497 N.E.2d 41 (1986)

THE USE OF FORCE IN SELF—DEFENSE MUST BE BASED ON A REASONABLY FORMED BELIEF THAT IT IS NECESSARY

■**INSTANT FACTS** Goetz (D) shot four youths who asked him for money and claimed that he acted in self-defense because he thought they intended to rob him.

■**BLACK LETTER RULE** The reasonableness of a belief in the need to use force is determined according to an objective standard of reasonableness, taking into account the circumstances or situation facing the defendant.

■ PROCEDURAL BASIS

Appeal from an order affirming the quashing a grand jury indictment for attempted murder, assault, and illegal weapon possession.

■ FACTS

Goetz (D) boarded a subway train in New York City, carrying a pistol in a holster. Four youths, who had boarded the train at a prior stop, approached Goetz (D), and one of them said, "Give me five dollars." None of the youths displayed a weapon, although two of them had screwdrivers under their coats. Goetz (D) took out his gun and began shooting. He hit three of the four youths (one of them in the back) and, after surveying the scene, he shot the fourth. The train stopped and Goetz (D) told the conductor that the youths had tried to rob him. Goetz (D) then fled and ultimately surrendered to police in New Hampshire nine days later. Goetz (D) made a statement to the police that he had been carrying a handgun for three years, since he was injured in a mugging. Goetz (D) stated that he knew none of the youths was armed, but that he knew from the smile on one of their faces that they wanted to "play" with him. He said he was afraid, based on his prior experiences, that he would be maimed. Goetz (D) stated that he wanted to kill the four youths and to make them suffer as much as possible. One youth, according to Goetz (D), acted like he didn't know the others, standing still and holding on to a hand strap. Goetz (D) shot him once and, after checking on the other youths, saw that he didn't look "so bad" so he shot him again. Goetz (D) stated that if he had been under more "self-control," he would have put his gun to the youth's forehead and fired. Goetz (D) also stated that he would have continued shooting if he had had more bullets. Goetz (D) was indicted by a grand jury for attempted murder, assault, and illegal weapons possession. The trial court quashed the indictment, holding that the prosecutor erroneously instructed the grand jury that it was to judge whether Goetz's (D) conduct was that of a reasonable man in Goetz's (D) situation. The trial court held that the standard to be used was whether Goetz's (D) beliefs were reasonable *to him*. The appellate division upheld the order of the trial court.

■ ISSUE

Was the grand jury properly instructed as to the standard to be applied in evaluating Goetz's (D) actions?

■ DECISION AND RATIONALE

(Wachtler, C.J.) Yes. The reasonableness of a belief in the need to use force is determined according to an objective standard of reasonableness, taking into account the circumstances or situation facing the defendant. A person may use deadly force if he or she reasonably believes that the force is necessary to protect him or her from death or serious bodily injury. The objective standard does not require that the actual circumstances of an incident be ignored. The circumstances may include not only the physical movements of the person who is the potential assailant, but also any relevant knowledge the defendant had, such as the physical attributes of the people involved (including the defendant), and the prior experiences the defendant had that could support a reasonable belief that another person had the intention to rob him or her, or that the use of deadly force was necessary under the circumstances. New York law has long provided that self-defense claims are to be evaluated according to an objective standard of reasonableness. But when the legislature revised the Penal Code, it rejected the objective standard set forth by the drafters of the Model Penal Code, which provided that a recklessly or negligently formed belief as to the necessity of using deadly force would result in a conviction for homicide that required a reckless or negligent intent. The New York rule is that self-defense provides a complete defense to a charge, but the use of force in self-defense must be based on a reasonable belief. Reversed, and the dismissed counts of the indictment are reinstated.

Analysis:

The rule announced by the court in this "Subway Vigilante" case is not a truly objective standard, but a hybrid objective/subjective standard. The actions of a defendant are to be evaluated according to an objective standard, but the circumstances of the defendant still must be considered. Query whether the court's reference to "prior experiences . . . which could provide a reasonable belief that another person's intentions were to injure or rob him" refers to a traumatically induced condition, akin to battered-woman syndrome, or whether it refers to a more generally held knowledge, or "street smarts." Although Goetz (D) ultimately was acquitted of most of the criminal charges against him, one of the youths he shot won a $43 million civil judgment against him in 1996. In more recent years, Goetz (D) has run unsuccessfully for Mayor of New York on a platform that espoused vegetarianism and kindness to animals (his campaign materials referred obliquely to the shootings as part of his work as an "activist" against crime).

■ CASE VOCABULARY

GRAND JURY: A body of (often twenty-three) people who are chosen to sit permanently for at least a month—and sometimes a year—and who, in ex parte proceedings, decide whether to issue indictments. If the grand jury decides that evidence is strong enough to hold a suspect for trial, it returns a bill of indictment (a *true bill*) charging the suspect with a specific crime.

INDICTMENT: The formal written accusation of a crime, made by a grand jury and presented to a court for prosecution against the accused person; the act or process of preparing or bringing forward such a formal written accusation.

QUASH: To annul or make void; to terminate.

Tennessee v. Garner

(Prosecuting Government) v. (Shooting Victim)

471 U.S. 1, 105 S.Ct. 1694 (1985)

DEADLY FORCE MAY NOT BE USED TO STOP A NON–VIOLENT SUSPECT FROM FLEEING

■**INSTANT FACTS** Garner (P) was shot by a police officer while fleeing from the scene of a break-in.

■**BLACK LETTER RULE** The Fourth Amendment to the U.S. Constitution prohibits the use of deadly force against a fleeing suspect who is not believed to pose a threat of serious physical harm to others.

■ **PROCEDURAL BASIS**

Appeal from an order of the court of appeals that reversed and remanded a district court judgment for Tennessee (D).

■ **FACTS**

Police officer Hymon (D) responded to a call that reported a prowler. When he arrived on the scene, he went around to the back of the house and saw Garner (P) stopped at the fence at the edge of the yard. Hymon (D) could see Garner's (P) hands and face in the light from his flashlight. Hymon (D) was "reasonably sure" that Garner (P) was unarmed. Hymon (D) thought Garner (P) was seventeen or eighteen years old and five feet, seven inches tall (in fact, Garner (P) was fifteen, five feet, four inches tall, and weighed around 100 to 110 pounds). Hymon (D) testified that he called to Garner (P) to stop, and Garner (P) began to climb over the fence. Hymon (D) was convinced that Garner (P) would escape, so he shot him, hitting him in the back of the head. Garner (P) died after being taken to the hospital. He was found to have ten dollars and a purse taken from the house from which he was fleeing. Hymon (D) shot Garner (P) pursuant to a Tennessee statute that allows an officer to use "all the necessary means to effect [an] arrest" if a suspect flees or resists an attempt to arrest him (case law in Tennessee held that the use of deadly force would be allowed only against fleeing felony suspects). The district court found the statute and Hymon's (D) actions to be constitutional.

■ **ISSUE**

Was the use of deadly force constitutionally permissible against an unarmed fleeing prowler?

■ **DECISION AND RATIONALE**

(White, J.) No. The Fourth Amendment to the U.S. Constitution prohibits the use of deadly force against a fleeing suspect who is not believed to pose a threat of serious physical harm to others. Shooting a fleeing suspect is a "seizure" within the meaning of the Fourth Amendment

---

prohibition of unreasonable searches and seizures. The state's interest in apprehending all fleeing felony suspects does not outweigh the suspect's interest in his own life. Using deadly force against a fleeing suspect also frustrates the mutual interest of the state and the suspect in judicial determination of guilt and punishment. There is no evidence that a meaningful threat of deadly force has resulted in the apprehension of more suspects by deterring escape attempts. In fact, most police departments have prohibited the used of deadly force against nonviolent suspects. The rule that allows the use of deadly force against fleeing felony suspects comes from a time when most felonies were punishable by death or involved violence, neither of which is true today. The rule also arose at a time when deadly force could be inflicted only at close quarters during a struggle, which means the police officer's life would have been in jeopardy. Deadly force may only be used to prevent the escape of a suspect who threatens an officer with a weapon, or if there is probable cause to believe the suspect has committed a crime that involves the infliction or threatened infliction of serious physical harm. There were no such facts in this case, so the use of deadly force was unreasonable. Affirmed.

Analysis:

The modern-day distinction between felonies and misdemeanors can be difficult to grasp until after the crime is committed and an arrest is made. For example, in many jurisdictions, the distinction between felony theft and misdemeanor theft depends on the value of the items stolen, a fact that ordinarily cannot be determined until after a suspect has been arrested and the stolen items investigated. It is unclear from the Court's opinion whether deadly force would be constitutionally permissible if used against a fleeing misdemeanor suspect who posed a threat of serious bodily harm (such as a drunk driver).

■ CASE VOCABULARY

FELONY: A serious crime usually punishable by imprisonment for more than one year or by death.

FOURTH AMENDMENT: The constitutional amendment, ratified with the Bill of Rights in 1791, prohibiting unreasonable searches and seizures and the issuance of warrants without probable cause.

MISDEMEANOR: A crime that is less serious than a felony and is usually punishable by fine, penalty, forfeiture, or confinement (usually for a brief term) in a place other than a prison (such as a county jail).

PROBABLE CAUSE: A reasonable ground to suspect that a person has committed or is committing a crime or that a place contains specific items connected with a crime. Under the Fourth Amendment, probable cause—which amounts to more than a bare suspicion but less than evidence that would support a conviction—must be shown before an arrest warrant or search warrant may be issued.

DEADLY FORCE MAY BE USED TO PREVENT A FELONY THAT CAUSES PERIL TO LIFE OR SAFETY

■**INSTANT FACTS** Ceballos (D) set up a trap with a gun to shoot intruders and was convicted of assault with a deadly weapon when the gunshot hit a person breaking in.

■**BLACK LETTER RULE** Deadly force may be used to defend against a forcible and atrocious crime that causes human life or personal safety to be in great peril, or to be presumed to be in great peril.

■ **PROCEDURAL BASIS**

Appeal from a conviction for assault with a deadly weapon.

■ **FACTS**

Ceballos (D) set up a trap in his garage after tools were stolen from his home; he noticed that the lock on his garage doors was bent and that there were pry marks on one of the doors. The trap consisted of a loaded .22 caliber pistol aimed at the center of the garage doors and wired so that the pistol would fire if the doors were opened. Two boys, Stephen and Robert, broke into the garage while Ceballos (D) was away. They were unarmed and entered the garage to look for property, and possibly to steal that property. The gun went off and the shot hit Stephen in the face. Ceballos (D) acknowledged setting the trap and said he did it to protect his property from being stolen. He was convicted of assault with a deadly weapon and contended on appeal that the trap gun only did in his absence what Ceballos (D) could have done if he had been at home at the time.

■ **ISSUE**

Did Ceballos (D) use excessive force?

■ **DECISION AND RATIONALE**

(Burke, J.) Yes. Deadly force may be used to defend against a forcible and atrocious crime that causes human life or personal safety to be in great peril, or to be presumed to be in great peril. Burglary is not always a forcible and atrocious crime. There are circumstances in which burglary will not cause a fear of great bodily harm. In this case, the burglars were unarmed and waited until no one else was on the premises. The California Penal Code appears to justify the use of deadly force against all felonies, but that provision only codifies the common law, which held that deadly force could be used only against crimes that are an attempt to commit a violent injury. The trap gun does not distinguish between intruders and those who might lawfully enter the property (e.g., firefighters), so a rule allowing the use of trap guns will not be adopted. Affirmed.

Analysis:

The rule regarding the use of deadly force against a burglar requires the actor to make a quick decision: does this burglar pose a threat? The physical threat posed by the burglars here is minimal, but even if Ceballos (D) had been home at the time, how would he have known that? The court's rule seems intended to prevent a "shoot first, ask questions later" rule. As a practical matter, deadly force would appear to be justified only if the burglar is confronted and then proceeds to do something that poses a threat.

■ CASE VOCABULARY

BURGLARY: The modern statutory offense of breaking and entering any building—not just a dwelling, and not only at night—with the intent to commit a felony. Some statutes make petit larceny an alternative to a felony for purposes of proving burglarious intent.

MANTRAP: A booby-trap; especially a device to catch a trespasser or burglar. A mantrap is not illegal if it is designed merely to sound an alarm and not cause bodily harm. Illegal mantraps include manufactured devices such as spring guns, and dangerous hidden conditions (manufactured or natural) that can injure a person, such as pitfalls.

The Queen v. Dudley & Stephens

(Prosecuting Government) v. (Sailors)

14 Q.B.D. 273 (1884)

NECESSITY DOES NOT EXCUSE HOMICIDE

■**INSTANT FACTS** Dudley and Stephens (D) killed and ate a boy while on the verge of starvation.

■**BLACK LETTER RULE** Necessity does not justify killing another person who poses no danger.

■ **PROCEDURAL BASIS**

Decision on a special verdict.

■ **FACTS**

Dudley (D) and Stephens (D), along with Parker and Brooks, were cast away on an open boat after their vessel sank. They had no water, except for such rainwater as they were able to gather, and very little food. On the twentieth day, they were without food and water of any kind. Parker, the smallest of them, was very weak and not expected to live much longer. The sailors were more than 1000 miles away from land. Dudley (D) indicated that Parker should be killed, but Brooks did not agree. Dudley (D) told Brooks to go to sleep, and Dudley (D) and Stephens (D) then killed Parker. Parker did not agree to be killed, and the sailors did not draw lots to see who should be killed. Parker was killed because he was the smallest and weakest of the four, and his condition was the worst. There was no likely prospect of rescue when Parker was killed, and there was no way of obtaining food, except by killing one of the four. If the sailors did not eat soon, they all would have died of starvation.

■ **ISSUE**

Was the killing of Parker justified under the circumstances?

■ **DECISION AND RATIONALE**

(Huddleston, B.) No. Necessity does not justify killing another person who poses no danger. The only type of necessity that justifies homicide is the necessity of self-defense. The extreme necessity of hunger has been held not to justify larceny, so it logically cannot justify homicide. American case law has suggested that necessity may excuse homicide if the victims are selected by lot, but this is not the rule in England. Lord Bacon's statement that homicide may be done to save the lives of several people is an error. There is no legal or moral duty for one person to give up his life to save another. Although the temptation faced by Dudley (D) and Stephens (D) was terrible, the fact that many in the same situation would have yielded to the

---

same temptation is no excuse. Dudley (D) and Stephens (D) are guilty and sentenced to death.

Analysis:

As horrific as the offense committed by Dudley (D) and Stephens (D) was, cannibalism was not an unusual occurrence aboard merchant ships at the time. Many owners sent vessels to sea that were inadequately provisioned for long voyages, or that were unseaworthy, and thus put the crew in constant danger of shipwreck. In fact, the vessel in this case was a racing yacht not intended for ocean voyaging, being delivered to a new owner in Australia. Among members of the maritime community, the practice of cannibalism was well known, but always officially denied. Dudley (D) and Stephens (D) were unique in that they confessed to their crime as soon as they were rescued, and never denied what took place. For more background on this case, *see* NEIL HANSON, THE CUSTOM OF THE SEA (2000).

■ **CASE VOCABULARY**

ASSIZE: A session of a court or council.

NECESSITY: A justification defense for a person who acts in an emergency that he or she did not create and who commits a harm that is less severe than the harm that would have occurred but for the person's actions.

SPECIAL VERDICT: A verdict in which the jury makes findings only on factual issues submitted by the judge, who then decides the legal effect of the verdict.

People v. Unger

(Prosecuting Government) v. (Prisoner)

362 N.E.2d 319 (Ill. 1977)

THE DEFENSE OF NECESSITY IS AVAILABLE TO A PRISONER WHO ESCAPES TO AVOID HARM

■ **INSTANT FACTS** Unger (D) escaped from prison after his life was threatened.

■ **BLACK LETTER RULE** Necessity is a defense if the defendant did not cause or develop the situation and if the defendant reasonably believed his or her actions were necessary to avoid a greater injury than the injury that might reasonably result from the defendant's actions.

■ PROCEDURAL BASIS

Appeal from an order of the court of appeals, reversing Unger's (D) conviction for escape.

■ FACTS

Unger (D) was a prisoner in a minimum-security prison. He walked away from the prison and was arrested two days later at a motel. Unger (D) testified at trial that another inmate had threatened him with a knife and that other inmates had assaulted and sexually molested him. He received threats from other inmates and escaped after he received a telephone call from an unknown inmate that threatened his life because he reported the sexual assault to prison authorities. None of the threats, however, were reported to the prison authorities. Unger (D) testified that he left the prison to save his life and that he intended to return, once he found someone who could help him. There was evidence that Unger's (D) excuses were pretextual, and that his motive in escaping was to gain publicity. At trial, Unger (D) requested jury instructions on the defenses of necessity and compulsion, but the trial court instructed the jury that the reasons for Unger's (D) escape were immaterial. The court of appeals reversed the conviction.

■ ISSUE

May Unger (D) raise the defense of necessity?

■ DECISION AND RATIONALE

(Ryan, J.) Yes. Necessity is a defense if the defendant did not cause or develop the situation and if the defendant reasonably believed his or her actions were necessary to avoid a greater injury than the injury that might reasonably result from the defendant's actions. The defense of necessity applies when a defendant is forced to choose between two evils, and the defense of compulsion applies when a defendant was unable to exercise a free choice at all. The defense of necessity applies to this case. Unger (D) was forced to choose between two evils, and he believed his escape was necessary to save himself from further harm. The facts that Unger

(D) did not report the assaults to the authorities and that he did not report to the authorities immediately after making his escape are relevant, but relate to the weight and credibility of his evidence, not to the issue of whether the defense may be raised.

The California court, in the case of *People v. Lovercamp,* 43 Cal. App. 3d 823, 118 Cal. Rptr. 110 (1974), recognized a limited necessity defense for prisoners who escape. The California court set out five conditions that must be met before the defense is allowed: (1) the prisoner is faced with a specific threat of death, forcible sexual attack, or substantial bodily harm in the near future; (2) there is either no time to complain to the authorities, or past complaints have been futile; (3) there is no time or opportunity to resort to the courts; (4) there is no evidence of violence used to effect the escape; and (5) the prisoner reports to the authorities as soon as he or she has reached a place of safety. The factors set out in *Lovercamp* go to the weight and credibility of a defendant's testimony and will be considered as relevant evidence, but will not be preconditions to raising the defense of necessity. And the absence of one or more of the *Lovercamp* factors does not by itself disprove a claim of necessity. Affirmed.

Analysis:

Courts have been reluctant to recognize a necessity defense for escaping prisoners, partly out of a concern that the availability of the defense will encourage more escapes. Prisons are, by their very nature, dangerous places for inmates, and excusing prisoners who escape because they claim to be in danger could lead to more prisoners attempting escapes. Allowing a necessity defense is at least an implicit recognition that prisoners do not forfeit all rights when they are confined and that they are entitled to a "last resort" remedy of escape. Note, too, that the *Lovercamp* court did not require that an escaped prisoner turn himself or herself in immediately, but allowed the prisoner to reach a "place of safety" first.

■ CASE VOCABULARY

COMPULSION: The act of compelling or the state of being compelled; an uncontrollable inclination to do something; objective necessity; duress.

DURESS: The use or threatened use of unlawful force—usually that a reasonable person cannot resist—to compel someone to commit an unlawful act. Duress is a recognized defense to a crime, contractual breach, or tort.

EIGHTH AMENDMENT: The constitutional amendment, ratified as part of the Bill of Rights in 1791, prohibiting excessive bail, excessive fines, and cruel and unusual punishment.

JUSTIFICATION: A lawful or sufficient reason for one's acts or omissions; any fact that prevents an act from being wrongful; a showing, in court, of a sufficient reason why a defendant did what the prosecution charges the defendant to answer for. Under the Model Penal Code, the defendant must believe that the action was necessary to avoid a harm or evil and that the harm or evil to be avoided was greater than the harm that would have resulted if the crime had been committed. Model Penal Code § 3.02. Also termed JUSTIFICATION DEFENSE; NECESSITY DEFENSE.

NECESSITY: A justification defense for a person who acts in an emergency that he or she did not create and who commits a harm that is less severe than the harm that would have occurred but for the person's actions. For example, a mountain climber lost in a blizzard can assert necessity as a defense to theft of food and blankets from another's cabin.

THE NECESSITY DEFENSE REQUIRES A SHOWING OF IMMINENT DANGER

■**INSTANT FACTS** Warshow (D) was arrested for trespass while protesting at a nuclear power plant and attempted to assert a defense of necessity.

■**BLACK LETTER RULE** The defense of necessity requires a showing that the threatened harm is imminent or reasonably appears to be imminent.

■ **PROCEDURAL BASIS**

Appeal from a conviction for unlawful trespass.

■ **FACTS**

Warshow (D) was part of a group of demonstrators who protested the reopening of a nuclear power plant. The plant had been shut down for repairs and refueling, and Warshow (D) and the other protesters tried to block access to the plant. They refused to leave the premises and were arrested. Warshow (D) sought to raise a necessity defense at trial. Warshow (D) offered evidence on the hazards of nuclear power and on the possibility of a nuclear accident and meltdown if the plant were allowed to resume operation. The trial court excluded the evidence and refused to grant compulsory process for the witnesses who would have presented the evidence for the defense.

■ **ISSUE**

May Warshow (D) assert a necessity defense?

■ **DECISION AND RATIONALE**

(Barney, J.) No. The defense of necessity requires a showing that the threatened harm is imminent or reasonably appears to be imminent. Low-level radiation and nuclear waste are not imminent dangers, but present a long-term threat. To be an imminent danger, the threat or perceived threat must be close at hand. Long-term hazards are not imminent because there is time to exercise other options besides breaking the law. Warshow (D) did not claim that he was acting to prevent an impending accident, but rather that he was acting to foreclose the "chance" or "possibility" of an accident. The necessity defense cannot be used to justify acts taken to prevent speculative and uncertain dangers. Affirmed.

■ CONCURRENCE

(Hill, J.) The state and federal governments have both approved the development and operation of nuclear power plants. Allowing a necessity defense here would be allowing the jury to redetermine policy questions that already have been decided. The majority is acting illogically in considering whether the necessary elements of the defense have been shown before considering whether the defense is available. Contrary to what the dissent states, there has been no showing of a danger not already considered by the legislative scheme.

■ DISSENT

(Billings, J.) Warshow (D) offered specific expert evidence of defects in the construction of the power plant that he believed could and would cause a meltdown within seven seconds of failure on the start-up of the plant. Warshow (D) also showed that all other methods of stopping the reopening of the plant had been exhausted. The concurrence relies on the existence of a regulatory scheme, but does not address the question of whether that scheme has been adequate to address the danger posed.

Analysis:

The majority bases its decision on the failure of Warshow (D) to show imminent harm and concludes that the danger threatened is not sufficiently imminent. Arguably, such a determination should be left to the jury. The immediacy of danger, or the reasonableness of the perception of immediate danger, would seem to be factual questions—something that would ordinarily be decided by the jury. The concurrence relies on an argument that the issue has been decided by the legislature, but ignores the possibility that the decision could be wrong, and Warshow (D) and others like him are left with no other option but to protest (akin to what the early American revolutionaries called an "appeal to heaven").

■ CASE VOCABULARY

CIVIL DISOBEDIENCE: A deliberate but nonviolent act of lawbreaking to call attention to a particular law or set of laws of questionable legitimacy or morality.

COMPULSORY PROCESS CLAUSE: The clause of the Sixth Amendment to the U.S. Constitution giving criminal defendants the subpoena power for obtaining witnesses in their favor.

THE DEFENDANT RAISING A COMPULSION DEFENSE MUST HAVE FEARED IMMINENT BODILY HARM

■**INSTANT FACTS** Crawford (D) was convicted of multiple crimes, and claimed that he was forced to commit them.

■**BLACK LETTER RULE** The defense of compulsion requires a showing that the defendant acted out of a fear that he or she would suffer imminent bodily harm, not from some future threat of bodily harm.

■ **PROCEDURAL BASIS**

Appeal from convictions for aggravated robbery, kidnapping, and aggravated burglary.

■ **FACTS**

Crawford (D) owed money to Bateman for drugs he purchased on credit. He testified that Bateman gave him a gun, drove him to a hospital parking lot, and told him to rob Overholt. Crawford (D) got out of the car and robbed and beat Overholt. Crawford (D) then approached Monhollon, threatened him with the gun, and made Monhollon drive him to Monhollon's home. While on the way to Monhollon's house, Crawford (D) took Monhollon's wallet and checkbook. When they arrived at Monhollon's house, Crawford (D) made Monhollon lie face down on the floor and crawl into another room. Crawford (D) took Monhollon's ring and cash and vandalized his house. Crawford (D) also took Monhollon's clothes and shoes and ate his food. Crawford (D) forced Monhollon to go to the other half of the duplex he lived in, and when there Crawford (D) handcuffed the resident to the bathroom sink and went through her jewelry and dresser drawers. He also ate her ice cream and cookies. Crawford (D) then forced Monhollon to drive him to another house, where Crawford (D) beat and robbed the resident and locked her in her basement. Crawford (D) then told Monhollon to drive him to an automatic teller machine, where he forced Monhollon to withdraw money. Crawford (D) put Monhollon in the trunk of the car and drove to another city. Crawford (D) testified that he then spoke to Bateman, who was not satisfied with the evening's take and threatened to hurt Crawford (D) and his son if Crawford (D) did not get more. Crawford (D) testified that Bateman told him to rob a hotel after midnight. In the interim, Monhollon managed to get free and reported the incident to police, who arrested Crawford (D) in the hotel. Crawford (D) claimed at trial that everything he did was out of fear of Bateman. He testified that Bateman had forced him to commit several crimes, and that he knew that he had to do what Bateman told him to do until the money Crawford (D) owed was paid off. Crawford (D) said that Bateman was a member of a violent group of drug dealers who would not hesitate to harm Crawford (D) and his son if Crawford (D) did not comply. Crawford (D) testified that he thought the police would not believe him because he was an addict, and that he was afraid of what might happen to him or his son if he informed on Bateman.

■ ISSUE

Did Crawford establish the defense of compulsion?

■ DECISION AND RATIONALE

(Allegrucci, J.) No. The defense of compulsion requires a showing of a threat of imminent bodily harm and a reasonable belief that death or great bodily harm will be inflicted on the defendant if he or she does not engage in the criminal activity. Threats to inflict some kind of harm in the future are not sufficient threats to establish compulsion. The belief that bodily harm will be inflicted must be a reasonable one, not a vague understanding that the person making the threats is dangerous. Compulsion requires a continuous threat, with no opportunity to escape. The threats made to Crawford (D) were not threats of imminent bodily harm, and Crawford (D) also had several opportunities to escape the threats. The federal compulsion defense, which requires only an immediate threat, a well-grounded fear that the threat will be carried out, and no reasonable opportunity to escape, is contrary to the state statutory definition of the defense of compulsion. The fear must be reasonable, but the statute also requires a showing that the defendant did not willingly put himself or herself in a position in which the compulsion was probable. Affirmed

Analysis:

The distinction between compulsion and necessity may seem unclear. Necessity, the "lesser of two evils" defense, refers to a choice between two harms caused by an emergency situation. Compulsion refers more to the choice between "harm or be harmed"—that is, to commit a criminal act or to suffer harm to oneself. The threat is caused by another person, not by other circumstances.

■ CASE VOCABULARY

AGGRAVATED KIDNAPPING: Kidnapping accompanied by some aggravating factor (such as a demand for ransom or injury of the victim).

COMPULSION: The act of compelling or the state of being compelled; an uncontrollable inclination to do something; objective necessity; duress.

KIDNAPPING: The crime of seizing and taking away a person by force or fraud.

State v. Hunter

(Prosecuting Government) v. (Hitchhiker)

740 P.2d 559 (Kansas 1987)

COMPULSION IS A DEFENSE TO FELONY MURDER

■INSTANT FACTS Hunter (D) was convicted of felony murder but claimed he was forced to participate in the criminal activity.

■BLACK LETTER RULE Compulsion is not a defense to a homicide charge, unless the charge is felony murder.

■ PROCEDURAL BASIS

Appeal from a conviction for felony murder.

■ FACTS

Hunter (D) was picked up by Remeta and others while hitchhiking. Hunter (D) stated that Remeta showed him some guns and made remarks about a hitchhiker he wished he had killed. Remeta refused to let Hunter (D) out of the truck when he requested to get out. Remeta fired a gun out of the car window while the car was moving; he showed Hunter (D) two bullets and asked Hunter (D) if he thought the bullets could kill him. Remeta also spoke of several people he had killed, including one man he had killed for forty dollars and a girl he shot five times. While Hunter (D) was in the truck, Remeta shot a police officer. Remeta drove to a grain elevator, shot another person and took two hostages with Hunter's (D) assistance. Remeta shot and killed the hostages and left their bodies by the side of the road. Hunter (D) testified that he thought he had no chance to escape. Remeta testified that he would have shot Hunter (D) if Hunter (D) did not comply with his directions. The trial court did not instruct the jury on the defense of compulsion.

■ ISSUE

Was Hunter (D) entitled to an instruction on the defense of compulsion?

■ DECISION AND RATIONALE

(Lockett, J.) Yes. Compulsion is not a defense to a homicide charge, unless the charge is felony murder. The traditional rule is that compulsion is never a defense to homicide, the rationale being that an individual ought to sacrifice his or her own life rather than escape by the murder of an innocent person. The better rule is that compulsion is not a defense to *intentional* homicide. Compulsion is a defense to any other felony, and a defendant should not lose the defense because the person making threats unexpectedly kills someone during the commission of another crime. The threat to Hunter (D) was continuous, and he had no

---

reasonable chance to escape. Remeta was a dangerous person, and it was up to the jury to determine if Hunter (D) was afraid for his life, and if that fear was reasonable. Reversed.

Analysis:

Although the court does not say so explicitly, it seems evident that the court would limit the application of the compulsion defense to felony murders in which the actual killing was done by the person who made the threats, or by some other participant in the crimes. The threatened defendant is thus not the one who is forced to make the choice between losing his or her own life and taking the life of another. Query whether an accidental killing committed by a person engaged in a felony under compulsion would be excused by the court's rule.

■ CASE VOCABULARY

FELONY MURDER: Murder that occurs during the commission of a dangerous felony (often limited to rape, kidnapping, robbery, burglary, and arson).

FELONY MURDER RULE: The doctrine holding that any death resulting from the commission or attempted commission of a dangerous felony is murder.

CHAPTER NINE

Mental Illness as a Defense

People v. Serravo

Instant Facts: Serravo (D) stabbed his wife while she slept; when she awoke, he blamed it on an intruder, but when arrested and tried for the attempted murder, he blamed his actions on "orders from God."

Black Letter Rule: In applying the statutory definition of insanity, "right" and "wrong" are measured by existing societal standards of morality rather than by defendant's personal and subjective understanding of the illegality of act in question.

Smith v. State

Instant Facts: The defendant was convicted of shooting a law enforcement officer with intent to kill, wound, or maim after leaving his post at an army base without permission.

Black Letter Rule: A person is not responsible for criminal conduct if at the time the act was committed, a mental disease or defect caused a lack of capacity to appreciate the wrongfulness of his conduct or conform his conduct to law.

People v. Serravo

(State of Colorado) v. (Wife Stabber)

823 P.2d 128 (Colo. 1992)

THE ABILITY TO "DISTINGUISH RIGHT FROM WRONG" IS BASED ON EXISTING SOCIETAL STANDARDS

■**INSTANT FACTS** Serravo (D) stabbed his wife while she slept; when she awoke, he blamed it on an intruder, but when arrested and tried for the attempted murder, he blamed his actions on "orders from God."

■**BLACK LETTER RULE** In applying the statutory definition of insanity, "right" and "wrong" are measured by existing societal standards of morality rather than by defendant's personal and subjective understanding of the illegality of act in question.

■ **PROCEDURAL BASIS**

On grant of certiorari to the state supreme court to review the decision of the court of appeals.

■ **FACTS**

Serravo (D) returned home from work, spent some time in the kitchen reading the Bible, then went upstairs and stabbed his sleeping wife in the back. When she awoke, he told her an intruder had stabbed her. He told her to wait in bed while he phoned for help. Serravo (D) told the police that he had gone to the store and left the garage door open. When he returned home, he heard the front door slam. Curious, he went upstairs to check on his wife and children and found his wife bleeding. Serravo (D) consented to a search of the home and voluntarily gave the police the clothing he was wearing. Days later, Mrs. Serravo discovered letters from her husband, confessing to the stabbing as an act to sever their marital bond. He told her he had gone to be with Jehovah for a while but would return. Mrs. Serravo phoned her husband to ask about the letters. He told her God had instructed him to stab her. Mrs. Serravo then phoned the police and her husband was arrested. Serravo (D) pleaded not guilty by reason of insanity to the charges against him. He was examined by several psychiatrists. At trial, the prosecution offered testimony from Dr. Seig, a psychiatric resident who had examined Serravo (D), to establish his sanity at the time of the stabbing. The defendant told Dr. Seig that he was working on a plan with God to establish a multimillion-dollar sports complex that would enable him to teach others about his path to perfection. On the night of the stabbing, Serravo was encouraged in his endeavor by some of his coworkers, but he continued to be discouraged by his wife's lack of support. Dr. Seig diagnosed Serravo (D) as having an organic delusional disorder caused by a brain injury or paranoid schizophrenia—either condition accounted for Serravo's (D) beliefs. The doctor believed these delusions drove Serravo's (D) actions when he stabbed his wife. Serravo (D) knew the stabbing was contrary to the law, but he believed his action was morally justified.

Serravo (D) presented testimony from five mental health experts. The first (Dr. Miller) opined that Serravo stabbed his wife as part of a divine mission that morally justified his actions. This psychiatrist believed Serravo's (D) mental illness prevented him from distinguishing between right and wrong, but he conceded that Serravo (D) probably knew his conduct was wrong. A second professional (Dr. Kaplan) suggested Serravo was a paranoid schizophrenic, laboring under a delusion that his wife posed a threat to his completing his divine mission. Dr. Kaplan believed Serravo (D) felt the stabbing was the right thing to do; but explained that his disease prevented him from knowing right from wrong. Two other doctors (Drs. Heron and Sundell) explained that at the time of the stabbing, Serravo's (D) delusion that he was communicating with God blurred his thinking and rendered him incapable of knowing right from wrong. Dr. Leslie Cohen conducted extensive testing of Serravo (D) and concluded Serravo had the false belief that he had magical powers and was unable to know right from wrong at the time he stabbed his wife. Since Serravo (D) believed that others did not understand his reasoning, he felt it best to not even attempt to explain things to the police. That is why he hid his actions from the police.

The sanity issue was presented to the jury. The jury was instructed that a person is not accountable when a disease or defect operating at the time of a crime renders the actor incapable of knowing right from wrong. The jury was told that one was "incapable of distinguishing right from wrong" even when a person knows his conduct is criminal, but, because of a mental disease or defect, he believes it is still morally right. The prosecution objected, arguing that the instruction permitted the jury to determine right and wrong subjectively. The trial court disagreed and the jury returned a verdict of not guilty by reason of insanity.

■ ISSUE

Was the jury appropriately instructed on the insanity standard as allowing a subjective determination of the incapability of distinguishing right from wrong?

■ DECISION AND RATIONALE

(Quinn, J.) No. At trial, the jury was instructed that the phrase "unable to distinguish right from wrong" includes a person who may know his conduct is illegal, but who also believes, because of the mental disease or defect, that the conduct is morally right. This statutory notion of "right from wrong" is based on the rule established in *M'Naghten's Case*, 8 Eng. Rpt. 718 (1843). There, the jury concluded M'Naghten was unable to appreciate that the act he committed was wrong. Therefore, he was not guilty due to his insanity. Looking back at the decisions and commentary following *M'Naghten's Case*, it can be said that *M'Naghten* holds that a person may be deemed legally sane if the person commits an act contrary to law and knows that the act is wrong—regardless of whether the person knows it is illegal. This is a sound expression.

Other cases using the right-wrong test have required the actor to be able to distinguish *legal right* from *legal wrong*. In those cases, if a defendant knows his actions are illegal, he may be held criminally responsible. The problem with that approach is that, while someone truly insane may know an act is illegal, the actor may not see the act as immoral. When an insane person is held responsible for an illegal action he believes is the "right thing," the goals of the law are not served. Judging conduct by a "moral wrong" standard has been endorsed by earlier cases. By using a "moral wrong" standard, the rule will also work in situations where the actor's delusion has him believing that God commanded him to commit the illegal act. If the construction of the word "wrong" was limited to a "legal wrong," the defense would be removed from insane actors whose disease has destroyed their ability to distinguish between the morality and immorality of their actions.

But whether an act is morally wrong or right must be determined by a societal standard. A personal belief that an act is moral cannot be used to exonerate a sane person. Jury Instruction Number 5 permitted the jury to make reference to a moral, as well as a legal, standard in this case. The instruction was so broad as to permit the jury to find morality both subjectively and objectively, which is inconsistent with the law requiring adoption of a societal standard of moral wrong. The court of appeals held that "orders from God," or a "deific-decree" delusion, constituted an exception to the societal standard of morality. When an actor's mental defect has him taking orders from God to commit an illegal act, whether the actor knows it is illegal or morally wrong is unimportant. While knowledge that an act is forbidden is generally sufficient to impose legal responsibility, when the act is performed under the belief that it is a direct order from God, it would be improper to expect the actor to understand the act to be wrong. The judgment of the court of appeals is accordingly approved in part and disapproved in part.

Analysis:

Following the trial of John Hinckley for his attempted assassination of President Reagan, this standard was modified and codified by Congress at 18 U.S.C.A. § 17: "It is an affirmative defense to a prosecution under any federal statute that, at the time of the commission of the acts constituting the offence, the defendant, as a result of a severe mental disease or defect, was unable to appreciate the nature and quality or the wrongfulness of his acts. Mental disease or defect does not otherwise constitute a defense."

■ CASE VOCABULARY

INSANE: Mentally deranged; suffering from one or more delusions or false beliefs that (1) have no foundation in reason or reality, (2) are not credible to any reasonable person of sound mind, and (3) cannot be overcome in a sufferer's mind by any amount of evidence or argument.

INSANITY: Any mental disorder severe enough that it prevents a person from having legal capacity and excuses the person from criminal or civil responsibility. Insanity is a legal, not a medical, standard.

INSANITY DEFENSE: An affirmative defense alleging that a mental disorder caused the accused to commit the crime.

M'NAGHTEN RULES: The doctrine that a person is not criminally responsible for an act when a mental disability prevented the person from knowing either (1) the nature and quality of the act or (2) whether the act was right or wrong. The federal courts and most states have adopted this test in some form.

NOT GUILTY BY REASON OF INSANITY: A not-guilty verdict, based on mental illness, that usually does not release the defendant but instead results in commitment to a mental institution; a criminal defendant's plea of not guilty that is based on the insanity defense.

Smith v. State

(Deserting Soldier) v. (State of Alaska)

614 P.2d 300 (Alaska 1980)

A MENTAL DISEASE OR DEFECT MAY RELIEVE AN ACTOR OF CRIMINAL
RESPONSIBILITY

It's $250 an hour for me to testify that you have mental problems. It's $550 an hour to testify that they caused you to shoot the officer.

stus.com

■**INSTANT FACTS** The defendant was convicted of shooting a law enforcement officer with intent to kill, wound, or maim after leaving his post at an army base without permission.

■**BLACK LETTER RULE** A person is not responsible for criminal conduct if at the time the act was committed, a mental disease or defect caused a lack of capacity to appreciate the wrongfulness of his conduct or conform his conduct to law.

■ **PROCEDURAL BASIS**

On appeal from jury verdict finding Smith (D) legally responsible for the crime charged.

■ **FACTS**

On September 28, 1977, Allen J. Smith (D), an army private at Fort Richardson, commandeered a vehicle at gunpoint and left the base. After being chased by the police, he shot and seriously wounded Judicial Services Officer Leon Jordan. He was charged with shooting with the intent to kill, wound, or maim. Smith (D) had purchased the gun two days earlier. On the day of this incident, Smith (D) was told he was being discharged from the military as an undesirable soldier. Smith (D) displayed no real reaction to being told he would be discharged. The Army had no knowledge of Smith (D) being diagnosed as a paranoid schizophrenic, and despite previous hospitalizations, Smith (D) gave no indication he posed any serious dangers. After learning of the discharge, Smith (D) went to the supply room at the base and said he needed a car to go to the airport. The clerk told Smith (D) he might know where he could find one. He took Smith (D) to see two sergeants who gave Smith (D) keys to a truck. Smith (D) asked the sergeant to drive him, but he refused. Smith (D) then took the keys and headed toward Anchorage. Smith (D) exchanged gunfire with one of the guards at the base as he left. Smith (D) was chased by the police; eventually Smith (D) abandoned his vehicle and ran into a wooded area. One of the officers pursued Smith (D) on foot. He found Smith(D) behind a tree, pointing his gun at him. Smith (D) then fired two shots, striking the officer in the chest and shoulder. The officer returned fire and then collapsed. Smith (D) was then captured.

■ **ISSUE**

On the evidence presented, could a jury determine that Smith (D) had substantial capacity to conform his conduct to the requirements of the law when he shot Officer Jordan?

■ DECISION AND RATIONALE

(Rabinowitz, C.J.) Yes. Smith (D) made two statements in custody, admitting to shooting the officer. The only defense raised at trial was insanity. Under Alaska law, that defense excuses a person from criminal liability "if at the time of the conduct, [due to a] mental disease or defect, he lacks substantial capacity either to appreciate the wrongfulness of his conduct or to conform his conduct to the requirements of law." To support his claim of insanity, Smith (D) was examined by three doctors, all of whom agreed Smith (D) suffered from chronic schizophrenia. The doctors disagreed, however, as to whether his disease fit the legal definition of insanity. Each doctor felt Smith (D) knew the difference between right and wrong. Two believed he was unable to conform his conduct to social norms; the third doctor felt he could. While interrogated, Smith (D) told police he knew his actions were illegal and immoral, but the experts agreed that even with a mental defect, Smith (D) may know his conduct is wrong. One of the medical experts, Dr. Rader, testified that the day of the shooting, Smith (D) displayed conduct that was not a product of his illness; rather, Smith (D) was simply acting as if he were insane to establish the defense (the "Ganzer syndrome"). Dr. Rader opined that even though Smith (D) was a schizophrenic, he could still commit acts for which he could be legally responsible. While some of his actions showed faulty judgment on his part, he did display reasonable behavior in many instances. In support of his conclusions, Dr. Rader identified eight examples of considered, rational judgment during the course of the illegal events.

In contrast with Dr. Rader, Dr. Langdon focused on the many delusions held by Smith (D). Langdon posited that all schizophrenics lack the ability from time to time to conform their conduct to the requirements of the law, but he explained that many people with mental illness could use reason to carry out their plans. Where rational actions fit his plans, Smith (D) would appear rational, but where societal norms ran contrary to his plans, he did not hesitate to violate them. The record reflects that the court could have been persuaded that Dr. Rader's opinion was the more compelling. Courts have always allowed the trier of fact to disregard the testimony of experts it finds not credible. The record establishes that Smith (D) suffered from some mental defect, but it is not clear that the mental defect prevented him from acting within the law. Based on the evidence presented at trial, substantial evidence was presented by the prosecution to prove beyond a reasonable doubt that Smith (D) was legally sane when he shot Officer Jordan. Affirmed.

■ DISSENT

(Boochever, J.) The only doctor who testified that Smith (D) was capable of conforming his conduct to the requirements of law based his conclusion on a theory that Smith (D) was motivated by the goal of getting out of the service. Looking at the incident itself, Dr. Rader concluded that Smith (D) intended to leave Alaska as quickly as possible. He hints at no explanation for Smith (D) engaging in this illegal adventure once Smith (D) had been advised that he was getting his discharge. It is true that during the course of his journey there were isolated meaningful acts; those actions, taken out of context, are not inconsistent with a general inability to conform conduct to the law. One frequently performs intelligent acts in the pursuit of delusionary goals.

Analysis:

The testimony of Dr. Rader was deemed the more reasonable explanation for Smith's (D) conduct. Because Smith (D) was able to act rationally and formulate what appeared to be a "plan," the doctor believed it was unlikely that, as Dr. Langdon's testimony suggested, he was insane for that split-second when he shot at the police officer. Compare Smith's (D) actions here with those of the defendant in *People v. Serravo*, 823 P.2d 128 (Colo. 1992). In *Serravo*, the court noted that after stabbing his wife, Serravo had the presence of mind to tell her a lie to avoid being arrested for the assault. The court concluded there that the rational actions between the criminal acts were still a part of the defendant's illness; as the dissent in this case also points out, a mentally ill person need not act mentally ill all the time.

■ CASE VOCABULARY

IRRESISTIBLE IMPULSE TEST: A test for insanity, holding that a person is not criminally responsible for an act if mental disease prevented that person from controlling potentially criminal conduct.

SUBSTANTIAL CAPACITY: The Model Penal Code's test for the insanity defense, stating that a person is not criminally responsible for an act if, as a result of a mental disease or defect, the person lacks substantial capacity either to appreciate the criminality of the conduct or to conform the conduct to the law. This test combines elements of both the *M'Naghten* rules and the irresistible-impulse test by allowing consideration of both volitional and cognitive weaknesses. This test was formerly used by the federal courts and many states, but since 1984 many jurisdictions (including federal courts)—in response to the acquittal by reason of insanity of would-be presidential assassin John Hinckley—have narrowed the insanity defense and adopted a new test resembling the *M'Naghten* rules, although portions of the substantial-capacity test continue to be used.

CHAPTER TEN

Attempt

State v. Lyerla

Instant Facts: Lyerla (D) fired three shots at a pick-up truck and one occupant of the truck was killed; Lyerla (D) was convicted of attempted second-degree murder and appealed.

Black Letter Rule: Under South Dakota's definition of second-degree murder, the offense of attempted second-degree murder does not exist since it is impossible to intend to commit an unintentional act.

People v. Stone

Instant Facts: Stone (D) went to a local carnival after hearing that some gang members, including some of his cohorts, had engaged in a verbal altercation there; when he got there, Stone (D) shot his gun out the window of the truck in which he was riding, in the direction of a group of about ten rival gang members, and he was convicted of the attempted murder of one of the group members.

Black Letter Rule: The mental state required for attempted murder is the intent to kill *a* human being, not a *particular* human being.

People v. Murray

Instant Facts: Murray (D) made plans to marry his niece and was charged with attempting to form an incestuous marriage.

Black Letter Rule: An attempt to commit a criminal offense must be manifested by acts that would end in the consummation of that offense but for the intervention of circumstances independent of the defendant's will.

McQuirter v. State

Instant Facts: The defendant was convicted of attempt to commit an assault with intent to rape and he appealed.

Black Letter Rule: To support a conviction for attempt, the prosecution must prove beyond a reasonable doubt that the defendant intended to commit the crime.

People v. Rizzo

Instant Facts: Charles Rizzo (D) and others were convicted of attempt to commit robbery in the first degree; Rizzo (D) appealed.

Black Letter Rule: Acts sufficient to establish an attempt must go beyond preparation and must bring the defendant closer to achieving the goal of committing the intended crime.

People v. Staples

Instant Facts: Staples (D) rented an office in a building over a bank, intending to drill through the floor and into the bank's vaults; before anything was taken from the bank, Staples (D) abandoned his plans, but he was arrested and charged with attempted bank robbery nonetheless.

Black Letter Rule: Regardless of whether the abandonment of a crime is voluntary or nonvoluntary, if sufficient acts have been performed toward commission of the crime, the defendant may be held responsible for an attempt.

People v. Lubow

Instant Facts: Lubow (D) owed Silverman $30,000 for diamonds he had purchased from him and tried to talk Silverman into participating in a scheme to defraud other stone salesmen in an effort to repay him; Lubow (D) was convicted of solicitation.

Black Letter Rule: Proof of the crime of solicitation is complete upon proof of the communication; it does not require an overt act in furtherance nor does it even require proof of delivery of the solicitation to the intended target.

Booth v. State

Instant Facts: Stanford was supposed to sell a stolen coat to his attorney, Booth (D), but was arrested before the sale; the police urged Stanford to go forward with the sale to catch Booth (D), who was also arrested and charged with attempting to buy stolen property.

Black Letter Rule: If a defendant could not be convicted of a substantive crime, he or she may not be convicted of an attempt to commit that crime.

People v. Dlugash

Instant Facts: Geller was shot multiple times by his roommate during an argument; several minutes later, thinking Geller may still be alive, Dlugash (D) shot him several more times.

Black Letter Rule: A defendant may be convicted of attempted murder even though the target of his or her crime already died from other causes.

People v. Thousand

Instant Facts: Thousand (D) was arrested after luring an undercover deputy posing as a fourteen-year-old girl to meet him for sexual relations.

Black Letter Rule: Absent a statutory recognition of the defense, impossibility is not a defense to a criminal act.

State v. Lyerla

(South Dakota) v. (Truck Driver)

424 N.W.2d 908 (S. Dak. 1988)

ATTEMPTED SECOND–DEGREE MURDER DOES NOT EXIST UNDER SOUTH DAKOTA LAW

■**INSTANT FACTS** Lyerla (D) fired three shots at a pick-up truck and one occupant of the truck was killed; Lyerla (D) was convicted of attempted second-degree murder and appealed.

■**BLACK LETTER RULE** Under South Dakota's definition of second-degree murder, the offense of attempted second-degree murder does not exist since it is impossible to intend to commit an unintentional act.

■ PROCEDURAL BASIS

On appeal from a conviction for second-degree murder and attempted second-degree murder.

■ FACTS

Lyerla (D) was traveling on the same road as a pickup truck. The vehicles passed each other a few times and then the truck driver began driving in such a manner that Lyerla (D) could not pass his vehicle. Lyerla (D) left the interstate to load his pistol. Seeing Lyerla (D) leave the highway, the pickup truck appeared to "wait" for him near the ramp leading back onto the freeway. Lyerla (D) reentered the freeway and passed the pickup truck. When the truck then attempted to pass him, Lyerla (D) fired his gun at it three times. Two girls riding in the back of the truck were injured, and one bullet entered the cab of the truck and killed a seventeen-year-old girl. Lyerla (D) was charged with first-degree murder and two counts of attempted murder in the first degree, or, alternatively, second-degree murder and two counts of attempted murder in the second degree. At trial, Lyerla (D) explained that he was being harassed by the occupants of the truck and feared for his life. He had fired the shots in an attempt to disable their vehicle. While the occupants of the truck told a different story than Lyerla (D), the prosecutor conceded that the truck appeared to be playing games with Lyerla (D). Lyerla (D) was convicted of second-degree murder and two counts of attempted murder in the second degree.

■ ISSUE

Can a defendant be convicted of attempting to commit murder in the second degree?

■ DECISION AND RATIONALE

(Konenkamp, Cir. J.) No. In order to be guilty of attempting to commit a crime, the actor must have the intention to commit the crime. For an actor to commit second-degree murder, death must result while in a criminally reckless state of mind and "without a design to kill any particular person." South Dakota has not previously prosecuted a defendant for such a crime.

In similar cases outside of South Dakota, other courts have declined to find an actor guilty of attempted murder when the statutes have been similarly phrased. Here, the jury found that Lyerla (D) did not intend to kill the seventeen-year old passenger, since he was convicted not of first-degree murder, but of second-degree murder. Since he did not intend to kill the girl who was actually shot, he could not have intended to kill the other passengers who were not shot. Under the definition of second-degree murder, it would seem impossible to *intend* to commit an *unintentional* act. Reversed.

■ **DISSENT**

(Sabers, J.) It was established that Lyerla (D) did not intend to kill the girl inside the truck, nor did he intend to kill the other girls in the truck. However, had his actions resulted in the deaths of the two girls in the truck bed, he would have been convicted of second-degree murder in their deaths. Because the death of the other two girls did not result, he should be held responsible for attempted murder. Second-degree murder under the statute does not require specific intent. The law simply requires a dangerous (or stupid) act. Lyerla's (D) act of pulling the trigger fulfilled the law's requirement, establishing attempted murder in the second degree. The defendant argues that it is impossible to intend to attempt to commit an unintentional killing and cites several cases in support of his contention. These cases fail to recognize that the South Dakota statute on attempt does not require an intentional act. All that is required is a voluntary, as opposed to an involuntary, act. Lyerla (D) intentionally pulled the trigger and shot his weapon in a dangerous manner. That act should constitute attempted second-degree murder under South Dakota law.

Analysis:

The majority concludes that a person cannot intend to commit a crime that does not require intent, whereas the dissent focuses on a different portion of the statute. The dissent would interpret the statute to cover any killing that occurs as a result of reckless conduct, whether killing was the intended goal of the conduct or not. Lyerla (D) did act recklessly. Because of his reckless actions, someone died. Others could have died, too. But the real issue in this case lies with the definition of "attempt," according to which one must make "an effort to accomplish something." Here it was not demonstrated that Lyerla made an effort to accomplish a killing.

■ **CASE VOCABULARY**

ATTEMPT: The act or an instance of making an effort to accomplish something, especially without success. In criminal law, an overt act that is done with the intent to commit a crime but that falls short of completing the crime. Attempt is an inchoate offense distinct from the attempted crime. Under the Model Penal Code, an attempt includes any act that is a substantial step toward commission of a crime, such as enticing, lying in wait for, or following the intended victim or unlawfully entering a building where a crime is expected to be committed.

FIRST–DEGREE MURDER: Murder that is willful, deliberate, or premeditated, or that is committed during the course of another dangerous felony.

GENERAL INTENT: The state of mind required for the commission of certain common-law crimes not requiring specific intent or not imposing strict liability. General intent usually takes the form of recklessness (involving actual awareness of a risk and the culpable taking of that risk) or negligence (involving blameworthy inadvertence).

HOMICIDE: The killing of one person by another.

MURDER: The killing of a human being with malice aforethought.

RECKLESS: Characterized by the creation of a substantial and unjustifiable risk of harm to others and by a conscious (and sometimes deliberate) disregard for or indifference to that risk; heedless; rash. Reckless conduct is much more than mere negligence; it is a gross deviation from what a reasonable person would do.

SECOND–DEGREE MURDER: Murder that is not aggravated by any of the circumstances of first-degree murder.

AN ATTEMPT TO KILL *ANYONE* IS ATTEMPTED MURDER

Did you mean to shoot that guy!?!

Not specifically...

stus.com

■**INSTANT FACTS** Stone (D) went to a local carnival after hearing that some gang members, including some of his cohorts, had engaged in a verbal altercation there; when he got there, Stone (D) shot his gun out the window of the truck in which he was riding, in the direction of a group of about ten rival gang members, and he was convicted of the attempted murder of one of the group members.

■**BLACK LETTER RULE** The mental state required for attempted murder is the intent to kill *a* human being, not a *particular* human being.

■ **PROCEDURAL BASIS**

State supreme court review of an intermediate appellate court decision reversing the defendant's conviction.

■ **FACTS**

A police officer observed a group of about ten to twenty-five youths roaming around at a parking-lot carnival. He recognized some of the group to be gang members, and he thought the group appeared to be "looking for trouble." Words were exchanged, including some gang-related slurs, and some of the youths left the carnival to avoid a fight. A group of gang members followed them and kicked their truck as they drove away. The truck owner returned home and told several people, including Stone (D), what had happened at the carnival. Stone (D) and some of the others returned to the carnival in the same truck, where they drove past a group of rival gang members a couple times. On the third pass, the driver made a gang sign at the group, and Stone (D) pointed his gun out the passenger-side window. Stone (D) shot in the direction of the group. The youths ducked and scattered. Stone (D) was charged with the attempted murder of Joel, one of the kids in the group that Stone (D) shot at. Joel testified that he did not think Stone (D) was pointing the gun at him, but that the shot was *near* him. He believed Stone (D) was just trying to scare them, but not really hurt anyone. A jury found Stone (D) guilty of attempted premeditated murder, and Stone (D) appealed. The court of appeal reversed, finding that when Stone (D) shot his gun toward the group, he intended to kill someone, but not Joel. The state supreme court granted review.

■ **ISSUE**

Can a person who shoots into a group of people, intending to kill one of the group but not knowing or caring which one, be convicted of attempted murder?

■ **DECISION AND RATIONALE**

(Chin, J.) Yes. The mental state required for attempted murder is the intent to kill *a* human being, not a *particular* human being. We have previously held that the fact that the defendant intended to kill a particular target does not mean he did not intend to kill someone else within the "kill zone." This is a reasonable inference a jury may draw, and no particular jury instruction is required. There was evidence in this case that Stone (D) used a means to kill the named victim that inevitably could result in the death of other victims within the zone of danger. In the *Scott* case, we held that the intent to kill an intended target transfers to the unintended target and could support a conviction for attempted murder of the unintended target. The social harm of murder is the killing of one human being by another, and the requisite intent is therefore the intent to kill *a*, not a specific, human being. Thus, a person who intends to kill can be guilty of attempted murder even if the person has no specific target in mind. An indiscriminate would-be killer is just as culpable as one who targets a specific person. There is a difference between intent to kill in murder and attempted murder cases: a person who intends to kill can be guilty of the murder of each person actually killed, even if he intended to kill just one. But guilt of attempted murder must be judged separately as to each alleged victim, whether the alleged victim was particularly targeted or randomly chosen. In other words, a defendant who intends to kill one person will be liable for multiple counts of murder when multiple victims die, but only one count of attempted murder if no one dies. But when no one dies, the defendant will be guilty of attempted murder even if he intended to kill a random person rather than a specific one. Reversed and remanded.

Analysis:

The information in this case specifically alleged that the defendant intended to kill Joel F. This allegation was problematic, given that the prosecution ultimately could not prove that the defendant targeted a specific person, rather than simply someone within the group. In hindsight, it may have been better if the case had been charged differently. The information does not necessarily need to name a specific victim. It is sufficient if the charge contains a statement that the accused has committed some offense, which may be in any words sufficient to give the accused a reasonable opportunity to prepare and present a defense. If the defendant is accused of attempted murder of someone, although not necessarily a specific person, it would be enough to allege facts that give notice of the incident referred to, and that the defendant is charged with attempted murder.

■ CASE VOCABULARY

ATTEMPTED MURDER: An overt act that is done with the intent to commit a crime but that falls short of completing the crime. Attempt is an inchoate offense distinct from the intended crime. Under the Model Penal Code, an attempt includes any act that is a substantial step toward commission of a crime, such as enticing, lying in wait for, or following the intended victim or unlawfully entering a building where a crime is expected to be committed.

People v. Murray

(State of California) v. (Incestuous Uncle)

14 Cal. 159 (1859)

AN ATTEMPT REQUIRES MORE THAN MERE PREPARATION

I plan to elope with my niece. Would you be our witness?

■**INSTANT FACTS** Murray (D) made plans to marry his niece and was charged with attempting to form an incestuous marriage.

■**BLACK LETTER RULE** An attempt to commit a criminal offense must be manifested by acts that would end in the consummation of that offense but for the intervention of circumstances independent of the defendant's will.

■ **PROCEDURAL BASIS**

On appeal to the California Supreme Court.

■ **FACTS**

Murray (D) made plans to marry his niece. He made statements to that effect and planned to elope. Murray (D) asked another individual to go with him to the magistrate's office to serve as a witness. Murray (D) was charged with attempting to form an incestuous marriage.

■ **ISSUE**

Is a declaration of intent, accompanied by minimal preparations, sufficient to constitute the offense of attempted incest?

■ **DECISION AND RATIONALE**

(Field, C.J.) No. The facts of this case establish the defendant's intent to marry his niece, but something beyond intent must be shown to constitute an attempt. An actor must step beyond merely preparing to commit the crime to be guilty of an attempt. All the steps taken by Murray (D) were preparations. No acts were manifested that would result in the commission of the offense of incest. Reversed and remanded.

Analysis:

The defendant in an attempt case must set in motion a chain of events from which there is no turning back in order to be found guilty. Thus, in *People v. Miller*, 42 P.2d 308 (Calif. 1935), the court explained that, for an attempt, "[t]here must be some appreciable fragment of the crime committed, and it must be in such progress that it will be consummated unless interrupted by circumstances independent of the will of the attempter." In this case, many things could have gotten in the way of the uncle's plans—not the least of which is that the uncle could have changed his mind.

■ CASE VOCABULARY

ATTEMPT: The act or an instance of making an effort to accomplish something, especially without success. In criminal law, an overt act that is done with the intent to commit a crime but that falls short of completing the crime. Attempt is an inchoate offense distinct from the attempted crime. Under the Model Penal Code, an attempt includes any act that is a substantial step toward commission of a crime, such as enticing, lying in wait for, or following the intended victim or unlawfully entering a building where a crime is expected to be committed.

INCEST: In this context, intermarriage between persons related in any degree of consanguinity or affinity within which marriage is prohibited.

(Convicted Attempted Rapist) v. (State of Alabama)

63 So. 2d 388 (Ala. App. 1953)

THE VICTIM'S FEAR OF BEING RAPED CAN ESTABLISH THE DEFENDANT'S INTENT

■**INSTANT FACTS** The defendant was convicted of attempt to commit an assault with intent to rape and he appealed.

■**BLACK LETTER RULE** To support a conviction for attempt, the prosecution must prove beyond a reasonable doubt that the defendant intended to commit the crime.

■ **PROCEDURAL BASIS**

On appeal from a conviction for attempted assault with intent to rape.

■ **FACTS**

Allen, a white woman, was enjoying a Coke with her children at a diner. As they started to walk toward home, Allen noticed the defendant, McQuirter (D), a black man, sitting in a parked truck. As they passed him, he muttered something and opened the door of the truck, following them down the street. She stopped at the house of an acquaintance and waited for McQuirter (D) to leave. When she resumed her walk home, McQuirter (D) appeared in front of her. She told her children to run to a neighbor for help. When McQuirter (D) saw the neighbor, he retreated, coming to rest at a stop sign across from Allen's house. Allen watched the defendant from the neighbor's porch for half an hour. McQuirter (D) eventually left and Allen went home. The incident was reported to the police and corroborated by Allen's daughter. A police officer testified that, upon his arrest, McQuirter (D) told him he had intended "to get himself a white woman" that night. The chief of police testified that McQuirter (D) told him he had been drinking and had intended to assault the first woman that passed his truck. He had planned to kill her if she screamed. McQuirter (D) testified at trial, however, that he did not make any comments to Allen, and he further denied making any statements to the police. He was found guilty of attempting to commit assault with intent to rape and fined $500.

■ **ISSUE**

Can evidence of an attempted rape be proven simply from the fact that the targeted victim feared the defendant intended to rape her?

■ **DECISION AND RATIONALE**

(Price, J.) Yes. Alabama law provides for conviction for an attempt to commit an assault with attempt to rape by a showing of an attempt to rape that has not progressed far enough to constitute an assault. Under that law, the jury must be satisfied that the defendant intended to rape the prosecutrix. Intent is to be determined by the jury from the evidence put forward at

---

trial and may include evidence as to current social customs, including the fact that the defendant was black and the potential victim was white. The defense argued that the testimony of the officers should have been excluded since there was shown no overt act committed in furtherance of the attempt, but once any facts are proven that lead to the inference that the crime has been committed, the confession is admissible. Affirmed.

Analysis:

In this case, McQuirter (D) was found to have committed an "act" in furtherance of his crime. The facts do not show that Allen was even physically touched by the defendant. Under *People v. Murray*, 14 Cal. 159 (1859), the act should have been one that, if uninterrupted, would have resulted in Allen being raped. Consider the court's explanation that intent could be determined from "social conditions and customs founded upon racial differences, such as that the prosecutrix was a white woman and defendant was a Negro man."

■ CASE VOCABULARY

PROSECUTRIX [Complainant]: The party who brings a legal complaint against another; especially the plaintiff in a civil suit.

(State of New York) v. (Attempted Robber)

246 N.Y.334, 158 N.E. 888 (1927)

ATTEMPTED ROBBERY REQUIRES PREPARATION BEYOND AN AGREEMENT TO ROB AND A DECISION TO SEARCH FOR A TARGET

This is so humiliating. Are we truly criminals if we can't even find the guy we want to rob?

stus.com

■INSTANT FACTS Charles Rizzo (D) and others were convicted of attempt to commit robbery in the first degree; Rizzo (D) appealed.

■BLACK LETTER RULE Acts sufficient to establish an attempt must go beyond preparation and must bring the defendant closer to achieving the goal of committing the intended crime.

■ PROCEDURAL BASIS

Appeal by the defendant from the judgment of the appellate division affirming his conviction.

■ FACTS

Rizzo (D) and three others planned to rob Charles Rao of the United Lathing Company's payroll, valued at about $1200. The four armed men rode around in search of Rao, going to the bank where he was supposed to get the cash and to several buildings being constructed by United Lathing Company. They discovered they were being followed by the police; all four men were arrested. Rao, the intended victim, was not at the location where the defendants were ultimately arrested; in fact, the defendants had never found the man they intended to rob.

■ ISSUE

Does the intent to commit a robbery, coupled with a search for the intended target, establish an attempt to commit robbery?

■ DECISION AND RATIONALE

(Crane, J.) No. Acts sufficient to establish an attempt must go beyond preparation and must bring the defendant closer to achieving the goal of committing the intended crime. Under New York law, "[a]n act, done with intent to commit a crime, and tending but failing to effect its commission, is 'an attempt to commit that crime." Although any act to prepare for the commission of a crime may be said to help achieve its accomplishment, and searching for Rao certainly was an act designed to commit the crime, the law considers some acts too remote to constitute an attempt. The acts must bring the defendants closer to achieving the goal of committing their intended crime. As the court stated in *Hyde v. U.S.*, 225 U.S. 347, an attempt has only been committed when the likelihood of the defendants' success is high. Since crimes may be committed in a multitude of ways, it is difficult to create a law to apply to all facts. The determination must be made based on the facts of each case. Here, the defendants were looking for the company's payroll agent in order to take his money. Under the laws of

---

New York, to commit a robbery, money must be taken by force or through fear. The question is, then, whether the actions of the defendants here came close to taking Rao's property. Rao could not be robbed until he was found. At the time the defendants were arrested, Rao had not even obtained the funds from the bank to cover the payroll. The defendants cannot be found to have attempted the robbery of a person they had not found, and who did not possess the funds to be stolen.

It should be noted that, of the four defendants, only Rizzo (D) appealed his conviction. Since all four men were tried together and convicted on the basis of the same evidence, if Rizzo's (D) conviction could not stand, neither may the conviction of his three "accomplices." However, absent their appeal, they are not entitled to a remedy and must serve their sentences. Since two of the men were guilty of illegally carrying weapons, their lack of appeal may be related to those charges. Nonetheless, the district attorney should bring this matter to the attention of the Governor to be dealt with as he sees fit. Reversed and remanded for a new trial.

Analysis:

Certainly, the defendants here did more than the defendant in McQuirter v. State, 63 So.2d 388 (Ala. App. 1953), in which the defendant's acts that instilled a fear of rape in the victim were sufficient to support an attempt conviction. Here, however, the court noted that it was not a certainty that the defendants would find their target—in fact, even if Rao had been found, he had not been to the bank to get the cash. One of the motivations for applying the "next to the last possible act" rule in attempt cases is to encourage those with criminal intentions to abandon their plans. If minor preparations placed potential criminals at risk for conviction, they would reap no benefit from abandoning their crime.

■ CASE VOCABULARY

INDISPENSABLE–ELEMENT TEST: A common law test for the crime of attempt, based on whether the defendant acquires control over any thing that is essential to the crime. Under this test, for example, a person commits a crime by buying the explosives with which to detonate a bomb.

LAST–PROXIMATE–ACT TEST: A common-law test for the crime of attempt, based on whether the defendant does the final act necessary to commit an offense (such as pulling the trigger of a gun, not merely aiming it). Most courts have rejected this test as being too lenient.

People v. Staples

(State of California) v. (Would–Be Bank Robber)

6 Cal. App. 3d 61, 85 Cal. Rptr. 589 (1970)

ABANDONING PLANS TO COMMIT A CRIME DOES NOT PRECLUDE AN ATTEMPT
CONVICTION

I wonder how many holes I have to drill before it counts as an attempt.

stus.com

■**INSTANT FACTS** Staples (D) rented an office in a building over a bank, intending to drill through the floor and into the bank's vaults; before anything was taken from the bank, Staples (D) abandoned his plans, but he was arrested and charged with attempted bank robbery nonetheless.

■**BLACK LETTER RULE** Regardless of whether the abandonment of a crime is voluntary or nonvoluntary, if sufficient acts have been performed toward commission of the crime, the defendant may be held responsible for an attempt.

■ **PROCEDURAL BASIS**

Appeal by the defendant from his conviction for attempted burglary.

■ **FACTS**

Staples (D) rented an office over a bank under an assumed name, brought in equipment, including gas tanks, torches, and drilling tools, and started drilling holes in the floor over the bank vault. He stopped short of having the holes go through the floor. Staples (D) did not pay the rental at the end of the first month and the landlord entered the office and discovered the tools. The landlord turned Staples's (D) tools over to the police. Staples (D) was arrested some months later. After being advised of his rights, the defendant gave the police a written statement in which he described his plan to drill into the bank. Staples (D) admitted that he intended to burglarize the bank and that he began drilling with an intent to enter the vault. He also explained that as he drilled, he began to reconsider, realizing that the life of a fugitive was not for him; he would prefer his life as a mathematician to being on the run. Although he had continued to ponder the bank robbery now and again, the plan seemed increasingly absurd.

■ **ISSUE**

When a defendant has gone beyond mere preparations to commit a crime, may he be prosecuted for an attempt even though he later reconsiders and abandons his plans?

■ **DECISION AND RATIONALE**

(Reppy, Assoc. J.) Yes. Many tests have been composed in an attempt to delineate when preparation for a crime is transformed into an attempt. None of the tests to date are without limitations, but the shortcomings of these tests are unimportant here. Staples's (D) actions went beyond mere preparation. Drilling was clearly a step toward accomplishing the burglary— it began the "breaking" of the "breaking and entering." Staples's (D) actions were detected when the landlord regained control over the office space and turned Staples's (D) equipment over to the police. Whether Staples's (D) abandonment was voluntary or not is unavailing.

What is important is whether Staples's (D) actions had proceeded far enough that they could be classified as an attempt. Once actions have been transformed into an attempt, there is no going back. Here, Staples (D) committed an act that presented the danger of harm. Affirmed.

Analysis:

The result here seems harsh. Staples (D) had abandoned the idea of robbing the bank. Unlike the would-be robbers in *People v. Rizzo*, 246 N.Y.334, 158 N.E. 888 (1927), however, Staples (D) *had* settled on his target and would have been successful had he chosen to proceed. Under the rule in this case, it seems unlikely a person could set a crime in motion and then voluntarily abandon the crime without the risk of prosecution for an attempt.

■ CASE VOCABULARY

ABANDONMENT: The relinquishing of a right or interest with the intention of never again claiming it; renunciation.

SOLICITATION IS COMPLETE UPON COMMUNICATION

■INSTANT FACTS Lubow (D) owed Silverman $30,000 for diamonds he had purchased from him and tried to talk Silverman into participating in a scheme to defraud other stone salesmen in an effort to repay him; Lubow (D) was convicted of solicitation.

■BLACK LETTER RULE Proof of the crime of solicitation is complete upon proof of the communication; it does not require an overt act in furtherance nor does it even require proof of delivery of the solicitation to the intended target.

■ PROCEDURAL BASIS

On appeal from convictions for criminal solicitation in the second degree.

■ FACTS

Lubow (D) and other defendants owed Max Silverman, a jeweler, $30,000 for diamonds. In an effort to make money to pay off this debt or have Silverman write it off, the defendants, all jewelers, contacted Silverman and presented him with a proposal under which Silverman would obtain precious stones on credit. Payment for the stones would be stalled. The stones would be sold at less than cost, with the proceeds used to buy more and more diamonds until the amount owed became substantial, at which time, under the scheme, Silverman would file bankruptcy, explaining he lost the money gambling. The cash from the sale of the diamonds would be split among Silverman and the defendants. Lubow (D) promised that they could each end up with upwards of a quarter of a million dollars. Silverman reported the scheme to the authorities and was given a tape recorder to record further conversations with the defendants.

■ ISSUE

May the crime of solicitation be proven without evidence of an act in furtherance of the crime being solicited?

■ DECISION AND RATIONALE

(Bergan, J.) Yes. The crime of solicitation prohibits one from getting another's assistance in the commission of a crime. Solicitation to commit a felony was a crime at common law and could constitute a separate crime though it had not reached the attempt state. The law does not require that the actors commit an act in furtherance of their future crime; all that is required is that the solicitation itself occur. Further, this crime may be committed even though the solicitation is not actually delivered to the intended cohort, such as when a phone message is left and not received. There is sufficient evidence in the record here to find the defendants intended to have Silverman defraud creditors in the purchase of diamonds and that the defendants actually approached Silverman with the plan and asked for his participation. This brings the conduct within the statute. In this case, the existence of the solicitation is supported by the tape recordings that Silverman made. In other cases, without this type of proof, the decision to prosecute could arguably be abused, in that an unscrupulous person need only tell the police that another had recruited him for the commission of a crime to expose another to criminal liability. However, that same risk exists with nearly every crime. Affirmed.

Analysis:

In solicitation cases, as compared to other attempt-crime cases, the point at which the crime is committed is objectively fixed. There is no need for hair-splitting as to whether the activities went beyond simple preparation and became part of the actual crime. The crime of solicitation serves to fill the gap between those criminal activities that do not reach the "attempt" state and those that do.

■ CASE VOCABULARY

CRIMINAL SOLICITATION: The criminal offense of urging, advising, commanding, or otherwise inciting another to commit a crime. Solicitation is an inchoate offense distinct from the solicited crime. Under the Model Penal Code, a defendant is guilty of solicitation even if the command or urging was not actually communicated to the solicited person, as long as it was designed to be communicated. Model Penal Code § 5.02(2).

(Arrested Attorney) v. (Prosecuting State)

398 P.2d 863 (Okla. Crim. App. 1964)

A DEFENDANT CANNOT RECEIVE "STOLEN PROPERTY" THAT IS NO LONGER STOLEN

■**INSTANT FACTS** Stanford was supposed to sell a stolen coat to his attorney, Booth (D), but was arrested before the sale; the police urged Stanford to go forward with the sale to catch Booth (D), who was also arrested and charged with attempting to buy stolen property.

■**BLACK LETTER RULE** If a defendant could not be convicted of a substantive crime, he or she may not be convicted of an attempt to commit that crime.

■ **PROCEDURAL BASIS**

On appeal by the defendant from his conviction in district court.

■ **FACTS**

Stanford, an informant with an illustrious criminal record, admitted to breaking into a parked car to steal a gray cashmere coat. He went home and phoned his attorney, Booth (D), telling him that he "had the coat he ordered." Stanford promised to deliver it for $20. The two men decided on a time and place to make the exchange; in the meantime, Stanford wore the coat himself. Based on the report of the car break-in, the police recognized the coat on Stanford and arrested him. He admitted having stolen the coat. The police encouraged Stanford to deliver the coat to Booth (D) and watched the transfer from a closet. They witnessed Stanford telling Booth (D) that the coat was "hot." Booth (D) then placed the coat in his car. The police returned Stanford to the police station and proceeded to Booth's (D) house with a warrant, found the coat, and arrested him. At trial, the judge concluded that once stolen goods are recovered by the police, they are no longer "stolen." The jury was instructed, however, that in order to convict Booth (D) of attempting to receive stolen property, it needed to find an intent to commit the crime and an act done in furtherance of the crime.

■ **ISSUE**

If a defendant cannot be convicted of the substantive crime, is it possible for him to be convicted of an attempt?

■ **DECISION AND RATIONALE**

(Nix, J.) No. The issue of whether an actor may be held responsible for the crime of receiving stolen property once that property has already been retrieved from the thief is one of first impression in Oklahoma. Other courts have held that, in order to be guilty of receiving stolen goods, the goods "must have retained their stolen character at the time they were received by the accused." These courts have conceded that when goods have been recovered by their owner, or the owner's agent (including the police), the goods are no longer "stolen." Booth (D)

---

here argues that since the owner of the coat had, technically, recovered it, he could not be convicted of receiving stolen property.

The earliest case on the matter, *Regina v. Collin*, 9 Cox C.C. 497, 169 Eng. Rep. 1477 (1864), held that a charge of attempt can only be allowed to stand when, if the defendant had not been interrupted, he would have committed the complete felony. Since then, courts in this country have held that a "legal impossibility" excuses an attempt, but a "factual impossibility" does not. Here, once the coat was recovered by the police, it was no longer stolen. It was thus legally impossible for Booth (D) to receive it as stolen property. The defendant here may be morally guilty, but the law does not punish a criminal mind without more. A criminal must commit an illegal act. One may purchase goods from someone with a reputation for stealing, thinking it likely the goods he or she takes are stolen. However, if the thief came by the goods honestly, the purchaser cannot be guilty of a crime, even though he believed he might be committing one. When a statute requires *knowledge,* that knowledge must be correct or there is no crime. Reversed.

Analysis:

The court here makes a logical argument. It focuses on the *knowledge* of the actor. *Assuming* a fact does not make it true. Thinking a coat is stolen is not knowledge of its character—it is, rather, a mistake. The court knows its argument is legally sound, but, morally, not very satisfying, which is likely why it ends its analysis of Booth's (D) conviction with a call to the legislature to adopt a new statute.

■ CASE VOCABULARY

IMPOSSIBILITY: A fact or circumstance preventing the commission of a crime.

FACTUAL IMPOSSIBILITY: Impossibility due to the fact that the illegal act cannot physically be accomplished, such as trying to pick an empty pocket. Factual impossibility is not a defense to the crime of attempt.

LEGAL IMPOSSIBILITY: Impossibility due to the fact that what the defendant intended to do is not illegal even though the defendant might have believed that he or she was committing a crime—this type of legal impossibility is a defense to the crimes of attempt, conspiracy, and solicitation; impossibility due to the fact that an element required for an attempt has not been satisfied, which is a defense to the crime of attempt.

People v. Dlugash

(State of New York) v. (Attempted Murderer)

41 N.Y.2d 725, 363 N.E.2d 1155 (1977)

ATTEMPTED MURDER MAY OCCUR EVEN IF THE VICTIM WAS ALREADY DEAD

Hmmm... I better shoot him a few more times, just in case he's not really dead.

stus.com

■**INSTANT FACTS** Geller was shot multiple times by his roommate during an argument; several minutes later, thinking Geller may still be alive, Dlugash (D) shot him several more times.

■**BLACK LETTER RULE** A defendant may be convicted of attempted murder even though the target of his or her crime already died from other causes.

■ **PROCEDURAL BASIS**

On appeal following a dismissal of the indictment.

■ **FACTS**

Geller was found dead, the victim of multiple gunshot wounds. Dlugash (D) was arrested for the murder and admitted to the police that he and Geller had been out that evening drinking. While they were out together, Geller began demanding that a third man, Bush, pay him $100 for rent and Bush refused, telling Geller he could end up with a bullet in him if he persisted. The three men went back to Geller's place and continued drinking. Geller renewed his demand for rent from Bush and Bush pulled a gun and shot Geller three times. A few minutes later, Dlugash (D) walked over to Geller's body and shot Geller several more times, even though Dlugash (D) admitted later that Geller already looked dead. Bush then collected the guns and left the apartment to dispose of them. Dlugash (D) gave the police no reason for his actions except that he perhaps feared Bush. Dlugash (D) was indicted on a single count of murder. Dlugash's (D) statements were admitted as evidence of the crime. Medical testimony could not establish with certainty how long it would have taken Geller to die from Bush's shots, but testimony did seem to support a finding that death would not have taken long. Dlugash (D) was found guilty of murder and moved to have to verdict set aside. His motion was denied. On appeal, the Appellate Division reversed the conviction and dismissed the indictment, based on the inability of the prosecution to prove that Geller was alive at the time Dlugash (D) shot him. Absent proof he was alive, Dlugash (D), the court held, could not have killed him.

■ **ISSUE**

May a defendant be held responsible for attempted murder even though the target of his crime was already dead?

■ **DECISION AND RATIONALE**

(Jasen, J.) Yes. Of course, to sustain a homicide conviction, it must be shown that the intended victim was alive at the time he was shot. It cannot be murder to shoot a dead body.

Attempted murder, however, presents a different scenario. While the Model Penal Code sought to eliminate the defense of impossibility in virtually all cases, it still holds actors criminally responsible when the end result they intended constitutes a crime. If the defendant believed the victim was alive at the time he shot him, it is not a defense that the victim was already dead. The record in this case shows that there was evidence that Dlugash (D) believed Geller was alive when he shot him—he shot him in vital areas of the body and did so at point-blank range. It is not beyond the realm of possibility that Dlugash (D) thought he was delivering the final, fatal blow to Geller. While Dlugash (D) later argued that he believed Geller was dead when he shot him, that is a self-serving statement which the jurors were free to disregard if they found it not credible. It is not necessary for the prosecution to establish, beyond a reasonable doubt, that the victim was alive. The only concern was whether the defendant believed the victim he was shooting was alive. Further, the court could have modified the judgment to reflect the conviction for attempted murder if they felt the evidence was insufficient, and it did not. The appellate division failed to take the proper corrective action. Reversed.

Analysis:

Here, in contrast with *Booth v. State*, 398 P.2d 863 (Okla. Crim. App. 1964), the court dealt with a statute that gave it substantially more leeway to ignore the defendant's actual knowledge and focus more closely on his intent. The court explains that the legislature drafted the statute in the manner it did to allow the focus to be on an actor's intent rather than the external circumstances. In the cases that have followed *Dlugash*, such as *People v. Leichtweis*, 59 A.D.2d 383, 399 N.Y.S.2d 439 (1977), the fact-finders continue to convict defendants of attempt based on intent.

■ CASE VOCABULARY

ATTEMPT: An overt act that is done with the intent to commit a crime but that falls short of completing the crime. Attempt is an inchoate offense distinct from the attempted crime. Under the Model Penal Code, an attempt includes any act that is a substantial step toward commission of a crime, such as enticing, lying in wait for, or following the intended victim or unlawfully entering a building where a crime is expected to be committed.

INTENT: The state of mind accompanying an act, especially a forbidden act. While motive is the inducement to do some act, intent is the mental resolution or determination to do it. When the intent to do an act that violates the law exists, motive becomes immaterial.

(Prosecuting State) v. (Criminal Defendant)

631 N.W.2d 694 (Mich. 2001)

IMPOSSIBILITY IS NOT A DEFENSE TO A CHARGE OF ATTEMPT

■INSTANT FACTS Thousand (D) was arrested after luring an undercover deputy posing as a fourteen-year-old girl to meet him for sexual relations.

■BLACK LETTER RULE Absent a statutory recognition of the defense, impossibility is not a defense to a criminal act.

■ PROCEDURAL BASIS

On appeal from a dismissal by the circuit court based on the doctrine of impossibility.

■ FACTS

A Michigan deputy participating in an undercover investigation on Internet crime posed as a minor when entering "chat rooms," in order to identify persons using these rooms for criminal purposes. At one point, the deputy, using the alias "Bekka," was approached by the defendant, whom he told he was a fourteen-year-old girl. During the "chat," the defendant, using the screen name "Mr. Auto–Mag," told Bekka his real name, Chris Thousand (D), and sent Bekka a photo of himself. For about a week, "Bekka" and Thousand (D) conversed in the chat room, and the content of the chats became more sexually explicit. Aware of her young age, Thousand (D) nonetheless invited Bekka to participate in various sexual acts with him. Thousand (D) also sent Bekka photos of male genitalia and asked Bekka to come to his home to engage in sexual activity. He asked if she looked older than sixteen, in case his roommates wondered about her age. The two eventually agreed to meet at a McDonald's parking lot. The police were waiting there for him and arrested Thousand (D). Thousand (D) brought a motion to quash the charges, arguing that, absent a real child victim, the evidence was insufficient to support a conviction. The circuit court agreed and dismissed the charges. The court of appeals affirmed.

■ ISSUE

Does the doctrine of impossibility provide a defense to the charge of distributing obscene material to a minor?

■ DECISION AND RATIONALE

(Young, J.) No. The doctrine of impossibility is the dilemma that arises when the defendant's mistake of fact or law renders it impossible for him or her to have committed the underlying crime or attempt to commit the crime. The distinction has been made between crimes that are factually impossible and those that are legally impossible. At common law, legal impossibility was a defense, while factual impossibility was not, even though the reasons for the distinctions have not been easy to articulate. A factual impossibility is created by a fact unknown to the actor that would prevent him or her from completing the crime. A legal impossibility arises when an actor intends to commit an act, thinking it to be a crime, even though it is not truly illegal. A "hybrid legal impossibility" occurs when the impossibility is created both by legal and factual misapprehensions. Because of the lack of clear lines distinguishing between these types of impossibility, most jurisdictions now consider them "logically indistinguishable" and no longer consider "impossibility" as a defense. Absent Michigan's recognition of the defense of impossibility at common law, there is no reason to do so here.

Turning then to the statute under which Thousand (D) was charged, an attempt is committed when intent is combined with an act committed in furtherance of the commission of the crime. The statute does not create an exception to prosecution for impossibility. Here, Thousand (D) sent an obscene photo, not to a fourteen-year-old girl but to an undercover police officer, but he has not been charged with having committed the actual crime. Instead, he has been charged with attempt. The absence of a minor child is not a defense to that crime. Reversed in part and remanded.

Analysis:

In *Booth v. State*, 398 P.2d 863 (Okla. Crim. App. 1964), the court concentrated on the concept of knowledge as opposed to simple assumption. True knowledge cannot exist based on "facts" that are simply wrong. The court in this case sought to refocus the attention of the parties on the idea of intent. Whether the defendant was misled as to the facts involved—such as the age of his victim—was not important. The fact remained that the defendant would have committed the crime had the facts been as he had presumed.

■ CASE VOCABULARY

OBSCENE: Extremely offensive under contemporary community standards of morality and decency; grossly repugnant to the generally accepted notions of what is appropriate. Under the Supreme Court's three-part test, material is legally obscene—and therefore not protected under the First Amendment—if, taken as a whole, the material (1) appeals to the prurient interest in sex, as determined by the average person applying contemporary community standards; (2) portrays sexual conduct, as specifically defined by the applicable state law, in a patently offensive way; and (3) lacks serious literary, artistic, political, or scientific value.

CHAPTER ELEVEN

Complicity

State v. Ochoa

Instant Facts: Ochoa (D) and two others were convicted of second-degree murder for aiding and abetting the person who actually shot and killed the victim.

Black Letter Rule: A person is an aider and abettor if he or she shares the criminal intent of the principal and acts in concert with the principal.

State v. Tally

Instant Facts: A telegram was sent to Ross, warning him that his life was in danger, and Tally (D) sent a subsequent telegram that directed that the warning not be delivered to Ross.

Black Letter Rule: The assistance rendered by an aider and abettor does not need to be essential to the commission of the crime, but only sufficient to make the crime easier to accomplish.

State v. Formella

Instant Facts: A student was charged and convicted for the conduct of other students in stealing math exams from his school, and he appealed.

Black Letter Rule: An individual is criminally liable for the conduct of another when he acts as an accomplice in the commission of an offense by promoting or facilitating the commission of the offense, or by aiding, or agreeing or attempting to aid, another person in planning or committing the offense.

People v. Beeman

Instant Facts: Beeman (D) was convicted as an aider and abettor and claimed that he did not intend to aid in the commission of the crime.

Black Letter Rule: Conviction for aiding and abetting requires proof that the defendant acted with the knowledge of the criminal purpose, and with the intent of committing, encouraging, or facilitating the offense.

Wilson v. People

Instant Facts: Wilson (D) helped Pierce to commit a burglary, and claimed he did so only to get Pierce arrested.

Black Letter Rule: In order to find a person guilty as an aider and abettor, he or she must have had the same criminal intent as the principal.

State v. Etzweiler

Instant Facts: Etzweiler (D) lent his car to Bailey, who was intoxicated, and Bailey caused a fatal motor vehicle accident.

Black Letter Rule: An accomplice will be liable only for crimes that he or she intended to facilitate.

State v. Christy Pontiac-GMC, Inc.

Instant Facts: Employees of Christy Pontiac—GMC, Inc. (Christy) (D) submitted forged documents to an automobile manufacturer in order to receive unearned customer rebates.

Black Letter Rule: A corporation may be convicted of a specific-intent crime when an agent of the corporation takes illegal acts in furtherance of the corporation's business interests.

United States v. Hilton Hotels Corp.

Instant Facts: Members of the hospitality industry in Portland, Oregon formed an association to promote the industry; as an incentive for its members to pay the association's dues, the association encouraged its members not to patronize other members not in good standing.

Black Letter Rule: A corporation cannot disown the criminal acts of its agents simply by making it company policy not to break the law; to do so would permit a corporate defendant to avoid responsibility for illegal conduct it actually condoned.

State v. Ochoa

(Government) v. (Rioter)

41 N.M. 589, 72 P.2d 609 (1937)

A PERSON WHO ACTS IN CONCERT WITH ANOTHER AND SHARES A CRIMINAL INTENT
IS GUILTY OF AIDING AND ABETTING

■**INSTANT FACTS** Ochoa (D) and two others were convicted of second-degree murder for aiding and abetting the person who actually shot and killed the victim.

■**BLACK LETTER RULE** A person is an aider and abettor if he or she shares the criminal intent of the principal and acts in concert with the principal.

■ **PROCEDURAL BASIS**

Appeal from convictions for murder in the second degree.

■ **FACTS**

Velarde (D), Avitia (D), and Ochoa (D) lived in a community that was in a state of considerable excitement regarding the eviction of Campos from his house and the prosecution of Navarro for breaking and entering that house. Five days before the killing that gave rise to this case, Velarde (D) told a gathering of people to meet the next day at Campos's house. The day before the killing, there was a meeting that appointed a committee to meet with Sheriff Carmichael. Ochoa (D) was chairman of the meeting, Velarde (D) was named to the committee, and Avitia (D) attended the meeting. The committee asked for Navarro's release, which was refused. The committee also asked to speak to Navarro, but this request was also refused by Carmichael, who said the committee could see Navarro the next day, at his trial. The next morning, Carmichael and his deputies brought Navarro to the Justice of the Peace. The proceedings against Navarro were postponed, and the Sheriff and his deputies attempted to take Navarro back to the jail. Concern had arisen that there would be an attempt to rescue Navarro. A crowd had gathered outside the Justice's office, so Carmichael and his deputies took Navarro out by the rear exit. The crowd realized that Navarro would emerge from the rear of the building into the alley, and Velarde (D) was seen motioning the crowd to the direction of the alley and going into the alley practically at the head of the crowd. Ochoa (D), Avitia (D), and Velarde (D) were all identified as being in the front of the crowd at the rear door. An unarmed deputy came out of the door and was confronted by the crowd, with Velarde (D) gesturing in a threatening manner and saying, "[n]ow you shall see what happens, disgraced [one]." The deputy withdrew and Carmichael, an undersheriff, and two deputies came out of the building with Navarro. Ochoa (D) struck at the undersheriff with a hammer. After the officers moved through the crowd, Avitia (D) drew a pistol from his pocket and rushed toward the officers. A tear gas bomb was thrown, and Deputy Boggess was knocked down. While he was down, Avitia (D) and Ochoa (D) were seen beating and kicking him. A number of gunshots were fired. Ignacio Velarde, the brother of defendant Velarde (D), shot and killed

---

Sheriff Carmichael. Avitia (D), Ochoa (D), and Velarde (D) were convicted of second-degree murder, as aiders and abettors in the death of Sheriff Carmichael.

■ **ISSUE**

Could the defendants be prosecuted as aiders and abettors?

■ **DECISION AND RATIONALE**

(Sadler, J.) Yes. A person is an aider and abettor if he or she shares the criminal intent of the principal and acts in concert with the principal. Avitia (D) and Ochoa (D) acted in concert with Ignacio Velarde when they kicked and beat Deputy Boggess. Although they may not have known beforehand that there was any plan or intention to kill Carmichael, Avitia (D) and Ochoa (D) became aware of it when shots were fired. Avitia (D) and Ochoa (D) continued to assault Boggess after the shots were fired, and it was permissible for the jury to infer that they shared the shooter's intent, because they kept Boggess from going to the aid of Carmichael. Avitia (D) and Ochoa (D) assisted the shooter, and so will be said to have adopted his intent. Velarde (D), however, was not seen to assault Boggess or otherwise assist in the shooting of the sheriff. The convictions of Avitia (D) and Ochoa (D) are affirmed, and the conviction of Velarde (D) is reversed.

Analysis:

The incident in which Carmichael was shot grew out of an already tense situation. Navarro was an active union member whose crime was re-entering his house after he had been evicted from it. Navarro had built the house some years earlier, but the land that it and several other similar houses stood on was bought by a powerful local politician, who proceeded to evict many of the residents in order to stop unionization activities at a nearby coal mine. Velarde's (D) actions in this case consisted mostly of words. His words were sufficiently ambiguous that, although they did nothing to calm the crowd, they did not overtly provoke or threaten violence.

■ **CASE VOCABULARY**

ABET: To aid, encourage, or assist (someone), especially in the commission of a crime; to support (a crime) by active assistance.

ACCESSORY: Something of secondary or subordinate importance; a person who aids or contributes in the commission or concealment of a crime. An accessory is usually liable only if the crime is a felony.

AID AND ABET: To assist or facilitate the commission of a crime, or to promote its accomplishment. Aiding and abetting is a crime in most jurisdictions.

INCITE: To provoke or stir up (someone to commit a criminal act, or the criminal act itself).

PRINCIPAL: One who authorizes another to act on his or her behalf as an agent; one who commits or participates in a crime.

RIOT: An unlawful disturbance of the peace by an assembly of usually three or more persons acting with a common purpose in a violent or tumultuous manner that threatens or terrorizes the public.

THE AID GIVEN BY AN AIDER AND ABETTOR MUST MAKE THE COMMISSION OF THE CRIME EASIER

■INSTANT FACTS A telegram was sent to Ross, warning him that his life was in danger, and Tally (D) sent a subsequent telegram that directed that the warning not be delivered to Ross.

■BLACK LETTER RULE The assistance rendered by an aider and abettor does not need to be essential to the commission of the crime, but only sufficient to make the crime easier to accomplish.

■ **PROCEDURAL BASIS**

Appeal from an order impeaching a judge for aiding and abetting murder.

■ **FACTS**

The Skeltons, relatives of Tally (D), set out on horseback in pursuit of Ross. The Skeltons were armed and were angry with Ross for seducing their sister. It was widely believed in the Skeltons' town that Ross's life was in danger. Tally (D) went to the railroad station, where the telegraph office was located, saying that he was waiting to see if a telegram would be sent. A witness testified that he suggested that a physician should be sent to assist any injured people, and Tally (D) replied that his people could take care of themselves. The witness also suggested that all of them should be arrested, but Tally (D) made no reply. A relative of Ross entered the telegraph office and was followed by Tally (D). The relative gave the telegraph operator a message to send to Ross, in the town of Stevenson, which said four armed men were following him on horseback. Tally (D) either saw the message or deduced what it said. He asked a friend if he should threaten the telegraph operator so that he would not send the message. The friend dissuaded Tally (D) from making threats. Tally (D) wrote out a telegram to Huddleston, the telegraph operator in Stevenson, which said not to let the warned party get away. Tally (D) told the telegraph operator that his message related to the one just sent, and that the telegraph operator should add the words "say nothing." Huddleston testified that he received the first message for Ross and attempted to find him, but could not locate him. He then received the message from Tally (D) and went to find a relative of Tally's (D), to decide what to do. Huddleston saw Ross approaching, but did not give him the message (he claimed that he did not have a copy of it, but it is noted that he did not have a copy when he went to find Ross earlier). The Skeltons surprised Ross and shot and killed him.

■ **ISSUE**

Was Tally (D) guilty of aiding and abetting Ross's murder?

■ **DECISION AND RATIONALE**

(McClellan, J.) Yes. The assistance rendered by an aider and abettor does not need to be essential to the commission of the crime, but only sufficient to make the commission of the crime easier to accomplish. An aider and abettor need not be physically present at the scene of the crime, but he or she must render some assistance in the commission of the crime. It was well known to everyone in Tally's (D) town that the Skeltons had gone in pursuit of Ross. It is apparent that Tally (D) sent his telegram in order to prevent the warning from reaching Ross, so that the Skeltons could have their revenge on him. Tally intended to aid the Skeltons and took steps that were calculated to aid them. Tally's (D) telegram deprived Ross of a chance he may have had to escape from the Skeltons. Tally (D) managed to delay Huddleston long enough for the Skeltons to find Ross and kill him. Ross did not know that there were four men after him, but he would have been so warned if he had received his telegram. It may have been possible for him to reach a place of safety if he had known the full danger that he faced. Judgment removing Tally (D) from office ordered.

■ **DISSENT**

(Head, J.) It has not been proven beyond a reasonable doubt that Tally (D) intended to aid and abet the murder of Ross. It has not been proven beyond a reasonable doubt that the warning telegram would have been delivered to Ross if Tally's (D) telegram had not been sent.

Analysis:

The court discusses only briefly the question of whether the Skeltons knew about the help they would receive from Tally (D). The court does not say so explicitly, but it is clear that knowledge of the principal is not necessary. From the court's discussion, in fact, it seems clear that nothing is required of the principal beyond the commission of the crime. He or she does not need to request the help or even know of the help. It is enough that the aider and abettor made the crime easier. Note that this case is a judicial discipline case, not a criminal prosecution. A portion of the opinion not reprinted says that the opinion is not intended to prejudice any future proceedings against any of those involved, but there is no record that Tally (D) was punished any further for his role in the crime, or that the Skeltons were ever prosecuted for the murder.

■ **CASE VOCABULARY**

ACCESSORY AFTER THE FACT: An accessory who was not at the scene of the crime but knows that a crime has been committed and who helps the offender try to escape arrest or punishment. An accessory after the fact may be prosecuted for obstructing justice.

ACCESSORY BEFORE THE FACT: An accessory who assists or encourages another to commit a crime but who is not present when the offense is actually committed. Most jurisdictions have abolished this category of accessory and instead treat such an offender as an accomplice.

ACCOMPLICE: A person who is in any way involved with another in the commission of a crime, whether as a principal in the first or second degree or as an accessory; a person who knowingly, voluntarily, and intentionally unites with the principal offender in committing a crime and thereby becomes punishable for it. Although the definition includes an accessory before the fact, not all authorities treat this term as including an accessory after the fact.

WITHDRAWING FROM COMPLICITY REQUIRES SOME AFFIRMATIVE ACT

Let's just steal the tests!

Sure! What's the worst that could happen?

stus.com

■INSTANT FACTS A student was charged and convicted for the conduct of other students in stealing math exams from his school, and he appealed.

■BLACK LETTER RULE An individual is criminally liable for the conduct of another when he acts as an accomplice in the commission of an offense by promoting or facilitating the commission of the offense, or by aiding, or agreeing or attempting to aid, another person in planning or committing the offense.

■ PROCEDURAL BASIS

Appeal by the defendant from his conviction as an accomplice.

■ FACTS

Formella (D), a high-school junior, and two friends were studying at the library. After a couple hours, they returned to school to retrieve some books from their lockers. When they got to school, they ran into another group of kids who said they were going to steal some math exams, and these kids asked Formella (D) and his friends to serve as lookouts, which they agreed to do. When they got to their second-floor lockers, Formella (D) and his friends looked around to see if anyone else was there, but then they had second thoughts once they had retrieved their books from their lockers, and they decided to leave the school. They ran into the janitor on their way out, but they did nothing to alert the others that someone was in the building, as they had promised they would do. Once outside, Formella (D) and his pals waited a few minutes for the other group, who exited a few minutes later with the math exams. All of the students shared the exam questions. News of the theft leaked and the school reported it to the police, who conducted an investigation. They ultimately interviewed Formella (D), who admitted his involvement. Formella (D) was charged with criminal liability for the conduct of another under a state statute and was convicted. He appealed, arguing that the statute required the court to making a finding of fact relating to the timing of his withdrawal from the theft and the completion of the theft.

■ ISSUE

Did the trial court err in failing to make findings of fact relating to the timing of Formella's (D) withdrawal from the theft and the completion of the theft?

■ DECISION AND RATIONALE

(Galway, J.) No. An individual is criminally liable for the conduct of another when he acts as an accomplice in the commission of an offense by promoting or facilitating the commission of the offense, or by aiding, or agreeing or attempting to aid, another person in planning or committing the offense. A person is not an accomplice, however, if he terminates his complicity prior to the commission of the offense and wholly deprives it of effectiveness in the commission of the offense, or gives timely warning to the law enforcement authorities or otherwise makes proper effort to prevent the commission of the offense. The relevant statute does not define what is required to wholly deprive oneself of complicity of effectiveness in the commission of an offense. The Model Penal Code suggests, however, that actions sufficient to deprive the prior complicity of its effectiveness vary with the type of accessorial behavior. Generally speaking, an accomplice must engage in some affirmative act, such as an overt expression of disapproval to the principals, in order to terminate his complicity.

According to Formella (D), the court here erred in failing to make findings of fact regarding the time he terminated his complicity and the time the theft occurred, because without such findings the court could not properly apply the statute. We disagree. Although timing is one consideration, in that the alleged accomplice must terminate his complicity prior to the commission of the offense, even assuming the timing was right here, Formella (D) did not wholly deprive his complicity of its effectiveness. He engaged in no affirmative act, such as communicating his withdrawal to the principal offenders. Nor did he discourage them from acting, inform the custodian, or do anything else to undo his complicity. Silently withdrawing from the scene did nothing to undermine the encouragement that the defendant had provided. It was therefore not error for the trial court to refuse to make findings on the timing of the offense, because such findings would not have altered the result.

Analysis:

Note that although Formella (D) was only a junior in high school, this is a criminal court, not a juvenile court, case. It is possible that he was eighteen years old, but it is also possible that Formella (D) was treated as an adult offender even if he was under eighteen. Adult offenders may include not only those who have committed a crime after reaching the age of majority, but also those who, having committed a crime while a minor, were convicted after reaching the age of majority. Formella (D) may have fallen into this latter category. Even if tried as an adult, a youthful offender like Formella (D) may be eligible for special programs not available to older offenders, including community supervision, the successful completion of which may lead to erasing the conviction from the offender's record. Offenders in late adolescence who commit particularly violent or egregious crimes may also be tried as adults, but that does not appear to be the case here, where the crime at issue was the theft of math examinations.

■ CASE VOCABULARY

MODEL PENAL CODE: A proposed criminal code drafted by the American Law Institute and used as the basis for criminal-law revision by many states.

People v. Beeman

(Government) v. (Friend of Robbers)

35 Cal. 3d 547, 199 Cal. Rptr. 60 (1984)

PROOF OF INTENT TO ASSIST IN THE CRIME IS REQUIRED FOR AIDING AND ABETTING

■**INSTANT FACTS** Beeman (D) was convicted as an aider and abettor and claimed that he did not intend to aid in the commission of the crime.

■**BLACK LETTER RULE** Conviction for aiding and abetting requires proof that the defendant acted with the knowledge of the criminal purpose, and with the intent of committing, encouraging, or facilitating the offense.

■ PROCEDURAL BASIS

Appeal from convictions for robbery, burglary, false imprisonment, destruction of telephone equipment, and assault with the intent to commit a felony.

■ FACTS

Gray and Burk assaulted Beeman's (D) sister-in-law, robbed her, and took several pieces of jewelry from her. They also cut the telephone lines while committing the robbery. Beeman (D) was arrested while in possession of some of the jewelry, and he provided information that led to the arrests of Burk and Gray. Burk and Gray testified that Beeman (D) assisted in the commission of the crime by providing them with the floor plan of his sister-in-law's house, by telling them of the contents of the house, and by agreeing to dispose of the loot. Gray testified that Beeman (D) said, shortly before the robbery, that he wanted no part of it and that he was angry that the robbery had been committed.

■ ISSUE

Was Beeman (D) entitled to a jury instruction regarding his state of mind?

■ DECISION AND RATIONALE

(Reynoso, J.) Yes. Conviction for aiding and abetting requires proof that the defendant acted with the knowledge of the criminal purpose and with the intent of committing, encouraging, or facilitating the offense. The instruction that was given to the jury stated only that knowledge is required, but this is an incorrect statement of the law. Intent is a necessary element of a conviction for acting as an aider and abettor, and while intent may sometimes be inferred from knowledge of a criminal purpose, knowledge and intent are not invariably the same thing. Substituting proof of knowledge for proof of intent would effectively eliminate intent as an element of the offense. If specific intent is required for a conviction of the principal offense, the aider and abettor must share the specific intent. An aider and abettor will share the specific intent when he or she knows the full extent of the principal's criminal purpose and gives aid or encouragement with the intent or purpose of facilitating the principal's commission of the crime. Intent was central to Beeman's (D) defense, so failure to give a jury instruction on proof of intent was reversible error. Reversed.

Analysis:

Intent usually must be inferred from actions, particularly when a defendant is charged as an aider and abettor, since defendants rarely explain their intentions to accomplices. Inferring intent from actions is common sense for most of us (it strains credibility to imagine that a person would knowingly aid in the commission of a crime if he or she did not intend to assist in the commission of a crime). The court does not argue with that inference, but instead says that such an inference should not be a presumption.

■ CASE VOCABULARY

BURGLARY: The common-law offense of breaking and entering another's dwelling at night with the intent to commit a felony; the modern statutory offense of breaking and entering any building—not just a dwelling, and not only at night—with the intent to commit a felony.

FALSE IMPRISONMENT: A restraint of a person in a bounded area without justification or consent. False imprisonment is a common-law misdemeanor and a tort. It applies to private as well as governmental detention.

INTENT: The state of mind accompanying an act, especially a forbidden act. While motive is the inducement to do some act, intent is the mental resolution or determination to do it. When the intent to do an act that violates the law exists, motive becomes immaterial.

MENS REA: [Latin. "guilty mind."] The state of mind that the prosecution, to secure a conviction, must prove that a defendant had when committing a crime; criminal intent or recklessness.

PRESUMPTION: A legal inference or assumption that a fact exists, based on the known or proven existence of some other fact or group of facts. A presumption shifts the burden of production or persuasion to the opposing party, who can then attempt to overcome the presumption.

ROBBERY: The illegal taking of property from the person of another, or in the person's presence, by violence or intimidation; aggravate larceny.

SPECIFIC INTENT: The intent to accomplish the precise criminal act that one is later charged with.

Wilson v. People

(Deputy D.A.'s Son) v. (Government)

103 Colo. 441 (1939), 87 P.2d 5

A PRINCIPAL AND AN AIDER MUST SHARE THE SAME INTENT

■**INSTANT FACTS** Wilson (D) helped Pierce to commit a burglary, and claimed he did so only to get Pierce arrested.

■**BLACK LETTER RULE** In order to find a person guilty as an aider and abettor, he or she must have had the same criminal intent as the principal.

■ **PROCEDURAL BASIS**

Appeal from convictions for aiding an abetting burglary and larceny.

■ **FACTS**

Pierce approached Wilson (D) and asked him to find a place where liquor could be purchased. Wilson (D) obtained a bottle of sloe gin, which the two men drank. Wilson (D) noticed that his wristwatch was missing and accused Pierce of taking it. Pierce denied taking the watch and the two men got into a prolonged quarrel. As they discussed the disappearance of the watch, Pierce mentioned that he had been involved in a number of burglaries, including a recent one at a local café. Pierce then drew up a list of burglary tools that would be needed at some time in the future, and Wilson (D) said he could obtain them. Wilson (D) suggested that they go to his father's office to start on the jobs, and the two arrived at the idea of burglarizing a drugstore. They went to the drugstore, and Wilson (D) boosted Pierce up to break the glass in the transom. After the glass was broken, Wilson (D) boosted Pierce through the transom. When Pierce got inside the store, Wilson (D) telephoned the police. He returned to the drugstore, and when the police arrived told them that Pierce was inside. Pierce fled, and Wilson (D) helped the police track him down. Wilson (D) told the police that he got involved with the burglary to get even with Pierce for taking his watch. Wilson (D) testified that he had no intent to steal. The trial court instructed the jury that a person who participates in a crime may not raise the defense that he or she was acting as a decoy or spy. The decoy or spy must stop short of lending assistance to the criminal.

■ **ISSUE**

Was Wilson (D) entitled to raise a defense that he was acting as a decoy or spy?

■ **DECISION AND RATIONALE**

(Beck, J.) Yes. In order to find an alleged aider and abettor guilty, it is necessary that he or she have the same criminal intent as the principal. The jury should have been allowed to determine whether Wilson (D) acted with a felonious intent. The evidence showed that Wilson

---

(D) believed that Pierce took his watch, and there was evidence that tends to support Wilson's (D) claim that he acted only as a decoy to apprehend Pierce in the act. Reversed and remanded for a new trial.

Analysis:

The court seems to be blurring the line between intent and motive. While Wilson (D) was motivated by a desire to see Pierce arrested, he also acted with the intent of having Pierce break into the drugstore. His motive (getting revenge on a drinking companion he suspected of stealing from him) does not negate his intent to help with the break in, although it may have some bearing on the intent behind the burglary charge (burglary is a specific intent crime). Note that Pierce was barred from raising an entrapment defense, because Wilson (D) was acting on his own, not in any capacity as a law enforcement officer.

■ **CASE VOCABULARY**

DECOY: To entice (a person) without force; to inveigle.

ENTRAPMENT: A law-enforcement officer's or government agent's inducement of a person to commit a crime, by means of fraud or undue persuasion, in an attempt to later bring a criminal prosecution against that person; the affirmative defense of having been so induced. To establish entrapment (in most states), the defendant must show that he or she would not have committed the crime but for the fraud or undue persuasion.

LARCENY: The unlawful taking and carrying away of someone else's personal property with the intent to deprive the possessor of it permanently.

MOTIVE: Something, especially willful desire, that leads one to act.

State v. Etzweiler

(Government) v. (Car Owner)

125 N.H. 57, 480 A.2d 870 (1984)

A PERSON CAN ONLY BE AN ACCOMPLICE TO THE CRIME HE INTENDED TO FACILITATE

Dude, you're totally drunk. Here are the keys to my car.

Good call. You won't regret this.

stus.com

■INSTANT FACTS Etzweiler (D) lent his car to Bailey, who was intoxicated, and Bailey caused a fatal motor vehicle accident.

■BLACK LETTER RULE An accomplice will be liable only for crimes that he or she intended to facilitate.

■ PROCEDURAL BASIS

Transfer to the supreme court of motions to quash indictments.

■ FACTS

Etzweiler (D) lent his car to Bailey. Etzweiler (D) allegedly knew that Bailey had been drinking and was intoxicated. Bailey drove away and collided with another car. As a result of the collision, two people were killed. Etzweiler (D) was charged with negligent homicide as an accomplice.

■ ISSUE

Can Etzweiler (D) be charged as an accomplice to negligent homicide?

■ DECISION AND RATIONALE

(Batchelder, J.) No. An accomplice will be liable only for crimes that he or she intended to facilitate. The liability of an accomplice does not extend beyond the shared criminal purpose. The charge of negligent homicide requires a showing that the defendant was unaware of the risk of death created by his or her conduct, and a conviction for aiding and abetting requires a showing of intent to assist in the commission of the crime. Etzweiler (D) cannot have intended to assist Bailey in the commission of a crime Bailey did not know he was going to commit. Indictment quashed.

Analysis:

The statutory definition of negligent homicide applied in this case is different from the usual definition of negligent homicide. Negligent homicide is usually defined as homicide that results from the careless performance of a legal or illegal act in which the danger of death is apparent. Under that definition, charging Etzweiler (D) with aiding and abetting negligent homicide would not be so far-fetched.

■ CASE VOCABULARY

NEGLIGENT HOMICIDE: Homicide resulting from the careless performance of a legal or illegal act in which the danger of death is apparent; the killing of a human being by criminal negligence.

State v. Christy Pontiac–GMC, Inc.

(Minnesota) v. (Car Dealership)

354 N.W.2d 17 (Minn. 1984)

A CORPORATION MAY BE CONVICTED OF CRIMES REQUIRING SPECIFIC INTENT

■**INSTANT FACTS** Employees of Christy Pontiac–GMC, Inc. (Christy) (D) submitted forged documents to an automobile manufacturer in order to receive unearned customer rebates.

■**BLACK LETTER RULE** A corporation may be convicted of a specific-intent crime when an agent of the corporation takes illegal acts in furtherance of the corporation's business interests.

■ PROCEDURAL BASIS

On appeal from a bench trial.

■ FACTS

In 1981, GM offered a rebate program for new car purchasers. The rebate was to be paid half by GM and half by the dealer, but GM frequently paid the customer the entire rebate and then charged the dealer for its half at a later date. It was not uncommon for dealers to extend their half of the rebate to the customers as a discount on the sale price, rather than as a cash payment to the customers. Employees at Christy's (D) forged customers' signatures on sales contracts on two occasions and deposited the customers' rebate to the account of Christy (D). Christy (D) was owned by Jim Christy, who was the sole shareholder, president, and director.

■ ISSUE

Under state criminal statutes, may a corporation be prosecuted and convicted for specific-intent crimes, such as theft and forgery?

■ DECISION AND RATIONALE

(Simonett, J.) Yes. Christy (D) argued that a corporation could not be criminally liable for committing a specific-intent crime, especially when the offender could be imprisoned, since a corporation can neither be imprisoned nor have a mental state. In defining the crimes here, the legislature did not specifically exempt corporations from liability. Corporations must, therefore, be considered persons under the criminal law. The dilemma posed by ascribing specific intent to a corporation is not as troubling as Christy (D) insists. If a corporation can be responsible under tort law for punitive damages, it is not incongruous to hold one responsible for specific-intent crimes. This is especially true for crimes such as theft and forgery that occur frequently in a business setting. Of course, to constitute the commission of a crime, a corporation must do something beyond just having an employee that takes criminal actions on his own. There must be a relationship between the act committed and the officials of the corporation. The jury must find, beyond a reasonable doubt, that the acts of the agent were intended as the acts of

---

the corporation, meaning that the agent's actions were (a) within the scope of his employment with the authority to transact the business that was seen as criminal; (b) intended, at least in part, to further the interests of the corporation; and (c) ratified, authorized, or tolerated by the company's management. This standard differs from the one applied in civil matters, imposing a heavier burden of proof and requiring a showing that the conduct furthered the goals of the corporation. Management approval may even be found to exist when the illegal conduct is specifically prohibited by corporate policy.

Here, the record shows that the employee committing the forgery had the corporate authority to commit the acts. Moreover, Christy (D) obtained the benefits of the cash rebates from GM, not some other individual. Management also tolerated the employee's actions. Even after a customer complained to management about the reduced rebate he received, Christy (D) took no steps to correct the problem. Nothing was done until the Attorney General's office made an inquiry. The acts committed were, therefore, acts of the company. As an additional matter, it should be noted that the state attempted to prosecute Jim Christy, in addition to the dealership, but was unsuccessful because there was insufficient evidence to establish Mr. Christy's separate involvement. Had this been a case in which the corporation was the alter ego of Mr. Christy, prosecution of both Christy (D) and Mr. Christy may have been unfair. Affirmed.

Analysis:

In this case, the court was satisfied that prosecution of both the corporation and its sole shareholder, Jim Christy, was unnecessary. Nearly a decade later, the court considered another case of illegal corporate conduct in *State v. Medibus–Helpmobile, Inc.*, 481 N.W.2d 86 (Minn. Ct. App.1992). In that case, there were multiple owners of the defendant corporation, only some of whom were shown to be involved in the illegal activity. The court concluded there was not double prosecution where they held the company responsible for theft, together with some of its individual owners.

■ CASE VOCABULARY

ALTER EGO: A corporation used by an individual in conducting personal business, the result being that a court may impose liability on the individual by piercing the corporate veil when fraud has been perpetrated on someone dealing with the corporation.

COMMERCIAL CRIME: A crime that affects commerce, especially a crime directed toward the property or revenues of a commercial establishment. Examples include robbery of a business, embezzlement, counterfeiting, forgery, prostitution, illegal gambling, and extortion.

CORPORATE CRIME: A crime committed either by a corporate body or by its representatives acting on its behalf. Examples include price-fixing and consumer fraud.

LEGAL FICTION: An assumption that something is true even though it may be untrue, made especially in judicial reasoning to alter how a legal rule operates.

SPECIFIC INTENT: The intent to accomplish the precise criminal act that one is later charged with.

SWINDLE: To cheat (a person) out of property.

United States v. Hilton Hotels Corp.

(U.S. Government) v. (Major Hotel Chain)

467 F.2d 1000 (9th Cir. 1972)

A STATED COMPANY POLICY WILL NOT SHIELD A CORPORATION FROM CRIMINAL LIABILITY

■**INSTANT FACTS** Members of the hospitality industry in Portland, Oregon formed an association to promote the industry; as an incentive for its members to pay the association's dues, the association encouraged its members not to patronize other members not in good standing.

■**BLACK LETTER RULE** A corporation cannot disown the criminal acts of its agents simply by making it company policy not to break the law; to do so would permit a corporate defendant to avoid responsibility for illegal conduct it actually condoned.

■ PROCEDURAL BASIS

On appeal from a conviction for a violation of the Sherman Antitrust Act.

■ FACTS

The operators of hotels and restaurants and hotel and restaurant suppliers in Portland, Oregon, formed an association together with other hospitality businesses to attract conventions to the city. The association was financed through the contributions of its members, based on their annual revenue. Member Hotels agreed to give preferential treatment to suppliers who paid their assessments. This kind of agreement, if proven, would violate the provisions of the Sherman Act. The president of the Hilton Hotels Corp. (Hilton) (D) testified that it would be contrary to the hotel's policy to condition purchases on a suppliers' payment of association dues. It was the hotel's policy to make purchases based on a combination of stated factors, including cost, quality, and service. Hilton (D) had expressly told its purchasing agent about this policy; however, the agent admitted pressuring a supplier to pay its association dues by threatening to cancel its contract. Based on the admissions of the purchasing agent, Hilton (D) requested that the jury receive specific instructions relating to the imposition of criminal liability on a corporation for unauthorized actions. Those instructions were denied.

■ ISSUE

Did the trial court err in instructing the jury on the attachment of corporate criminal liability notwithstanding the fact that the employee's actions may be contrary to the corporations stated policies or actual instructions?

■ DECISION AND RATIONALE

(Browning, Cir. J.) No. At the conclusion of the trial, the court told the jury that a corporation was liable for the actions of its agents acting within the scope of their employment. The court explained that this meant not only that the corporation would be responsible for actions taken in connection with work, that is, authorized by the company, but also for actions that others would reasonably assume the agents could do. According to the trial judge, the corporation could be responsible for criminal activity, even though the activity was contrary to its stated instructions or policies.

It is not clear whether the Sherman Act permits the court to impose liability for implied condoning of illegal behavior. However, the Act is best able to achieve its goals if an employer is held responsible for its employee's actions, even when the actions violate company policy. The Sherman Act deals primarily with commercial crimes that are typically driven by greed, and offending companies are typically large conglomerates without central management. Because of the internal structure of these companies, it is difficult to identify the agents directly responsible for violating the Sherman Act, but it is often the case that the senior and high management participated in some way in the policies that led to the Sherman Act violations. While management may tell their employees it is important to obey all laws, including the Sherman Act, when the pressure is on to increase profits the orders are frequently ignored. When the Sherman Act is violated, it is most often the company that benefits. These considerations make it more appropriate to punish the entity. Here, despite being told not to participate in the boycott of non-paying members of the hospitality industry, Hilton's purchasing agent was permitted to buy all of the company's supplies with total discretion. He used that authority to pressure a supplier. Hilton (D) cannot be excused for the purchasing agent's conduct absent evidence of steps it took to enforce the contrary instructions. Affirmed.

Analysis:

The upshot of the holding of this case is that a business must do more than just issue a policy statement discouraging certain types of illegal behavior. Much earlier, in *Vulcan Last Co. v. State*, 217 N.W. 412 (Wis. 1928), a company was charged with attempting to influence the outcome of an election and argued it could not be responsible for the actions of its employees if they chose to act outside of their orders. The court, contrarily, found ample support for imposing liability on the corporation for the criminal acts of its employees, holding that "[a] corporation is held responsible for acts not within the agent's corporate powers strictly construed, but which the agent has assumed to perform for the corporation when employing the corporate powers actually authorized."

■ **CASE VOCABULARY**

SHERMAN ANTITRUST ACT: A federal statute, passed in 1890, that prohibits direct or indirect interference with the freely competitive interstate production and distribution of goods. This Act was amended by the Clayton Act in 1914.

CHAPTER TWELVE

Conspiracy

State v. Verive

Instant Facts: Verive (D) was convicted of attempt to dissuade a witness and conspiracy to dissuade a witness and claimed that he was being punished twice for the same act.

Black Letter Rule: A conviction for conspiracy requires an agreement to commit a criminal act and some overt act in furtherance of the conspiracy.

Griffin v. State

Instant Facts: Griffin (D) and others attacked two police officers, and Griffin was convicted of conspiracy.

Black Letter Rule: A conspiracy may be proven inferentially by showing that two or more persons pursued the same unlawful object, even if it appears that they acted independently.

United States v. Recio

Instant Facts: Recio (D) attempted to deliver drugs after they had been seized by law enforcement officers and was convicted of conspiracy to distribute illegal drugs.

Black Letter Rule: A conspiracy does not automatically terminate because the object of the conspiracy has been defeated without the knowledge of the conspirators.

People v. Lauria

Instant Facts: Lauria (D) ran an answering service that had prostitutes as customers and was indicted for conspiracy to commit prostitution.

Black Letter Rule: A supplier of goods or services used for unlawful purposes will be deemed a conspirator only if the supplier knew of the illegal purpose and intended to further the illegal use.

United States v. Diaz

Instant Facts: Diaz (D) was convicted of the use of a firearm in relation to a conspiracy to distribute illegal drugs, but the gun was carried by another participant in the conspiracy.

Black Letter Rule: A participant in a conspiracy is criminally liable for all acts that are done by other members in furtherance of the conspiracy and that are reasonably foreseeable as a necessary consequence of the unlawful agreement.

United States v. Neapolitan

Instant Facts: Neapolitan (D) was convicted of a RICO violation, based on one solicitation of a bribe in connection with the operation of a racketeering enterprise.

Black Letter Rule: A defendant will be convicted for engaging in a RICO conspiracy if the defendant committed only a single RICO violation.

State v. Verive

(Prosecuting Government) v. (Conspirator)

128 Ariz. 570, 627 P.2d 721 (Ct. App. 1981)

CONSPIRACY REQUIRES AN AGREEMENT TO COMMIT A CRIMINAL ACT

Yes, they look similar, but "conspiracy" and "attempt" are different enough to be separate crimes.

conspiracy charge

attempt charge

stus.com

■**INSTANT FACTS** Verive (D) was convicted of attempt to dissuade a witness and conspiracy to dissuade a witness and claimed that he was being punished twice for the same act.

■**BLACK LETTER RULE** A conviction for conspiracy requires an agreement to commit a criminal act and some overt act in furtherance of the conspiracy.

■ PROCEDURAL BASIS

Appeal from convictions on charges of attempting to dissuade a witness and conspiracy to dissuade a witness.

■ FACTS

Verive (D) agreed to go to Galvin's house and beat Galvin, in an effort to dissuade Galvin from testifying against Woodall. Woodall agreed to give Verive (D) $900 and a motorcycle in exchange for beating Galvin. Verive (D) went to Galvin's house and started to beat him. Galvin's son intervened to rescue him. Verive was convicted of both conspiracy to dissuade a witness and attempt to dissuade a witness, and argued that he was being prosecuted twice for the same offense, in violation of the double jeopardy clause of the U.S. Constitution.

■ ISSUE

Can Verive (D) be convicted of both conspiracy and attempt to commit the same crime?

■ DECISION AND RATIONALE

(Haire, J.) Yes. A conviction for conspiracy requires an agreement to commit a criminal act and some overt act in furtherance of the conspiracy. The offense is distinct from the crime of attempt and is not a lesser-included offense of attempt. The overt act required for a conspiracy conviction is any action that is sufficient to corroborate the existence of the agreement. It is not necessary that the act constitute an attempt to commit the crime. The focus of the crime of conspiracy is the agreement. The indictment against Verive (D) alleged the commission of two separate overt acts: the act of beating Galvin, and the act of going to Galvin's house. Either of these two acts would be sufficient for a conspiracy conviction. There is also sufficient evidence, apart from the evidence that supports a conspiracy conviction, to convict Verive (D) of attempt. Affirmed.

Analysis:

The overt act in furtherance of the conspiracy does not need to be an unlawful act. The court says that the proof that Verive (D) went to Galvin's house is evidence of an overt act sufficient to support a conviction for conspiracy. There was nothing inherently unlawful in going to Galvin's house. It is the agreement, followed by the act, that is unlawful.

■ **CASE VOCABULARY**

CONSPIRACY: An agreement by two or more persons to commit an unlawful act; a combination for an unlawful purpose.

CORROBORATION: Confirmation or support by additional evidence or authority.

DOUBLE JEOPARDY: The fact of being prosecuted twice for substantially the same offense.

DOUBLE JEOPARDY CLAUSE: The Fifth Amendment provision stating, "nor shall any person be subject for the same offense to be twice put in jeopardy of life or limb."

IMMUNITY: Freedom from prosecution granted by the government in exchange for the person's testimony.

PERJURY: The act or instance of a person's deliberately making material false or misleading statements while under oath.

Griffin v. State

(Assailant) v. (Prosecuting Government)

455 S.W.2d 882 (Ark. 1970)

CONSPIRACY MAY BE PROVEN BY INDIRECT EVIDENCE

Looks like a conspiracy waiting to happen.

stus.com

■**INSTANT FACTS** Griffin (D) and others attacked two police officers, and Griffin was convicted of conspiracy.

■**BLACK LETTER RULE** A conspiracy may be proven inferentially by showing that two or more persons pursued the same unlawful object, even if it appears that they acted independently.

■ **PROCEDURAL BASIS**

Appeal from a conviction for conspiracy.

■ **FACTS**

Police officers Vines and Ederington came on the scene of a motor vehicle accident. When Vines asked who was driving the vehicle, Griffin (D) said that he was; he challenged Vines to "[t]ake me . . . if you can" and started toward Vines with his fists. Vines attempted to stop Griffin (D), and when he could not, tried to defend himself. A group of people then attacked Vines and Ederington. The crowd was "hollering" and backed away after Vines shot Griffin (D). Vines told the crowd that they had better come get Griffin if they didn't want him shot again. The crowd continued to make noise, saying that they were going to "get" the officers. Griffin (D) was convicted of conspiracy.

■ **ISSUE**

Was the evidence sufficient to support a conviction for conspiracy?

■ **DECISION AND RATIONALE**

(Fogelman, J.) Yes. A conspiracy may be proven by inference, by showing that two or more persons pursued the same unlawful object, even if it appears that they acted independently. Direct evidence of an agreement is not necessary. It is enough to show facts and circumstances that, taken together, apparently indicate that they are mere parts of some complete whole. Affirmed.

Analysis:

There seldom will be direct evidence of an unlawful agreement in a prosecution for conspiracy. The testimony of co-conspirators is regarded by most as inherently suspect, and most courts require corroboration before the testimony of a co-conspirator is used to support a conspiracy

---

conviction. The court here does not even refer to an agreement as being essential to a finding of conspiracy, but mentions instead a "common object or intent pursuant to a common plan."

■ **CASE VOCABULARY**

CIRCUMSTANTIAL EVIDENCE: Evidence based on inference and not on personal knowledge or observation.

DIRECT EVIDENCE: Evidence that is based on personal knowledge or observation and that, if true, proves a fact without inference or presumption.

United States v. Recio

(Federal Government) v. (Drug Seller)

537 U.S. 270, 123 S.Ct. 819 (2003)

A CONSPIRACY DOES NOT END WHEN THE OBJECT OF THE CONSPIRACY BECOMES IMPOSSIBLE

■INSTANT FACTS Recio (D) attempted to deliver drugs after they had been seized by law enforcement officers and was convicted of conspiracy to distribute illegal drugs.

■BLACK LETTER RULE A conspiracy does not automatically terminate because the object of the conspiracy has been defeated without the knowledge of the conspirators.

■ PROCEDURAL BASIS

Appeal from an order of the Ninth Circuit Court of Appeals reversing Recio's (D) conviction.

■ FACTS

Law enforcement officers seized a truck that was carrying illegal drugs. With the assistance of the drivers of the truck, officers set up a sting operation. The truck was driven to its destination and a contact was paged; the contact said that someone would come to pick up the truck. Recio (D) and Lopez–Meza arrived, and Recio (D) drove away in the truck. Police arrested both Recio (D) and Lopez–Meza and they were charged with conspiracy to possess and distribute illegal drugs. They were convicted of the charge, as were the original drivers of the truck. After their conviction, the trial court ordered a new trial and instructed the jury that Recio (D) could not be convicted unless the jury believed that he joined the conspiracy before the police stopped the truck and seized the drugs. Recio (D) was convicted again and appealed, claiming that the evidence was insufficient to support a finding that he joined the conspiracy before the truck was stopped. The Ninth Circuit reversed his conviction.

■ ISSUE

Can Recio (D) be convicted of conspiracy, even if he joined after the drugs were seized?

■ DECISION AND RATIONALE

(Breyer, J.) Yes. A conspiracy does not automatically terminate because the object of the conspiracy has been defeated without the knowledge of the conspirators. The essence of a conspiracy is the agreement to commit an unlawful act. The agreement is a threat to the public not only because of the underlying crime, but because of the likelihood that other crimes will be committed, and because it diminishes the likelihood that the participants will stop their criminal behavior. Most authorities hold that the impossibility of realizing the goal of the conspiracy is irrelevant. The Ninth Circuit based its rule in part on the theory that finding that a conspiracy continues after law enforcement has made the object of the conspiracy impossible could lead to police misconduct. The court posited a situation in which an arrested conspirator was ordered to enlist co-conspirators, and the co-conspirators were then arrested. Such a situation could be entrapment, and existing law forbids convictions based on entrapment. Law enforcement sting operations are not necessarily the same as entrapment. Reversed.

Analysis:

Many commentators and defense attorneys have criticized federal drug and conspiracy prosecutions as focusing on the lower-level members of the conspiracy. In this case, we see only that the drivers of the truck and the two individuals who were sent to retrieve the drugs were convicted, but nothing in the case indicates that these four were the entire conspiracy (who was the "contact" who was paged to send someone to pick up the drugs?), or even the leaders of the conspiracy. Although all members of the conspiracy are equally guilty, it is the ones who commit the overt act who bear the greatest risk of prosecution for that crime.

■ CASE VOCABULARY

ENTRAPMENT: A law-enforcement officer's or government agent's inducement of a person to commit a crime, by means of fraud or undue persuasion, in an attempt to later bring a criminal prosecution against that person; the affirmative defense of having been so induced. To establish entrapment (in most states), the defendant must show that he or she would not have committed the crime but for the fraud or undue persuasion.

STING: An undercover operation in which law-enforcement agents pose as criminals to catch actual criminals engaging in illegal acts.

(Prosecuting Government) v. (Answering Service Owner)

251 Cal. App. 2d 471, 59 Cal. Rptr. 628 (1967)

SUPPLIERS OF GOODS OR SERVICES USED IN A CONSPIRACY MAY BE PART OF THE CONSPIRACY

I admit a few hookers used my answering service. But, I didn't charge them any differently than my other clients of questionable morals, like politicians.

stus.com

■**INSTANT FACTS** Lauria (D) ran an answering service that had prostitutes as customers and was indicted for conspiracy to commit prostitution.

■**BLACK LETTER RULE** A supplier of goods or services used for unlawful purposes will be deemed a conspirator only if the supplier knew of the illegal purpose and intended to further the illegal use.

■ PROCEDURAL BASIS

Appeal by the state from an order setting aside the indictment against Lauria (D).

■ FACTS

Lauria (D) operated a telephone answering service that was used by four women under investigation for prostitution. An undercover police officer set up an account with Lauria's (D) service, hinting that she was engaged in prostitution. She was assured that the service was discreet. On two occasions, the officer complained to Lauria (D) that she had missed telephone calls from "tricks." Lauria (D) was arrested and complained that he did not deserve to be because he had only nine or ten customers who were prostitutes, whereas another answering service had sixty to seventy. Lauria (D) told police that he always cooperated with law enforcement, and that he kept separate records for customers who were prostitutes, which were available to law enforcement if the police furnished him with a specific name. Lauria (D) testified before the grand jury that he knew some of his customers were prostitutes; in fact, he knew a particular customer was a prostitute because he had used her services. Lauria (D) was indicted for conspiracy to commit prostitution, but the trial court set aside the indictment as having been brought without reasonable or probable cause.

■ ISSUE

Were there sufficient grounds to charge Lauria (D) with conspiracy to commit prostitution?

■ DECISION AND RATIONALE

(Fleming, J.) No. A supplier of goods or services used for unlawful purposes will be deemed a conspirator only if the supplier knew of the illegal purpose and intended to further the illegal use. It is a legitimate inference that Lauria (D) knew that his customers were using his service to engage in prostitution, but the intent to further the criminal activity cannot be inferred from the facts in this case. Intent may be inferred from knowledge if the supplier has a stake in the criminal venture, such as charging an inflated price for the goods or services. There is no evidence that the prices Lauria (D) charged to prostitutes were any higher than those charged to other customers. Intent may also be inferred from knowledge if there is no legitimate purpose for the goods or services supplied, but there is nothing in the furnishing or use of a telephone answering service that necessarily implies illegal activities. If the volume of business is disproportionate to lawful demand, or if sales for illegal purposes amount to a large proportion of a supplier's business, knowledge will likewise support a finding of intent, but there was no showing here of an unusually large volume of calls made to the customers who were prostitutes. Finally, intent may be inferred from knowledge if the supplier knows that the goods or services will be used to commit a felony. In this case, prostitution is a misdemeanor, not a felony, so intent will not be inferred from the nature of the offense. Affirmed.

Analysis:

The court mentions, but refrains from deciding, the issue of whether all felonies will support an inference of intent from knowledge, or only those that are "inherently immoral." For most purposes, there is no distinction between felonies that involve "moral turpitude" and those that do not. If an offense is deemed serious enough to be classified as a felony, it typically will be regarded as involving "moral turpitude," or the kind of aggravated criminal conduct referred to by the court. Few, if any, felonies are considered "victimless crimes," as many regard prostitution.

■ CASE VOCABULARY

FELONY: A serious crime usually punishable by imprisonment for more than one year or by death.

GRAND JURY: A body of (often 23) people who are chosen to sit permanently for at least a month—and sometimes a year—and who, in ex parte proceedings, decide whether to issue indictments. If the grand jury decides that evidence is strong enough to hold a suspect for trial, it returns a bill of indictment (a *true bill*) charging the suspect with a specific crime.

INDICT: To charge (a person) with a crime by formal legal process, especially by grand-jury presentation.

MALUM IN SE: [Latin, "evil in itself."] A crime or an act that is inherently immoral, such as murder, arson, or rape.

MALUM PROHIBITUM: [Latin, "prohibited evil."] An act that is a crime merely because it is prohibited by statute, although the act itself is not necessarily immoral.

MISDEMEANOR: A crime that is less serious than a felony and is usually punishable by fine, penalty, forfeiture, or confinement (usually for a brief term) in a place other than a prison (such as a county jail).

MISPRISION: Concealment or nondisclosure of a serious crime by a person who did not participate in the crime.

United States v. Diaz

(Federal Government) v. (Drug Seller)

864 F.2d 544 (7th Cir. 1988)

PARTICIPANTS IN A CONSPIRACY ARE RESPONSIBLE FOR ALL CRIMES COMMITTED IN FURTHERANCE THEREOF

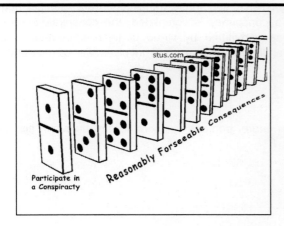

■INSTANT FACTS Diaz (D) was convicted of the use of a firearm in relation to a conspiracy to distribute illegal drugs, but the gun was carried by another participant in the conspiracy.

■BLACK LETTER RULE A participant in a conspiracy is criminally liable for all acts that are done by other members in furtherance of the conspiracy and that are reasonably foreseeable as a necessary consequence of the unlawful agreement.

■ PROCEDURAL BASIS

Appeal by Diaz (D) from a conviction for conspiracy to distribute illegal drugs and use of a firearm in relation to the commission of a drug trafficking crime.

■ FACTS

Diaz (D) supplied illegal drugs on multiple occasions to Perez. On September 9, 1987, Perez and Rodriguez met with Diaz (D) in order to sell cocaine to a Drug Enforcement Agency (DEA) agent. The drugs were physically delivered by Periallo, who brought the drugs to Chicago from Miami on the day of the planned sale. Diaz (D) and Periallo arrived at the scene of the sale separately and waited for the arrival of the DEA agent. When she arrived, Perez went to get the drugs from Periallo. Periallo told Perez that he had a gun that he intended to use if anyone tried to steal the drugs. Perez delivered the drugs to the DEA agents, and the signal was given to make the arrests. Diaz (D) was convicted of possession and distribution of cocaine, conspiracy to distribute cocaine, and use of a firearm in relation to the commission of a drug trafficking crime. The conviction for use of a firearm added an additional five years to Diaz's (D) sentence.

■ ISSUE

Is Diaz (D) guilty of using a firearm, even though he is not the one who carried the gun?

■ DECISION AND RATIONALE

(Ripple, J.) Yes. A participant in a conspiracy is criminally responsible for all acts that are done by other members in furtherance of the conspiracy and that are reasonably foreseeable as a necessary consequence of the unlawful agreement. A conspirator is liable for all substantive offenses in furtherance of the conspiracy even if he or she did not commit the offense, and even if he or she had no knowledge of the commission of the offense. The illegal drug trade is dangerous and violent. It is reasonable to assume that a gun will be carried

---

H I G H   C O U R T   C A S E   S U M M A R I E S

during a drug sale, particularly one involving a large quantity of drugs worth a considerable amount of money. Affirmed.

Analysis:

Conspiracies revolve around unlawful transactions, and those transactions are criminal acts that are seldom committed in isolation. If a conspiracy is completed, the conspirators have committed a crime in addition to the crime committed by virtue of their agreement. The illegality of the drug trade in particular generally means that those involved will commit other crimes, as well.

■ **CASE VOCABULARY**

CONSPIRACY: An agreement by two or more persons to commit an unlawful act; a combination for an unlawful purpose.

United States v. Neapolitan

(Federal Government) v. (Deputy)

791 F.2d 489 (7th Cir. 1986)

A PERSON IS GUILTY OF A RICO CONSPIRACY IF THERE IS AN AGREEMENT TO VIOLATE THE RICO STATUTE

■**INSTANT FACTS** Neapolitan (D) was convicted of a RICO violation, based on one solicitation of a bribe in connection with the operation of a racketeering enterprise.

■**BLACK LETTER RULE** A defendant will be convicted for engaging in a RICO conspiracy if the defendant committed only a single RICO violation.

■ **PROCEDURAL BASIS**

Appeal by Neapolitan (D) from a conviction for conspiracy.

■ **FACTS**

Neapolitan (D), Cadieux, and Sapit were law enforcement officers who were involved in a conspiracy involving the solicitation of bribes from car thieves in exchange for police protection. Neapolitan was charged with four counts of mail fraud relating to his solicitation of bribes and with conspiracy to run the affairs of the sheriff's office through a pattern of racketeering activity, in violation of the RICO statute. The predicate acts alleged for the RICO violation were the four counts of mail fraud and eleven acts of bribery. Neapolitan (D) was alleged to have participated in only one of the acts of bribery. He was acquitted of the mail fraud charges before trial and stood trial only on the RICO conspiracy charge. Neapolitan (D) was convicted. He argued that he could be convicted of a RICO conspiracy only if he conspired to commit two predicate acts, and he was alleged to have committed only one such act.

■ **ISSUE**

Can Neapolitan (D) be convicted of engaging in a RICO conspiracy if he conspired to commit only one predicate act?

■ **DECISION AND RATIONALE**

(Flaum, J.) Yes. A conviction for engaging in a RICO conspiracy may be had if the defendant committed only a single RICO violation. The RICO statute expressly prohibits conspiracies to violate the statute. The plain language of the statute thus makes it unlawful to be a part of any agreement to participate in or conduct the affairs of an enterprise through a pattern of racketeering activity. A RICO conspiracy requires two agreements: an agreement to participate in the affairs of an enterprise and agreement to the commission of at least two predicate acts. There is substantial evidence that Neapolitan (D) agreed to participate in the enterprise and that he agreed to the commission of two or more predicate acts. Sapit and Cadieux identified Neapolitan (D) as being involved in the operation of the auto theft conspiracy. When Neapolitan (D) received the bribe, he made numerous statements that indicated that he was associated with others. Cadieux was present when the bribe was received, and Cadieux arranged the meeting. Evidence of other crimes, while not constituting predicate acts, was evidence of Neapolitan's (D) link to the other officers involved. Finally, the indictment listed other bribes that were made during Neapolitan's (D) participation in the enterprise. There was sufficient evidence from which a jury could infer agreement to the commission of two of the predicate acts. Affirmed.

Analysis:

A conspiracy to violate RICO can look something like a conspiracy to conspire. There is an agreement to engage in an enterprise that involves racketeering, or unlawful acts, which is a common law conspiracy. There is an additional agreement, on top of the initial conspiracy, to violate particular criminal statutes. Both agreements must be present before a defendant will be found guilty of a RICO conspiracy.

■ CASE VOCABULARY

ENTERPRISE: Under federal anti-racketeering law, an individual, partnership, corporation, association, union, other legal entity, or group of individuals associated in fact, although not a legal entity. The enterprise must be ongoing and must exist as an entity separate from the allegedly illegal activity that it engages in.

PATTERN OF RACKETEERING ACTIVITY: Two or more related criminal acts that amount to, or pose a threat of, continued criminal activity.

PREDICATE ACT: Under RICO, one of two or more related acts of racketeering necessary to establish a pattern.

RACKETEERING: A system of organized crime traditionally involving the extortion of money from businesses by intimidation, violence, or other illegal methods.

RICO: Racketeer Influenced and Corrupt Organizations Act. A law designed to attack organized criminal activity and preserve marketplace integrity by investigating, controlling, and prosecuting persons who participate or conspire to participate in racketeering. Enacted in 1970, the federal RICO statute applies only to activity involving interstate or foreign commerce.

CHAPTER THIRTEEN

Rape

Brown v. State

Instant Facts: Brown (D) was convicted of rape, but the complainant said only that she tried to escape, and there was no evidence of resistance on Brown (D).

Black Letter Rule: A conviction for rape requires a showing that the victim used every physical power to resist the offense.

People v. Dorsey

Instant Facts: Dorsey (D) was convicted of raping a woman while in a stalled elevator, but Dorsey (D) made no explicit threats of physical violence to the complainant.

Black Letter Rule: A conviction for rape requires a showing of "earnest resistance," defined as the type of resistance to be reasonably expected from a person who genuinely refuses to participate, under all the attendant circumstances.

People v. Barnes

Instant Facts: Barnes (D) was convicted of rape with no proof that the complainant resisted or that he used force to overcome her resistance.

Black Letter Rule: A conviction for rape requires a showing that the act was committed against the victim's will by means of force or fear of immediate and unlawful bodily injury.

State v. Smith

Instant Facts: Smith (D) was convicted of sexual assault and claimed that he believed the complainant consented.

Black Letter Rule: A defendant may not be convicted of rape if the words and conduct of the complainant would justify a reasonable belief that the complainant consented.

In the Interest of M.T.S.

Instant Facts: M.T.S (D) had nonconsensual sexual intercourse with the complainant, but did not use force to overcome her resistance.

Black Letter Rule: Sexual assault consists of any act of sexual penetration done without the affirmative and freely given permission of the victim.

State v. Moorman

Instant Facts: Moorman (D) had sexual intercourse with a woman who was asleep and he was convicted of rape.

Black Letter Rule: The crime of rape is complete upon a showing of sexual intercourse with a person who is asleep, unconscious, or otherwise incapacitated and so incapable of giving consent or resisting.

Commonwealth v. Mlinarich

Instant Facts: Mlinarich (D) was convicted of raping a fourteen-year-old girl whom he had threatened to send to juvenile detention if she did not submit.

Black Letter Rule: If a victim has the ability to make a deliberate choice to avoid a sexual encounter, there is no forcible compulsion.

Boro v. People

Instant Facts: Boro (D) induced a woman to consent to sexual intercourse by telling her that the intercourse was for medical treatment.

Black Letter Rule: Consent to an act of sexual intercourse will bar a prosecution for rape, even when the consent was obtained by fraud, if the victim knew that she was consenting to an act of sexual intercourse.

Commonwealth v. Fischer

Instant Facts: Fischer (D) engaged in sexual activity with a woman and claimed that he believed the victim consented to his actions.

Black Letter Rule: A reasonable mistake of fact regarding a victim's consent is not a defense to a rape charge.

(Farmer) v. (Prosecuting Government)

127 Wis. 193, 106 N.W. 536 (1906)

A RAPE CONVICTION REQUIRES EVIDENCE OF PHYSICAL RESISTANCE

■INSTANT FACTS Brown (D) was convicted of rape, but the complainant said only that she tried to escape, and there was no evidence of resistance on Brown (D).

■BLACK LETTER RULE A conviction for rape requires a showing that the victim used every physical power to resist the offense.

■ PROCEDURAL BASIS

Appeal from a conviction for rape.

■ FACTS

Brown (D) was convicted of raping Nethery, a woman who lived on a neighboring farm. Nethery stated that she was crossing fields near the place where Brown (D) was working when she called out to him; Brown (D) came over to her, tripped her to the ground, and had sexual intercourse with her. Nethery said that she told Brown (D) to let her go, and that she tried to get away, but could not. Nethery screamed, but Brown (D) held his hand over her mouth until she almost strangled. She did not say that she used her hands, and there were no marks of a struggle on Brown (D). When Brown (D) was finished, he allowed Nethery to rise only after she promised not to tell anyone, a promise she made because she was afraid of Brown (D). Brown's (D) testimony denied any resistance on Nethery's part. On appeal, Brown (D) claimed there was insufficient evidence to support his conviction.

■ ISSUE

Was the evidence sufficient to support Brown's (D) rape conviction?

■ DECISION AND RATIONALE

No. A conviction for rape requires a showing that the victim used every physical power to resist the offense. It is not enough to show an absence of consent. There must be evidence that the victim put up the utmost physical resistance. There is no evidence here of physical resistance. Nethery's testimony was that she told Brown (D) to let her go, and that she screamed, but there were no other verbal protests. There was evidence that she tried to escape, but resistance is opposing force to force, not retreating from force. It is not credible that Brown (D) should have come away from the encounter with no signs of a struggle on his person or his clothing if Nethery had resisted. Reversed.

Analysis:

The court does not explain why an attempt to escape is not resistance. For many, flight may seem like a better, safer response to an attack than standing one's ground and not retreating. The court also does not say how much verbal protestation is necessary to show non-consent. The fact that Nethery only stopped screaming when Brown (D) put his hand on her mouth would seem to show that she made whatever verbal protests she could. The harshness of the result here was obliterated by later decisions, which required a showing or reasonable rather than all-out resistance.

■ **CASE VOCABULARY**

COMPLAINANT: The party who brings a legal complaint against another.

RAPE: At common law, unlawful sexual intercourse committed by a man with a woman not his wife through force and against her will; unlawful sexual activity (especially intercourse) with a person (usually a female) without consent and usually by force or threat of injury.

VIS MAJOR: [Latin, "a superior force."] A greater or superior force; also termed FORCE MAJEURE.

RESISTANCE TO RAPE MUST BE REASONABLE UNDER THE CIRCUMSTANCES

■INSTANT FACTS Dorsey (D) was convicted of raping a woman while in a stalled elevator, but Dorsey (D) made no explicit threats of physical violence to the complainant.

■BLACK LETTER RULE A conviction for rape requires a showing of "earnest resistance," defined as the type of resistance to be reasonably expected from a person who genuinely refuses to participate, under all the attendant circumstances.

■ PROCEDURAL BASIS

Decision on a post-trial motion to dismiss an indictment for insufficient trial evidence.

■ FACTS

Dorsey (D) was fifteen years old, five feet, seven inches tall, and weighed over two hundred pounds. He got on an elevator with the complainant, a five-foot tall forty-one-year-old woman who weighed one hundred thirty pounds. Dorsey (D) stopped the elevator between floors and told the victim twice to take her clothes off. The complainant did so, and Dorsey had sexual intercourse with her. The complainant testified that she did not scream because she thought that there was no one who could help her. The only explicit threat of physical violence came after Dorsey had finished, when he told her that his friends would "get" the complainant if anything "happened" to him in the next few days. Dorsey (D) was convicted of rape and moved to quash the indictment, claiming that the evidence was insufficient to support his conviction.

■ ISSUE

Was the evidence sufficient to support Dorsey's (D) rape conviction?

■ DECISION AND RATIONALE

(Shackman, J.) Yes. A conviction for rape requires a showing of "earnest resistance," defined as the type of resistance to be reasonably expected from a person who genuinely refuses to participate, under all the attendant circumstances. The former rule was that a victim of a rape had to show resistance to the utmost limit of the victim's power. This standard, however, focused attention on the victim of the crime, rather than on the actor or the crime itself. Legislation modified the standard for rape prosecutions to require "earnest resistance." The amount of resistance must be proportional to the circumstances of the attack, such as the relative strength of the parties and the apparent futility of further resistance. The resistance must be such as would be expected from a woman in the victim's circumstances. The victim's opinion is not an issue, but the concern is with what would reasonably appear necessary to a woman in her position. In this case, while there was no explicit physical threat from Dorsey (D), there was definitely an implied threat. Dorsey (D) was younger and much bigger than the complainant, and there was no place to which the complainant could retreat and no one likely to come to her assistance. The law does not require that a victim ascertain what an assailant might do if she does not comply with his directions. There was sufficient evidence for the jury to conclude that Dorsey (D) engaged in sexual acts with the complainant by means of forcible compulsion, in that there was an implied threat of imminent death or serious physical injury. No physical resistance could reasonably be expected from the complainant in these circumstances. Dorsey (D) also used "physical force" in committing the rape, by manipulating the elevator so that it stopped between floors. Total compliance by the complainant was all that earnest resistance reasonably could require. Affirmed.

Analysis:

The earnest resistance standard still places some focus on the actions of the victim, changing only the standard to which she will be held. The standard of resistance is determined with reference to the particular circumstances in which a victim finds herself. It no longer matters if there was more that a victim was physically capable of doing. The important inquiry is whether the victim did what was reasonable under the circumstances.

■ **CASE VOCABULARY**

ASSAILANT: One who physically attacks another; one who commits an assault.

People v. Barnes

(Prosecuting Government) v. (Marijuana Seller)

42 Cal. 3d 284, 228 Cal. Rptr. 228 (1986)

PROOF OF RESISTANCE IS NO LONGER REQUIRED IN A RAPE PROSECUTION

I only came here to buy pot and I want to leave now.

stus.com

■**INSTANT FACTS** Barnes (D) was convicted of rape with no proof that the complainant resisted or that he used force to overcome her resistance.

■**BLACK LETTER RULE** A conviction for rape requires a showing that the act was committed against the victim's will by means of force or fear of immediate and unlawful bodily injury.

■ **PROCEDURAL BASIS**

Appeal from an order of the court of appeals that overturned Barnes's (D) conviction for rape.

■ **FACTS**

Barnes (D) invited the victim to come to his home for drinks, but she told him that she only wanted to buy some marijuana from him. Barnes (D) persuaded her to come inside, and the complainant continued to tell him that she wanted to leave. Barnes started to hug and kiss the complainant, but she pushed him away, and repeated that she wanted to leave. Barnes (D) continued to make advances, and the complainant started to leave. As the complainant approached the gate to leave Barnes's (D) house, Barnes (D) became angry, told her she couldn't leave, and started arguing with her. The complainant asked Barnes (D) to open the gate, but he did not. Barnes (D) reared back as though he was going to hit the complainant. He and the complainant continued arguing for approximately twenty minutes. Barnes (D) told the complainant he would let her leave after he put his shoes on. The complainant followed Barnes (D) into the house and Barnes (D) closed the door to the room they were in. The complainant was concerned about what Barnes (D) would do. He lectured her, displayed his muscles, and said that she would now see the bad side of him. After approximately forty more minutes, Barnes (D) suddenly began to hug the complainant. She thought she was with a "psychotic" person who changed personalities suddenly, and she decided to feign compliance with Barnes (D). Barnes (D) told the complainant to take her clothes off, and she refused. Barnes (D) said she was going to upset him and made some kind of gesture. The complainant complied, and Barnes (D) had sexual intercourse with her. The complainant testified that she complied because she thought Barnes (D) would become violent if she did not. She left afterwards and did not report the incident to the police right away. Barnes (D) tried to telephone the complainant after the incident, but she hung up on him. Barnes (D) claimed that the complainant consented to the intercourse. His conviction for rape was overturned by the court of appeals, which held that there was no showing that the complainant resisted and that her resistance was overcome by force or violence.

■ ISSUE

Was proof of resistance required to convict Barnes (D) of rape?

■ DECISION AND RATIONALE

(Bird, C.J.) No. A conviction for rape requires a showing that the act was committed against the victim's will by means of force or fear of immediate and unlawful bodily injury. The legislature eliminated the requirement that prosecutions for rape show that a victim resisted the crime. In many cases, resistance can be futile, or even dangerous, as the resistance could provoke even greater violence. Some victims may be paralyzed with fear, and so incapable of resisting. It is impossible to say that a lack of resistance indicates consent, and so there is no blanket requirement that a victim of a sexual assault resist. The court will look at all of the circumstances of the case, including verbal or nonverbal threats, or the kind of force that might induce fear. Resistance, or the absence of resistance, may be relevant evidence in deciding if the accused reasonably and honestly believed there was consent. In this case, the totality of the circumstances could have led the jury to conclude that the complainant's compliance was the result of force, fear, or both, and that she truly did not consent. Reversed.

Analysis:

Resistance is now considered evidence, not a required element of proof. The resistance requirement is an outgrowth of the requirement that rape accusations be corroborated by other evidence. That requirement is itself based on the old (and now, much discredited) maxim that rape accusations are easily made, but hard to disprove. Rape is the only charge regarded with such suspicion at common law.

■ CASE VOCABULARY

ACQUAINTANCE RAPE: Rape committed by someone known to the victim, especially by the victim's social companion.

DATE RAPE: Rape committed by a person who is escorting the victim on a social occasion. Loosely, date rape also sometimes refers to what is more accurately called *acquaintance rape* or *relationship rape*.

State v. Smith

(Prosecuting Government) v. (Accused Rapist)

210 Conn. 132, 554 A.2d 713 (1989)

A CLAIM THAT THE VICTIM CONSENTED MUST BE REASONABLE

■**INSTANT FACTS** Smith (D) was convicted of sexual assault and claimed that he believed the complainant consented.

■**BLACK LETTER RULE** A defendant may not be convicted of rape if the words and conduct of the complainant would justify a reasonable belief that the complainant consented.

■ **PROCEDURAL BASIS**

Appeal from a conviction for sexual assault.

■ **FACTS**

Smith (D) met the complainant at a bar and went with her and others to a nearby restaurant. Smith (D) paid for the complainant's meal and then suggested that the group go to his apartment. The complainant accompanied Smith (D) to his apartment and sat with him, watching television. Smith (D) asked the complainant to kiss him, and she did, but Smith (D) continued to make advances. The complainant spit in Smith's (D) face, tried to kick him off, told him she had to leave to pick up her child, and insulted him. Smith (D) told the complainant that he could make it hard for her if she resisted. The complainant decided it would better to give in and pretend to enjoy the act. After Smith (D) engaged in sexual intercourse with the complainant, he told her that she could not prove she had been raped and that she had really enjoyed herself. The complainant gave Smith (D) a false telephone number and ate some sherbet that he offered her. She left Smith's apartment, went to the police station, and reported that she had been raped. Smith (D) claimed that he was mistaken as to the complainant's consent.

■ **ISSUE**

Is mistake as to consent a defense to a rape charge?

■ **DECISION AND RATIONALE**

(Shea, J.) Yes. A defendant may not be convicted of rape if the words and conduct of the complainant would justify a reasonable belief that the complainant consented. Consent is not made an affirmative defense to sexual assault, but, if consent is raised, the burden is on the state to prove lack of consent beyond a reasonable doubt. A finding of consent depends upon a reasonable interpretation of the manifestations of consent. If the conduct of the complainant under all of the circumstances should reasonably be viewed as indicating consent, a defendant should not be found guilty. In this case, however, there was ample indication that the

---

complainant did not consent. The evidence is sufficient to prove that a reasonable person would not have believed that the complainant had consented. Affirmed.

Analysis:

The focus shifts slightly here, from an analysis (or second-guessing) of a complainant's actions to consideration of how the defendant interpreted those actions. A complainant's subjective wishes are not relevant unless they are somehow communicated, with some degree of clarity, to the defendant. The quantum of proof for an affirmative defense is lower than the proof required for an element of an offense. Elements of an offense must each be proven beyond a reasonable doubt, whereas an affirmative defense generally must be proven by the lower preponderance of the evidence standard.

■ CASE VOCABULARY

AFFIRMATIVE DEFENSE: A defendant's assertion raising new facts and arguments that, if true, will defeat the plaintiff's or prosecution's claim, even if all allegations in the complaint are true.

GENERAL INTENT: The state of mind required for the commission of certain common law crimes not requiring a specific intent or not imposing strict liability.

MISTAKE OF FACT: The defense asserting that a criminal defendant acted from an innocent misunderstanding of fact rather than from a criminal purpose.

PREPONDERANCE OF THE EVIDENCE: The greater weight of the evidence; superior evidentiary weight that, although not sufficient to free the mind wholly from all reasonable doubt, is still sufficient to incline a fair and impartial mind to one side of the issue rather than the other.

REASONABLE DOUBT: The doubt that prevents one from being firmly convinced of a defendant's guilt, or the belief that there is a real possibility that a defendant is not guilty. "Beyond a reasonable doubt" is the standard used by a jury to determine whether a criminal defendant is guilty.

SPECIFIC INTENT: The intent to accomplish the precise criminal act that one is later charged with.

A SHOWING OF FORCE IS NOT REQUIRED IF THERE IS NO CONSENT

■**INSTANT FACTS** M.T.S (D) had nonconsensual sexual intercourse with the complainant, but did not use force to overcome her resistance.

■**BLACK LETTER RULE** Sexual assault consists of any act of sexual penetration done without the affirmative and freely given permission of the victim.

■ **PROCEDURAL BASIS**

Appeal from an order of the appellate division that reversed the trial court's disposition of delinquency.

■ **FACTS**

M.T.S. (D) was staying in the house in which the complainant lived. The complainant claimed that M.T.S. (D) came into the complainant's bedroom while she was asleep and began having sexual intercourse with her. The complainant slapped M.T.S. (D) and told him to get off of her. The complainant said that, earlier that day, M.T.S. (D) had told her that he would come up to her bedroom. When she woke during the night, M.T.S. (D) was standing in her bedroom doorway but she thought nothing of it. She said that he had made advances toward her on other occasions, but she always rejected him. M.T.S. (D) testified that he and the complainant had been kissing and necking and also discussing sexual intercourse. M.T.S. (D) also testified that the complainant repeatedly invited him to her bedroom and that she consented to sexual intercourse, but then told him to stop. M.T.S. (D) testified that he stopped when the complainant told him to do so. The trial court found that the complainant had consented to kissing and heavy petting, but not to intercourse. The appellate division reversed, holding that there was no evidence that M.T.S. (D) used force.

■ **ISSUE**

Was the state required to show the use of force in order to find M.T.S. (D) delinquent?

■ **DECISION AND RATIONALE**

(Handler, J.) No. Sexual assault consists of any act of sexual penetration done without the affirmative and freely given permission of the victim. The sexual assault statute does not refer to overcoming the will of the victim or overcoming the victim's resistance. The only level of force required is the force necessary to achieve penetration. Sexual assault is likened to criminal battery, which does not require any particular degree of force beyond that necessary to accomplish the battery. Physical force, for the purposes of the sexual assault statute, is any amount of force against another person in the absence of what a reasonable person would believe to be affirmative and freely given permission. An express announcement of consent is not, however, required, and consent may be manifested by conduct. The common-law rule held that a woman had to make some affirmative withdrawal of consent before a rape prosecution could be had. Resistance was considered the outward manifestation of non-consent. Although the requirement of resistance "to the uttermost" was done away with, resistance was used to demonstrate not only non-consent, but also that the force was sufficient to overcome the victim's will. Contemporary rape laws focus attention on the conduct of the actor, rather than that of the victim. The goal has been to eliminate the burden on the victim of proving non-consent. In this case, there was no requirement that the state prove that M.T.S. (D) used force. The trial court found non-consent, and that, coupled with the act of sexual penetration, was sufficient for a conviction of sexual assault. Reversed.

Analysis:

The modern trend in criminal law is to enact statutes that relate to "sexual assault" or, in some states, "criminal sexual conduct," rather than rape. These statutes tend to focus on the assaultive nature of the conduct. Most of them also relate to conduct that formerly would have been regarded, at most, as assault or battery, such as nonconsensual touching of some parts of the body. Sexual touching is regarded as different from common law rape only in degree, and is not regarded as an entirely different type of crime.

■ CASE VOCABULARY

JUVENILE DELINQUENCY: Antisocial behavior by a minor; especially, behavior that would be criminally punishable if the actor were an adult, but instead is usually punished by special laws pertaining only to minors.

SEXUAL ASSAULT: Sexual intercourse with another person who does not consent; offensive sexual contact with another person, exclusive of rape. Several state statutes have abolished the crime of rape and replaced it with the offense of sexual assault.

State v. Moorman

(Government) v. (Rapist of Sleeper)

358 S.E.2d 502 (N.C. 1987)

A SLEEPING VICTIM CANNOT CONSENT

Pssst--Lynn.

stus.com

■**INSTANT FACTS** Moorman (D) had sexual intercourse with a woman who was asleep and he was convicted of rape.

■**BLACK LETTER RULE** The crime of rape is complete upon a showing of sexual intercourse with a person who is asleep, unconscious, or otherwise incapacitated and so incapable of giving consent or resisting.

■ **PROCEDURAL BASIS**

Appeal from an order of the appellate court that reversed Moorman's (D) conviction for rape.

■ **FACTS**

Moorman (D) had sexual intercourse with the victim while she was asleep. The victim testified that she woke up while Moorman (D) was having intercourse and tried to sit up, but Moorman (D) pushed her back down. The victim further testified that she was afraid to offer any further resistance. After Moorman (D) was finished, the victim turned on the light; Moorman said that he thought the victim was actually the victim's roommate, and that he would not have assaulted her if he had known it was the victim and not her roommate. Moorman (D) testified that the victim told him not to worry, that it could happen to anyone. Moorman (D) was convicted of rape on an indictment that defined rape as intercourse committed by force and against the will of the victim. The court of appeals arrested judgment, holding that the rape of a victim who was asleep should proceed under the statutory section that refers to the rape of a person who was "physically helpless," and that there was a fatal variance between the indictment and the proof at trial.

■ **ISSUE**

Can Moorman (D) be convicted of raping a sleeping victim?

■ **DECISION AND RATIONALE**

(Exum, C.J.) Yes. The crime of rape is complete upon a showing of sexual intercourse with a person who is asleep, unconscious, or otherwise incapacitated and so incapable of giving consent or resisting. The evidence supports both a finding of force and lack of consent. If a victim is incapable of consenting or offering resistance, the common law implied both force and lack of consent. Reversed.

Analysis:

The court does not require proof of knowledge of incapacity, or even a reason to suspect incapacity. Although the facts here are quite clear that Moorman (D) should have realized that his victim was asleep and so incapable of giving consent, the question of knowledge could become an issue in other instances of incapacity, such as involuntary intoxication or mental incapacity. Some types of incapacity may not be as clear as unconsciousness or sleeping. For some types of incapacity, such as for victims who are underage, mistake regarding the capacity of the victim to consent is not a defense.

■ CASE VOCABULARY

ARREST OF JUDGMENT: The staying of a judgment after its entry; especially, a court's refusal to render or enforce a judgment because of a defect apparent from the record.

FATAL VARIANCE: A variance that either deprives the defendant of fair notice of the charges or exposes the defendant to the risk of double jeopardy. A fatal variance is grounds for reversing a conviction.

Commonwealth v. Mlinarich

(Prosecuting Government) v. (Guardian)

518 Pa. 247, 542 A.2d 1335 (1988)

THE VICTIM'S ABILITY TO AVOID AN ENCOUNTER NEGATES THE FORCIBLE COMPULSION ELEMENT

■**INSTANT FACTS** Mlinarich (D) was convicted of raping a fourteen-year-old girl whom he had threatened to send to juvenile detention if she did not submit.

■**BLACK LETTER RULE** If a victim has the ability to make a deliberate choice to avoid a sexual encounter, there is no forcible compulsion.

■ **PROCEDURAL BASIS**

Appeal from an order of the superior court that reversed convictions for rape and attempted rape.

■ **FACTS**

Mlinarich (D), aged sixty-three, had sexual intercourse with a fourteen-year-old girl in his care. Mlinarich (D) was convicted of rape and attempted rape under a statutory provision that defined rape as involving "forcible compulsion" or the "threat of forcible compulsion that would prevent resistance by a person of reasonable resolution." The forcible compulsion alleged was Mlinarich's (D) threat to have the victim returned to a juvenile detention facility if she did not comply with his demands. The superior court reversed Mlinarich's (D) conviction, holding that the threats he made did not involve a threat of physical violence, and so there was no forcible compulsion.

■ **ISSUE**

Did Mlinarich's (D) threats to return the victim to juvenile detention constitute forcible compulsion?

■ **DECISION AND RATIONALE**

(Nix, C.J.) No. If a victim has the ability to make a deliberate choice to avoid a sexual encounter, there is no forcible compulsion. Forcible compulsion does not, however, necessarily involve a threat of physical violence. Forcible compulsion involves a situation in which the compulsion overwhelms the will of the victim, and in which the result produced was non-voluntary. There was no such compulsion here. The victim had a choice, even though the choice was an unpleasant one. Her choice was a product of her free will and reason. The standard for compulsion is an objective one, based on a reasonable person, and does not take into account any special factors in the emotional or psychological make-up of the victim. The

---

age of the victim is relevant only regarding the statutory rape laws, and has no reference to forcible compulsion. Affirmed.

■ **DISSENT**

(Larsen, J.) Mlinarich (D), who was sixty-three years old, engaged in repeated acts of sexual abuse with a fourteen-year-old child. The victim had low mental abilities, cried during the abuse, and pleaded with Mlinarich (D) to stop. A fourteen-year-old child should not be placed in the position of making such a "choice." The majority leaves unclear the level of intensity that will satisfy the criteria for forcible compulsion. Would any kind of threat that involves any kind of a choice satisfy this standard?

Analysis:

The majority in this case returns the focus of the prosecution to the victim. The type of coercion involved here—an unpleasant choice—is common in cases that involve acquaintance rape. Formerly, there was a belief that a woman raped by a stranger felt more shame, and suffered greater emotional injuries, than a woman raped by an acquaintance. Recent studies have concluded that the opposite is true—that women raped by strangers tend to recover more quickly, and that women raped by acquaintances continue to blame themselves for the encounter (particularly where, as here, there is a "choice" not to submit).

■ **CASE VOCABULARY**

COMPULSION: The act of compelling; the state of being compelled. "Compulsion can take other forms than physical force; but in whatever form it appears the courts have been indisposed to admit that it can be a defence for any crime committed through yielding to it and the law of the matter is both meagre and vague. It can best be considered under the heads of obedience to orders, martial coercion, duress *per minas*, and necessity." *J.W. Cecil Turner, Kenny's Outlines of Criminal Law* 54 (16th ed. 1952).

SEXUAL ABUSE: An illegal sex act, especially one performed against a minor by an adult.

Boro v. People

(Doctor Impersonator) v. (Prosecuting Government)

163 Cal. App. 3d 1224, 210 Cal. Rptr. 122 (1985)

"CONSENT" MAY BE FRAUDULENTLY OBTAINED

Lying, fraud, and trickery by men are reproachable, but have gone on since the beginning of time and are not crimes.

Are we still talking about men seeking sex, or have we switched to men seeking political office?

stus.com

■**INSTANT FACTS** Boro (D) induced a woman to consent to sexual intercourse by telling her that the intercourse was for medical treatment.

■**BLACK LETTER RULE** Consent to an act of sexual intercourse will bar a prosecution for rape, even when the consent was obtained by fraud, if the victim knew that she was consenting to an act of sexual intercourse.

■ PROCEDURAL BASIS

Petition for a peremptory writ of prohibition.

■ FACTS

A person who called himself "Dr. Stevens" called the victim at work and told her that she was ill with a dangerous, highly infectious, and perhaps fatal disease. She was told that it could be cured either by an expensive, painful surgical procedure that would require her to be in the hospital for six weeks, or, for less money, she could have sexual intercourse with an anonymous donor who had been injected with a serum that would cure the disease. The victim agreed to have intercourse with the donor, believing that it was her only option. The victim withdrew $1000 as down payment for the "procedure" and went to a hotel room. The "donor"—Boro (D)—came to the hotel room and had sexual intercourse with the victim. Boro (D) was charged with rape, pursuant to a statute that defined rape as intercourse with a victim "who was at the time unconscious of the nature of the act." Boro (D) argued that the victim was aware of the nature of the act in which she engaged, so her motive for engaging in the act was irrelevant.

■ ISSUE

Will consent obtained by fraud bar a prosecution for rape?

■ DECISION AND RATIONALE

(Newsom, J.) Yes. Consent to an act of sexual intercourse will bar a prosecution for rape, even when the consent was obtained by fraud, if the victim knew that she was consenting to an act of sexual intercourse. The victim here clearly understood the nature of the act, and she understood that she was consenting to an act of intercourse. To say that a victim was unconscious of the nature of the act is to say that she did not know that she was consenting to intercourse. The legislature has drafted other statutes that make specific types of fraud in the inducement (such as impersonating a spouse) a basis for a charge of rape, but there is no such statute here. Peremptory writ of prohibition issued.

Analysis:

Statutes that apply the idea of fraud in the inducement to rape are quite specific in the types of false statements they prohibit. For example, Cal. Pen. Code § 266c, enacted after this case was decided, refers to a false statement that causes fear "that would cause a reasonable person in like circumstances to act contrary to the person's free will." A blanket prohibition against consent brought about by fraud in the inducement would be, at best, unworkable: would a person be guilty of rape if consent were obtained by false proclamations of undying affection?

■ CASE VOCABULARY

FRAUD IN THE FACTUM: Fraud occurring when a legal instrument as actually executed differs from the one intended for execution by the person who executes it, or when the instrument may have had no legal existence. Compared to fraud in the inducement, fraud in the factum occurs only rarely, as when a blind person signs a mortgage when misleadingly told that it's just a letter.

FRAUD IN THE INDUCEMENT: Fraud occurring when a misrepresentation leads another to enter into a transaction with a false impression of the risks, duties, or obligations involved; an intentional misrepresentation of a material risk or duty reasonably relied on, thereby injuring the other party without vitiating the contract itself, especially about a fact relating to value.

PROHIBITION: An extraordinary writ issued by an appellate court to prevent a lower court from exceeding its jurisdiction or to prevent a nonjudicial officer from exercising a power.

Commonwealth v. Fischer

(Prosecuting Government) v. (College Student)

721 A.2d 1111 (Pa. Super. 1998)

A MISTAKE REGARDING A VICTIM'S CONSENT IS NOT A DEFENSE

■INSTANT FACTS Fischer (D) engaged in sexual activity with a woman and claimed that he believed the victim consented to his actions.

■BLACK LETTER RULE A reasonable mistake of fact regarding a victim's consent is not a defense to a rape charge.

■ PROCEDURAL BASIS

Appeal from a conviction for involuntary deviate sexual intercourse, aggravated indecent assault, and other charges.

■ FACTS

Fischer (D) was convicted of involuntary deviate sexual intercourse and aggravated indecent assault. Fischer (D) and the victim both testified that, a few hours before the incident for which Fischer (D) was convicted, the two of them went to Fischer's (D) dormitory room and engaged in intimate contact. Fischer (D) testified that the contact included oral sex, with sexually aggressive actions by the victim. The victim testified that the contact was limited to kissing and fondling. After this encounter, Fischer (D) and the victim separated, but both later found themselves in Fischer's (D) room again. The victim testified that Fischer (D) locked the door and forced her to have oral sex. The victim also testified that she struggled with Fischer (D), told him she had to leave, and said repeatedly that she did not want to have sex with Fischer (D). The victim testified that she was able to leave the room only after she kneed Fischer (D) in the groin. Fischer (D) testified that when he and the victim arrived at his room, she told him that it would have to be "a quick one." Once in the room, Fischer testified that he was acting in the same manner as he had during his prior encounter with the victim, but that the victim said no, to which Fischer (D) replied that "no means yes." The victim said she had to leave, but Fischer (D) told her that she "wanted it." Fischer (D) testified that he stopped when the victim said that she honestly did not want to engage in sexual activity. Fischer (D) testified that the victim enjoyed the contact, but that she left abruptly after saying she was getting angry with Fischer (D). At trial, Fischer's (D) counsel argued that Fischer (D) believed that the victim was a willing participant and that, given the victim's prior conduct and Fischer's (D) sexual inexperience, the belief was reasonable. Fischer (D) appealed his conviction based on ineffective assistance of trial counsel, for failure to request a jury instruction that said that Fischer (D) could not be convicted if he made a reasonable mistake as to the consent of the victim. Fischer (D) argued that the statutory language that defines "forcible compulsion" as including intellectual or moral force links consent to a defendant's *mens rea,* and that a defendant's mental state should be considered in determining if he used force.

■ ISSUE

Was Fischer (D) entitled to a jury instruction regarding mistake of fact as to the victim's consent?

■ DECISION AND RATIONALE

(Beck, J.) No. A reasonable mistake of fact regarding a victim's consent is not a defense to a rape charge. The court is bound by earlier precedent, *Commonwealth v. Williams,* 294 Pa. Super. 93, 439 A.2d 765 (1982), which held that a reasonable mistake of fact regarding a rape victim's consent is not a defense to a rape charge. The rule may be inconsistent with statutory law, which provides that ignorance or mistake of fact is a defense if it negates the *mens rea* necessary to establish an element of the offense. Other jurisdictions have adopted the rule that mistake regarding consent is a defense, but this rule has not been adopted in Pennsylvania. Fischer (D) is not alleged to have engaged in intellectual or moral force, but is alleged to have used force to overpower the victim. Furthermore, Fischer's (D) attorney did not render ineffective assistance of counsel by failing to request the jury instruction. The requested instruction would have been a change in the existing law, and a failure to anticipate a change in the law as it does exist is not inadequate assistance of counsel. Affirmed.

Analysis:

Leave to appeal was granted in this case by the Pennsylvania Supreme Court, *see Commonwealth v. Fischer,* 556 Pa. 620, 730 A.2d 485 (1999), but leave was dismissed without opinion as improvidently granted, *Commonwealth v. Fischer,* 560 Pa. 410, 745 A.2d 1214 (2000). Although the court clearly does not like the rule that governs this case, it does not seem to think that this is a case in which a mistake regarding consent was made. By Fischer's own testimony, he did not let the victim leave when she first asked him to let her go, but continued to insist that she "wanted it." Furthermore, even if his attorney did not request a jury instruction, counsel argued to the jury that Fischer (D) believed that the victim consented to the conduct. The jury seems to have believed the victim, rather than Fischer (D).

■ CASE VOCABULARY

MENS REA: [Latin, "guilty mind."] The state of mind that the prosecution, to secure a conviction, must prove that a defendant had when committing a crime; criminal intent or recklessness.

CHAPTER FOURTEEN

Theft Offenses

Commonwealth v. Mitchneck

Instant Facts: Mitchneck (D) was convicted of fraudulently converting the money of another.

Black Letter Rule: Failing to pay money to a creditor under an agreement to pay the debt of another does not constitute fraudulent conversion, since the money at issue never belonged to the creditor.

The Case of the Carrier Who Broke Bulk Anon v. The Sheriff of London

Instant Facts: A common carrier failed to deliver goods he was asked to transport and instead kept them for himself.

Black Letter Rule: One who has been given possession of goods cannot later be deemed to have obtained those goods feloniously.

Rex v. Chisser

Instant Facts: A salesperson was helping Chisser (D) select ties when, as Chisser (D) was inspecting two of them, he picked them up and ran from the store.

Black Letter Rule: Taking goods without paying for them is treated as a felony even though the store clerk voluntarily handed the merchandise to the customer for inspection as part of an anticipated transaction.

The King v. Pear

Instant Facts: Pear (D) rented a horse; instead of returning it to its owner at the designated time, he sold the horse and kept the money.

Black Letter Rule: If one rents property under false pretenses and fails to return it at the end of the lease time, and instead sells the property and keeps the money, he has committed a felony.

People v. Sattlekau

Instant Facts: Sattlekau (D) placed an ad in the paper pretending to look for a housekeeper— possibly a wife. After he won the affections of Kaiser, he asked her for a sizeable amount of money, which he took with no intention of repaying it.

Black Letter Rule: A charge of grand larceny by false representations may be maintained even though not all of the representations made by the defendant are misstatements of existing facts, but refer to hopes or intentions to do things in the future.

Durland v. United States

Instant Facts: Durland (D) was charged with running a dishonest investment trust.

Black Letter Rule: A crime involving dishonesty or misrepresentations need not be established solely by proof of the misrepresentation of facts or past acts; promises of future performance made without regard to their truth can establish such a crime.

People v. Dioguardi

Instant Facts: Defendants were charged with extorting $4,700 from the officers of two corporations.

Black Letter Rule: In order to establish the crime of extortion, it need not be proven that the defendant actually created fear in the mind of his prospective victim, so long as the defendant was successful in persuading the victim that he had the power to create fear and threatens to use that power to extract payment of a tribute.

McCormick v. United States

Instant Facts: A state legislator was convicted of extortion for taking money under color of official right in violation of the Hobbs Act.

Black Letter Rule: Proof of extension of a quid pro quo is necessary to support a conviction under the Hobbs Act when an elected official receives campaign contributions; money or property is "extorted" only when the elected official exchanges the performance of his duties for money.

Lear v. State

Instant Facts: Lear (D) was convicted of robbery after he took a bag of coins from a clerk opening a shop and filling the cash register.

Black Letter Rule: Under Arizona law, robbery requires proof of taking property against the will of its owner by use of force or the creation of fear, and absent proof of these elements, a conviction will not stand.

State v. Colvin

Instant Facts: While under an order for protection (OFP), Colvin (D) entered the home of his ex-wife, sat down, and drank a beer; when asked to leave, he did so, but he was charged with burglary.

Black Letter Rule: A violation of an order for protection (OFP) is insufficient to establish first-degree burglary because there is an absence of a separately committed crime, or even the intent to commit a crime, other than violating the OFP.

Commonwealth v. Mitchneck

(Pennsylvania) v. (Purported Thief)

130 Pa. Super. 433 (1938), 198 A. 463

FAILING TO PAY MONEY OWED IS NOT THEFT

Stop that thief! He failed to pay for merchandise other people bought on credit.

Hmm. I really love arresting people, but I'm not sure this one is going to stick.

VAGNONI'S

stus.com

■**INSTANT FACTS** Mitchneck (D) was convicted of fraudulently converting the money of another.

■**BLACK LETTER RULE** Failing to pay money to a creditor under an agreement to pay the debt of another does not constitute fraudulent conversion, since the money at issue never belonged to the creditor.

■ **PROCEDURAL BASIS**

On appeal from the defendant's conviction for fraudulent conversion.

■ **FACTS**

Mitchneck (D) operated a coal mine in Beaver Township and employed several workers at the mine. These workers had accounts at a local store owned by Vagnoni and had signed orders directing Mitchneck (D) to deduct amounts from their paychecks and pay those amounts to Vagnoni. Mitchneck (D) agreed to make the accommodation for his employees. He then deducted the agreed amount from their wages but neglected to pay the money to Vagnoni. At trial, Mitchneck (D) was convicted of fraudulent conversion.

■ **ISSUE**

Is it fraudulent conversion to take money from an employee and fail to pay it over to another pursuant to written instructions?

■ **DECISION AND RATIONALE**

(Keller, P.J.) No. The offense of fraudulent conversion requires that a defendant take property or money from another person and use that property or money for his own benefit. While it cannot be denied that, pursuant to the agreement, Mitchneck (D) owed Vagnoni money, Mitchneck (D) did not take that money from Vagnoni. The agreement was a novation of the obligation between Vagnoni and his customers, making Vagnoni Mitchneck's (D) creditor. The defendant no longer owed the money to his employees; he owed it to Vagnoni. But failing to pay a debt is not fraudulent conversion. Mitchneck's (D) liability for the debts of his employees is a civil, not a criminal, matter. Reversed and defendant discharged.

Analysis:

Not every bad act is criminal in nature. Compare the actions of the employer here with the actions of an attorney in State v. Davis, 689 P.2d 5 (Utah 1984). In *Davis,* the defendant-attorney received a payment for property from a third party that should have been paid out to his clients. Instead of turning over the entire amount, Davis held some back as payment for his services and was convicted of theft. The court decided that Davis had received the money "as the attorney for the partnership," and his use of the property, even to pay himself for the partnership's debts to him, constituted conversion.

■ **CASE VOCABULARY**

CONVERSION: The wrongful possession or disposition of another's property as if it were one's own; an act or series of acts of willful interference, without lawful justification, with an item of property in a manner inconsistent with another's right, whereby that other person is deprived of the use and possession of the property.

NOVATION: The act of substituting for an old obligation a new one that either replaces an existing obligation with a new obligation or replaces an original party with a new party. A novation may substitute (1) a new obligation between the same parties, (2) a new debtor, or (3) a new creditor.

The Case of the Carrier Who Broke Bulk Anon v. The Sheriff of London

(Thief) v. (Prosecution)

YB. Pasch. 13 Edw. IV, f. 9, pl.5 (1473), 64 Selden Soc. 30 (1945)

FELONIOUS CONVERSION DOES NOT EXIST WHEN THE GOODS WERE DELIVERED VOLUNTARILY

■INSTANT FACTS A common carrier failed to deliver goods he was asked to transport and instead kept them for himself.

■BLACK LETTER RULE One who has been given possession of goods cannot later be deemed to have obtained those goods feloniously.

■ PROCEDURAL BASIS

Before the King's Council in the Star Chamber.

■ FACTS

A man made a bargain with another to carry certain bales of woad (a dye) and other things to Southampton and misdelivered them. The carrier then broke open the bales and converted the contents to his own use. He was prosecuted for a felony.

■ ISSUE

Can one be prosecuted for felony conversion when a carrier misdirects the delivery of his customer's goods and then retains the customer's property for his own use?

■ DECISION AND RATIONALE

(Bryan, C.J.C.P.) No. The carrier cannot be guilty of felony conversion of the customer's goods when the carrier had lawful possession of the goods and did not use any violence to obtain them. The only action for these goods may be an action of detinue.

■ CONCURRENCE

(The Chancellor.) The majority of the justices have decided that when goods are delivered to someone, they cannot be said to have obtained them feloniously. The lone dissenter argues that whether the goods were delivered or not is unavailing. He contends that one in possession of goods may still determine to take them feloniously just as one can take his or her own goods feloniously, such as where one removes goods delivered to another in hopes of filing a false claim for damages. But this did not happen here. One cannot be said to have taken goods feloniously when they were entrusted to him in the first place.

■ DISSENT

(Chokke, J.C.P.) If goods have been delivered as part of a bailment, the carrier cannot be said to have gained possession feloniously. However, there may still be a felony committed. The items in the containers were not his; they were his merely to be carried and delivered to another. If the carrier had given the containers away, he would not have been guilty of a felony, but he broke them open and took the articles for his own use. Such an action was a felony.

Analysis:

While the common carrier here is by no means innocent, the judges here are arguing about the level of his offense. Whether a crime is classified as a misdemeanor or a felony has serious implications when it comes to punishment. Unlike the employer in *Commonwealth v. Mitchneck*, 130 Pa. Super. 433, 198 A. 463 (1938) who by retaining a portion of his employee's pay was found not to have converted their property for his own, here there is no question but that the common carrier kept property that was not his. Where the question of wrongfully keeping property is resolved, the next issue becomes how blameworthy the actor's conduct is so that the proper punishment can be delivered.

■ CASE VOCABULARY

CHOSE: A thing, whether tangible or intangible; a personal article; a chattel.

DETINUE: A common law action to recover personal property wrongfully taken by another.

WARRANT: A writ directing or authorizing someone to do an act, especially one directing a law enforcer to make an arrest, a search, or a seizure.

Rex v. Chisser

(Prosecution) v. (Thief)

T. Raym 275, 83 Eng. Rep. 142 (King's Bench) (1678)

TAKING MERCHANDISE WITHOUT PAYING FOR IT, EVEN WHEN OFFERED FOR INSPECTION, IS THEFT

■**INSTANT FACTS** A salesperson was helping Chisser (D) select ties when, as Chisser (D) was inspecting two of them, he picked them up and ran from the store.

■**BLACK LETTER RULE** Taking goods without paying for them is treated as a felony even though the store clerk voluntarily handed the merchandise to the customer for inspection as part of an anticipated transaction.

■ PROCEDURAL BASIS

On indictment for theft.

■ FACTS

Chisser (D) came to the shop of Charteris and asked to see two cravats (ties). The shopkeeper showed him the ties and told him they sold for seven shillings. Chisser (D) told Charteris he would pay only three shillings. He then ran out of the shop with the ties.

■ ISSUE

When a shopkeeper voluntarily hands merchandise to a customer and the customer takes the items without paying for them, has he committed a felony?

■ DECISION AND RATIONALE

(Opinion author not identified.) Yes. The defendant committed a felony. He took the goods *felleo animo*, and his intent was supported by his decision to run. While Charteris "gave" the ties to the defendant, she intended that they remain in her possession until the defendant perfected their contract by paying for them. It made no difference that the shopkeeper handed the merchandise to the defendant; his leaving with the ties was the same as if he had taken them on his own.

Analysis:

The common carrier in *The Case of the Carrier Who Broke Bulk Anon v. The Sheriff of London*, YB. Pasch. 13 Edw. IV, f. 9, pl.5 (1473), 64 Selden Soc. 30 (1945), kept the goods he was hired to deliver. He was held not to have feloniously taken the goods because the owner of the goods had voluntarily delivered them to him. Here, the clerk handed the ties to her customer as part of the sale process, but not with any intention of entrusting them to him for any long-term purpose, and the felony conviction stood. This case seems to reach the more logical conclusion.

■ CASE VOCABULARY

FELLEO ANIMO: Felonious intent.

INCHOATE: Partially completed or imperfectly formed; just begun.

The King v. Pear

(Government) v. (Horse Thief)

1 Leach 212, 168 Eng. Rep. 208 (1779)

TAKING ANOTHER'S PROPERTY UNDER FALSE PRETENSES IS A FELONY

■**INSTANT FACTS** Pear (D) rented a horse; instead of returning it to its owner at the designated time, he sold the horse and kept the money.

■**BLACK LETTER RULE** If one rents property under false pretenses and fails to return it at the end of the lease time, and instead sells the property and keeps the money, he has committed a felony.

■ PROCEDURAL BASIS

On appeal from a jury's finding that the taking of the horse was a felony.

■ FACTS

The prisoner was indicted for stealing a horse belonging to Finch. Finch was a stable keeper and Pear (D) hired the horse to ride to Sutton and back. He gave Finch his address in town and told him he would return around eight that evening. Pear (D) did not return. It was discovered that Pear (D) sold Finch's horse the same day to a man in Smithfield Market. It was also discovered that Pear (D) had given Finch a false address.

■ ISSUE

Was the stablekeeper's delivery of the horse to the defendant such a voluntary act as to preclude the defendant from being held guilty of a felony in his conversion of the horse?

■ DECISION AND RATIONALE

(Ashhurst, J.) No. If one rents property under false pretenses and fails to return it at the end of the lease time, and instead sells the property and keeps the money, he has committed a felony. Here, the horse was hired to help Pear (D) take a journey. Pear (D) never left town; instead, he sold the horse. It was up to the jury to determine what Pear's (D) intentions were at the time he borrowed the horse from Finch. If Pear (D) rented the horse truly intending to take a trip and decided later to sell the horse, he cannot be convicted of feloniously taking the horse. If the jury determines that Pear's (D) leasing of the horse was simply a pretense for getting the horse so that he might sell it, and that he never intended to take his trip, the commission of a felony is for the judges. The jury found that Pear (D) intended to take the horse from the beginning and the question was then referred to the judges. They differed as to their opinion. The majority held that based on the jury's finding that the horse was rented solely for the purpose of converting it, the fact that the stablekeeper willingly parted with the horse did not make Pear's (D) actions any less felonious.

Analysis:

When dealing with the theft of property, early courts were concerned with whether the actor took the property with the intent to steal it or formed the intent to steal later on. When there is an innocent transfer of property, the thief cannot be said to have "forcefully" taken the property from its owner. In this case, while there was no "force" in taking the horse, the force was found in the defendant's lie that he would return the animal. The fact that the defendant gave the stablekeeper a phony address to frustrate attempts to find him tended to prove his intent.

■ CASE VOCABULARY

FALSE PRETENSES: The crime of knowingly obtaining title to another's personal property by misrepresenting a fact with the intent to defraud. Although unknown to English common law, false pretenses became a misdemeanor under a statute old enough to make it common law in the United States. Modern American statutes make it either a felony or a misdemeanor, depending on how valuable the property is. Also termed OBTAINING PROPERTY BY FALSE PRETENSES; FRAUDULENT PRETENSES.

FALSE REPRESENTATIONS MAY INCLUDE HOPES FOR THE FUTURE

So you see, my soon-to-be wife, you will actually benefit by lending me $1,000!

stus.com

■**INSTANT FACTS** Sattlekau (D) placed an ad in the paper pretending to look for a housekeeper—possibly a wife. After he won the affections of Kaiser, he asked her for a sizeable amount of money, which he took with no intention of repaying it.

■**BLACK LETTER RULE** A charge of grand larceny by false representations may be maintained even though not all of the representations made by the defendant are misstatements of existing facts, but refer to hopes or intentions to do things in the future.

■ **PROCEDURAL BASIS**

On appeal from a conviction for grand larceny.

■ **FACTS**

The defendant placed an ad looking for a housekeeper with the potential for marriage. He met Kaiser when she responded to the ad. The defendant wrote to her on stationery from the Uncle Sam Hotel and asked her to meet him for an interview. He told Kaiser his name was E. Paul. The two talked at length and had eight or nine more meetings. The defendant told Kaiser that he was single and that he owned the Uncle Sam Hotel in Pennsylvania. He said he had received an offer to buy his hotel for $6000 and that he had an option to lease a different hotel in New York. He told Kaiser that if he was able to get the New York property, the hotel could provide a home for the two of them once they married. The defendant wrote to Kaiser and laid out his plans for the new hotel. He gave her a short financial statement that appeared to support his ability to begin the New York business. He told her that he would be able to raise the last of the money soon, but that the person he was dealing with on the New York hotel was looking to speed things up, so he was $2000 short. While he said he could scrape together $1000, he asked her if she could lend him the last $1000. He promised to memorialize the loan with a note and to pay interest at six percent. Sattlekau (D) reminded Kaiser that, while she was helping him, she was also helping herself to better the position of the man who would be her husband. Kaiser withdrew $1000 and gave it to Sattlekau (D). He promised to see her later that day. Instead, Kaiser got a telegram telling her that Sattlekau's (D) hotel was on fire. Sattlekau (D) had to leave, he said, and would see her the next day. Of course, the "fire" ruined his prospects of selling the hotel, but he promised she would see her $1000 again. Kaiser never saw the defendant again until he was arrested—in the midst of trying the same scheme with a different woman. The defendant was indicted and convicted of first-degree grand larceny for taking $1000 from Kaiser by false pretenses.

■ ISSUE

May a charge of obtaining money under false pretenses be maintained even though not all of the defendant's statements were misrepresentations of existing facts, but rather referred to hopes or intentions for the future?

■ DECISION AND RATIONALE

(Clarke, J.) Yes. At trial, the defendant testified at length on his own behalf. The jury returned a verdict of guilty, finding the evidence sufficient to support a finding of false representations and use of false representations to defraud Kaiser of $1000. The jury concluded that the defendant's actions constituted a classic case of grand larceny by false pretenses. The intent to cheat and defraud was abundantly proven. The statements made by the defendant to Kaiser were almost all false and were made with the intention of getting her to part with $1000. When she parted with her money, she did so based on his promises. The defendant argues that his stated intentions to repay the money were sincere, so he did not commit fraud, but it is not necessary to establish in a case for false pretenses that all statements made in the course of the fraud were false. Affirmed.

Analysis:

This case presents the same problem often seen in insanity defense cases. The prosecution will frequently point to stretches of lucid or "sane" conduct engaged in by the defendant to dissuade the jury that the defendant was truly insane. Of course, as the court recognized in *Smith v. State*, 614 P.2d 300 (Alaska 1980), even insane people seem sane at times; and even defrauders occasionally make true statements. Here, Sattlekau (D) had stationery printed for a nonexistent hotel and used a false name as part of his intricate plan to take money from Kaiser. While he may have made truthful statements along the way, most his promises were false.

■ CASE VOCABULARY

DEFRAUD: To cause injury or loss to (a person) by deceit.

FALSE PRETENSES: The crime of knowingly obtaining title to another's personal property by misrepresenting a fact with the intent to defraud.

MISREPRESENTATION MAY BE FOUND FOR FUTURE, AS WELL AS PAST, FACTS

■**INSTANT FACTS** Durland (D) was charged with running a dishonest investment trust.

■**BLACK LETTER RULE** A crime involving dishonesty or misrepresentations need not be established solely by proof of the misrepresentation of facts or past acts; promises of future performance made without regard to their truth can establish such a crime.

■ PROCEDURAL BASIS

On appeal from the District Court of the United States for the Eastern District of Pennsylvania following a conviction.

■ FACTS

The indictment charged Durland (D) with running a dishonest "tontine" under the name of Provident Bond and Investment Company. Using this company, Durland (D) tricked individuals into investing small amounts each month in exchange for large returns—as high as fifty percent in six months. In his sales brochure, he denied that any "lottery" element entered into the company's business practices and stated that every investment would steadily increase in value.

■ ISSUE

Is the crime of running a dishonest tontine established on proof of misrepresentations not concerning existing facts, but rather concerning future promises?

■ DECISION AND RATIONALE

(Brewer, J.) Yes. Durland (D) operated a scheme to defraud investors, intending to pay the investors nothing at "maturity." Durland (D) argued that the statute at issue here was designed only to address those cases in which there is a misrepresentation of an existing fact, and it could not apply to promises of future events. Durland's (D) counsel argues that the charges here represent nothing more than a crime of an intention to breach a contract at some point in the future. It is true that one of the few settled principles of criminal law is that fraud must be charged based on misrepresentation of an existing fact, not on a future intention to break a contract. But the statute in this case is broader than counsel recognizes. The statute prohibits any scheme to defraud. The law distinguishes between facts that simply fail to materialize, though they were believed to be true at the time, and statements that were never true, such as when one buys goods on credit, believing the money will be there to pay for them when the bill comes due, as compared to one who purchases goods knowing he will not be able to pay, even in the future. The statute seeks to remedy the evil of luring investors with the promise of large returns. The thought of these gains is essential to all schemes of this type. As a result, the statute here is to be read as applying to misrepresentation of things both past and present. If testimony showed the business principals had a good faith belief they could make the payouts they had promised, there would be no crime. There was a crime, however, if the defendant is shown to have devised a scheme to defraud and, in furtherance of that scheme, mailed letters to potential victims so he could benefit from the scheme.

Analysis:

The unscrupulous con man in *People v. Sattlekau*, 120 App. Div. 42, 104 N.Y.S. 805 (1907), tried to avoid responsibility for his misrepresentations, claiming that while he may have told lies, most of his statements concerned his future desires and hopes. Here, Durland (D) tried a similar defense. He pointed to all the sales literature and argued that they contained legally enforceable promises to pay back the investors. The problem, of course, is that while the documents looked legitimate, they were not backed up by any intention to make good on the promises therein.

■ **CASE VOCABULARY**

TONTINE: A financial arrangement in which a group of participants share in the arrangement's advantages until all but one has died or defaulted, at which time the whole goes to that survivor.

A FEAR OF RETRIBUTION MAY BE EXTORTION

■INSTANT FACTS Defendants were charged with extorting $4,700 from the officers of two corporations.

■BLACK LETTER RULE In order to establish the crime of extortion, it need not be proven that the defendant actually created fear in the mind of his prospective victim, so long as the defendant was successful in persuading the victim that he had the power to create fear and threatens to use that power to extract payment of a tribute.

■ PROCEDURAL BASIS

On appeal from dismissal of the defendants' conviction for extortion and conspiracy.

■ FACTS

Two nonunion corporations engaged in the wholesale stationery business were forced to deal with organizational activities by four unions. Their premises were picketed and their truck drivers refused to cross the picket lines. Having deliveries in and out of the companies stopped for even two weeks would have forced them out of business. The picketing activities escalated until the attorney for the companies advised management to hold a consent election. The companies contacted McNamara (D), an important official in the Teamsters Union, to set it up. McNamara (D) discouraged the election, suggesting there was another way to handle things. McNamara (D) warned it would be expensive. McNamara (D) and a man named Holt met with one of the companies' officers and told him the union problems would stop if the corporations "joined up" with the local union, paid Equitable Research Associates (Equitable) $3500 to defray the expenses associated with organizing the corporations' employees, and hired Equitable as labor consultant. Defendant Dioguardi (D) was the sole officer of Equitable.

Equitable was to be paid $100 per month by each corporation for the term of the collective bargaining contract. In exchange for the $100, the corporations would receive counsel and advice on labor matters. Reluctantly, the companies agreed to McNamara's (D) terms and the following Monday pickets and organizers were absent from the corporations' premises. The companies wrote checks for $3500 and delivered them to McNamara. The checks were deposited in Equitable's bank account and paid back out to Dioguardi (D) as "salary." The corporations' management convinced their employees to join the union and a collective bargaining agreement was signed. Equitable, however, took no part in the negotiation of the contract and its consulting services were never used. Nonetheless, Equitable received a total of $4700 from the two companies at $200 per month each. The companies continued making payments to Equitable until they were notified to stop by the District Attorney's office. McNamara (D) and Dioguardi (D) were charged with conspiracy and extortion.

■ ISSUE

To prove the crime of extortion, is it sufficient to show that the defendant succeeded in persuading his victim that he has the power to cause harm, regardless of whether the victim was actually fearful of that harm?

■ DECISION AND RATIONALE

(Froessel, J.) Yes. Fear of economic loss or financial harm has long been recognized as satisfying the element of fear in a charge of extortion. But it is not required that a defendant create actual fear, so long as the defendant is successful in convincing his victim that he possesses the power to cause it. The important thing is that, in extorting the money, the defendant relied on his or her ability to generate fear. In this case, the stationery companies feared without a doubt that so long as the picketing of their facilities continued, they could be forced out of business. The threat was presented when McNamara (D) refused to intervene on the companies' behalves unless they assented to the terms of his proposal. The exact words are unimportant. When McNamara (D) professed to have the ability to affect the corporations' labor problems and demanded a payment for his exercise of control, he effectively communicated a threat to commit unlawful injury and he, as well as those acting with him, may be appropriately convicted of extortion.

The testimony at trial established that the officers of the two corporations met reluctantly with the unions and only did so because they believed these unions held the power to resolve the labor crisis threatening their business. All the officers of the two companies testified that McNamara led them to believe they would have guaranteed peace with their employees by making the payments they required. The power to stop picketing implies the power to resume it. A jury could have reasonably concluded that companies continued making payments because of McNamara's (D) insinuation that labor unrest would be restored as quickly as it has disappeared. The orders appealed from should be reversed, the indictments reinstated, and a new trial ordered.

Analysis:

The court here was not concerned with the exact language used by the defendants in order to convince their victims to pay the compensation they demanded. The defendants appeared cautious about saying the wrong thing, promising the wrong results, or making claim to having too much power—all of which may simply indicate experience with extortion. The defendants offered legitimate reasons for the "payments" they were requesting here, though the evidence at trial showed that none of these so-called needs for the money were legitimate.

■ CASE VOCABULARY

EXTORTION: The act or practice of obtaining something or compelling some action by illegal means, as by force or coercion.

TRIBUTE: Money paid by an inferior [sovereign or state] to a superior one to secure the latter's friendship and protection.

McCormick v. United States

(West Virginia State Legislator) v. (Prosecuting Government)

500 U.S. 257, 111 S.Ct. 1807 (1991)

PROOF OF A QUID PRO QUO IS REQUIRED TO ESTABLISH A VIOLATION OF THE
HOBBS ACT BY AN ELECTED OFFICIAL

■**INSTANT FACTS** A state legislator was convicted of extortion for taking money under color of official right in violation of the Hobbs Act.

■**BLACK LETTER RULE** Proof of extension of a quid pro quo is necessary to support a conviction under the Hobbs Act when an elected official receives campaign contributions; money or property is "extorted" only when the elected official exchanges the performance of his duties for money.

■ **PROCEDURAL BASIS**

On appeal to the U.S. Supreme Court on grant of certiorari.

■ **FACTS**

McCormick (D) was a member of the West Virginia House of Delegates, representing a district that had long suffered from a shortage of doctors. To address the shortage, West Virginia developed a practice of allowing foreign medical school graduates to practice medicine with temporary permits while they studied for their local board exams. Some doctors practiced this way for years while they repeatedly failed their exams. McCormick (D) was one of the plan's biggest supporters. When the legislature considered terminating this program, many foreign-educated doctors organized to lobby against the measure and hired Vandergrift to help them. The doctors were successful in having the program extended another year. As part of the legislation, many of the doctors that had been practicing under the program for years were to be given their medical licenses based on the experience they gained under the legislation. At McCormick's (D) next election, he told Vandergrift that his campaign was expensive and had not heard anything from these "foreign doctors." Vandergrift collected money from the doctors and paid it over to McCormick (D). McCormick (D) did not list any of those "donations" as either campaign contributions or income. In the financial records kept by the doctors' association, the payments were not shown as campaign contributions—the only notations made were that the money went to McCormick (D).

The following year, McCormick (D) introduced legislation to permit foreign-educated medical doctors to practice in the state without first having to pass state licensing tests. The bill eventually became law and afterwards, McCormick (D) received more cash from the doctors. Following a grand jury investigation, McCormick (D) was indicted and charged with five counts of violating the Hobbs Act. At the close of McCormick's (D) trial, the jury was instructed that, to establish a violation of the Hobbs Act, the prosecution needed to prove McCormick (D) induced the cash payment and did so knowingly and willfully by extortion. Of the five counts, McCormick (D) was found guilty of only one; the court declared a mistrial on the remaining four. The court of appeals affirmed the decision, holding that a conviction under the Hobbs Act

---

did not require proof of an exchange of promises between non-elected officials and their "benefactors." The court concluded that elected officials should be held to the same standards as other government officials when accepting money that was not a legitimate campaign contribution. The court of appeals rejected McCormick's contention that a Hobbs Act violation must be established by proof of a quid pro quo, and held that the statute only required a showing that the parties did not intend the money to be "legitimate campaign contributions."

■ ISSUE

Did the court of appeals properly decide that the conviction of an elected official for extortion of property under the Hobbs Act did not require a quid pro quo?

■ DECISION AND RATIONALE

(White, J.) No. It is the everyday business of a legislator to serve his constituents. Campaigns must be financed with contributions, and the contributions are frequently made based on what the candidate states he has done and on what he or she promises to do when elected. It is not a proper exercise of the Hobbs Act to hold a legislator responsible for illegal activity when he or she fulfills campaign promises. Activity like this was not what Congress had in mind when making it a "crime to obtain property from another, with his consent, 'under color of official right.' " An elected official cannot commit extortion in order to have his campaign financed. Contributions certainly cannot be solicited using threats of force, violence or fear; however, the Act prohibits soliciting donations in exchange for an *explicit promise* to perform an act or refrain from performing an act. A quid pro quo is necessary for conviction. Reversed and remanded for further proceedings.

Analysis:

Bribery and extortion are similar causes of action with overlapping elements and generally, when a defendant is charged with bribery, he cannot also be charged with extortion. In *People v. Kacer*, 448 N.Y.S.2d 1002, 113 Misc. 2d 338 (1982), the court was concerned with the difference between extortion and bribery. The court explained that the offenses are different in that "[i]t is compulsion that distinguishes extortion from bribery. Bribery is unqualified 'voluntary giving.' "

■ CASE VOCABULARY

BRIBERY: The corrupt payment, receipt, or solicitation of a private favor for official action. Bribery is a felony in most jurisdictions.

EXTORTION: The offense committed by a public official who illegally obtains property under the color of office, especially an official's collection of an unlawful fee.

HOBBS ACT: A federal anti-racketeering act making it a crime to interfere with interstate commerce by extortion, robbery, or physical violence.

QUID PRO QUO: [Latin, "something for something."] An action or thing that is exchanged for another action or thing of more or less equal value; a substitute.

ABSENT FORCE OR FEAR, A DEFENDANT MAY NOT BE CONVICTED OF ROBBERY

■**INSTANT FACTS** Lear (D) was convicted of robbery after he took a bag of coins from a clerk opening a shop and filling the cash register.

■**BLACK LETTER RULE** Under Arizona law, robbery requires proof of taking property against the will of its owner by use of force or the creation of fear, and absent proof of these elements, a conviction will not stand.

■ **PROCEDURAL BASIS**

On appeal from a conviction for robbery.

■ **FACTS**

George Gross testified for the prosecution that, when he opened the Campbell Quality Shop one morning, Lear (D) came in looking to purchase shirts and shoes. As Gross went about the tasks of opening the store for business, Gross took money from the store's safe, put the cash in the register, and began unrolling coins. Lear (D) grabbed the bag of coins from Gross and ran out of the store. Lear (D) had no weapons and used no force to take the money other than simply grabbing the bag. It was conceded the bag contained $33.

■ **ISSUE**

Do the facts support a finding that Lear (D) committed robbery?

■ **DECISION AND RATIONALE**

(Ross, J.) No. Under Arizona law, robbery is defined as the taking of personal property against the will of its owner, accompanied by means of force or fear. The fear may be shown by injury to the person or property, including injury to a family member or to anyone in the area at the time the robbery is committed. In this case, there is no element of fear. No threats were made. The bag was simply grabbed from the shop owner and Lear (D) then ran off with it. The "force" used was not the kind of force required under the law. Other cases have required the force to be of such a nature as to show the party being robbed was overpowered and his resistance was prevented. Simple "snatching" does not have the same force, nor does stealth. The prosecutor urged that this case was like *Brown v. State*, 34 Ariz. 150, 268 P. 618, where two robbers posed as prohibition officers who threatened to turn the victim in after she sold them beer. In exchange for not prosecuting her, one of the actors suggested that the victim pay a bribe. While the victim was counting the money to pay them, they reached for her entire amount of cash and left. *Brown* does not apply here, since the "force" provided was the

---

threat of legal action, which many courts have found sufficient to support a charge of robbery. Judgment reversed; cause remanded for further proceedings.

Analysis:

In *People v. Dioguardi*, 8 N.Y.2d 260, 203 N.Y.S.2d 870 (1960), the court did not require direct proof that the business owners were actually "in fear"—rather, all that was required was, in essence, a belief that the perpetrators had the power to instill fear or to follow through with a threat. The result in this case is likely not inconsistent with *Dioguardi*. The defendant here gave the sales clerk *no* reason whatsoever to be apprehensive. In fact, the sales clerk here went about his regular morning routine while Lear (D) was in the store, seemingly unafraid of the "threat" he posed.

■ CASE VOCABULARY

PUTTING–IN–FEAR: The threatening of another person with violence to compel the person to hand over property. These words are part of the common-law definition of robbery.

State v. Colvin
(State of Minnesota) v. (Order for Protection Violator)

645 N.W.2d 449 (Minn. 2002)

VIOLATION OF AN OFP IS INSUFFIENT TO SUPPORT A CHARGE OF FIRST—DEGREE BURGLARY

They're charging you with burglary.

But I was just having a beer at her house!

stus.com

■**INSTANT FACTS** While under an order for protection (OFP), Colvin (D) entered the home of his ex-wife, sat down, and drank a beer; when asked to leave, he did so, but he was charged with burglary.

■**BLACK LETTER RULE** A violation of an order for protection (OFP) is insufficient to establish first-degree burglary because there is an absence of a separately committed crime, or even the intent to commit a crime, other than violating the OFP.

■ PROCEDURAL BASIS

On appeal to the state supreme court following the appellate court's affirmance of the defendant's conviction for burglary.

■ FACTS

Colvin's (D) former wife received an ex parte OFP against her ex-husband. The order was valid for a year and a day and required that Colvin (D) not enter her home during that time. The order also prohibited Colvin (D) from committing any acts of violence against her and from having any contact with her elsewhere, including at her work. A girl staying with the former wife returned home to find Colvin (D) sitting in the house, watching television, and drinking a beer. The teenager asked him to leave and he complied. Colvin (D) was subsequently arrested and charged with first-degree burglary and violation of the OFP. Since he had been charged with two previous violations of the OFP, this violation came before the court as a felony. Colvin (D) was found guilty of first-degree burglary on a finding that his actions fulfilled all the elements of the crime: he entered the home without consent; another person was found to have been present in the home (the teenage girl); he entered the home intending to commit a crime; the crime he committed was the violation of the OFP.

■ ISSUE

Does a criminal defendant's violation of an OFP constitute a sufficient basis for holding him responsible for first-degree burglary in the absence of an intent to commit another crime once inside his ex-wife's home?

■ DECISION AND RATIONALE

(Lancaster, J.) No. In order to support a conviction for the crime of burglary, the state must show that the defendant intended to commit some crime beyond the trespass to the property. Whether the violation of the OFP is sufficient to constitute an independent crime under the burglary statute depends on how Colvin (D) violated the OFP. The prosecution argues that

Colvin (D) committed two separate violations of the OFP. First, he entered his ex-wife's house in violation of the order. Second, he intended to contact his wife, in violation of the order. By committing the second violation, Colvin (D) has provided the independent crime required by the charge of burglary. Unfortunately, insufficient evidence was adduced at trial to find that Colvin (D) intended to contact his ex-wife. The district court's written findings state simply that Colvin's (D) independent act was his violation of the OFP—his entry into her home. There was no evidence put forth at trial that Colvin (D) intended, by violating the OFP, to contact Michele.

Previous cases have found that trespass cannot be used to support a charge of burglary, since to do so would be to allow a simple trespasser to be charged as a burglar when the only intention was to remain in the building without the owner's consent. Here, the violation of the OFP's no-entry provision is similar. The violation of the OFP serves to fulfill the first element of burglary—unlawful entry. The same act cannot also be used to fulfill the independent-crime requirement. The legislature has already done much to address the problems of domestic abuse and provide for increasing penalties for multiple violations; multiple violations can be prosecuted as felonies and punished more severely than, for example, multiple counts of trespass. If even stronger penalties are necessary, it should be up to the legislature to amend the sentencing portions of the law. Reversed

■ DISSENT

(Anderson, J.) The concern of the majority is over the court's ability to penalize a violation of an OFP as a more serious crime. If the state abused its discretion in charging Colvin (D) with the crime here, the majority should address that. Absent that, the district court properly found the felony underlying the burglary to be separate from the breaking and entering through a violation of the OFP. The matter should be affirmed.

Analysis:

Courts frequently struggle with cases, like this one, that try to make a single act fulfill multiple requirements. The inability of the prosecution to make multiple use of criminal acts has been similarly shown, for example, in felony murder cases, where the same facts that establish the existence of a felony murder have also been urged at sentencing to justify the imposition of the death penalty. *See, e.g., Olsen v. State*, 67 P.3d 536 (Wyo. 2003). Often, these multi-purpose efforts are unsuccessful.

■ CASE VOCABULARY

BURGLARY: The modern statutory offense of breaking and entering any building—not just a dwelling, and not only at night—with the intent to commit a felony. Some statutes make petit larceny an alternative to a felony for purposes of proving burglarious intent.

ORDER FOR PROTECTION [STAY AWAY ORDER]: In a domestic-violence case, an order forbidding the defendant to contact the victim. A stay-away order usually prohibits the defendant from coming within a certain number of feet of the victim's home, school, work, or other specific place. Stay-away orders are most often issued in criminal cases.

TRESPASS: An unlawful act committed against the person or property of another, especially wrongful entry on another's real property.

CHAPTER FIFTEEN

Perjury, False Statements, and Obstruction of Justice

Bronston v. United States

Instant Facts: Under oath, a witness evaded the precise question asked but nonetheless testified truthfully.

Black Letter Rule: To support a perjury conviction, a witness must actually willfully state a material matter that he does not believe to be true.

United States v. Moore

Instant Facts: Moore (D) signed a false name when a postal inspector delivered a package to him, and he was charged with making a materially false statement about a matter within the jurisdiction of the federal government; he appealed his conviction, arguing that there was nothing "material" enough about his signing a fake name to satisfy the statute under which he was charged.

Black Letter Rule: A statement is material if it has a natural tendency to influence, or is capable of influencing, either a discrete decision or any other function of the agency to which it was addressed.

Brogan v. United States

Instant Facts: Brogan (D) was charged with and convicted of knowingly making a false statement to a federal agent by merely denying the receipt of illegal cash payments from an employer.

Black Letter Rule: A "false statement" under 18 U.S.C. § 1001 includes *any* false statement knowingly and willfully made within the jurisdiction of a federal agency, encompassing even a mere false denial of criminal wrongdoing.

United States v. Aguilar

Instant Facts: A federal judge was convicted of obstruction of justice when he lied to the FBI about the disclosure of a wiretap authorization to the targeted individual.

Black Letter Rule: The utterance of a false statement to an investigating agent—who may or may not testify before a grand jury—does not constitute an endeavor to interfere with the due administration of justice.

United States v. Cueto

Instant Facts: An attorney was convicted of obstruction of justice in connection with numerous court filings made on behalf of a criminal defendant.

Black Letter Rule: Otherwise lawful conduct violates 18 U.S.C. § 1503 if employed with the corrupt intent to interfere, obstruct, or impede the due administration of justice.

Arthur Andersen LLP v. United States

Instant Facts: During an informal investigation of Enron's financial activities, Arthur Andersen (D) instructed its employees to destroy material documents pertinent to Enron when otherwise called for by its document retention policies.

Black Letter Rule: One knowingly corruptly persuades another person with intent to cause that person to withhold documents from, or alter documents for use in, an official proceeding only when the person is conscious of his wrongdoing in contemplation of a particular official proceeding to which the documents might be material.

Bronston v. United States

(Film Producer) v. *(Prosecuting Authority)*

409 U.S. 352 (1973)

PERJURY BY IMPLICATION IS NOT RECOGNIZED

Wow, it's really you! Your technically nonperjurious, yet super-sneaky testimony left me breathless with admiration!

stus.com

■**INSTANT FACTS** Under oath, a witness evaded the precise question asked but nonetheless testified truthfully.

■**BLACK LETTER RULE** To support a perjury conviction, a witness must actually willfully state a material matter that he does not believe to be true.

■ **PROCEDURAL BASIS**

Certiorari to review a federal court of appeals decision affirming the defendant's perjury conviction.

■ **FACTS**

Bronston (D), the sole owner of a movie production company, opened numerous bank accounts throughout Europe to finance his projects. In 1964, Bronston's (D) company filed for Chapter 11 bankruptcy, and a hearing was held to determine the extent and location of the company's assets. At the hearing, Bronston (D) was asked, under oath, whether he had any bank accounts in Swiss banks, whether he ever had any such accounts, and whether he had any nominees who have Swiss bank accounts. In response, Bronston (D) answered that he did not have Swiss bank accounts, that his company had a Swiss bank account for about six months, and that he had no nominees having Swiss bank accounts. In fact, Bronston's (D) responses were literally true. However, his response to whether he ever had a Swiss bank account did not answer the question asked, for he maintained a personal Swiss bank account for many years in which he held considerable assets.

Bronston (D) was charged with perjury. At trial, the jury was instructed that perjury required an examination of the state of mind of the defendant and that he could be convicted of willfully providing false testimony if he fully understood the question and nonetheless provided a false statement. However, the court noted that the defendant could also be convicted based on a true statement that, in the context in which it was given, nevertheless constituted a false statement. Bronston (D) was convicted of perjury. On appeal, the court of appeals affirmed, holding that "an answer containing half of the truth which also constitutes a lie by negative implication, when the answer is intentionally given in place of the responsive answer called for by a proper question, is perjury." Bronston (D) appealed to the Supreme Court.

■ **ISSUE**

Can a witness be convicted of perjury for an answer, under oath, that is literally true but not responsive to the question asked and is arguably misleading by negative implication?

■ DECISION AND RATIONALE

(Burger, C.J.) No. To support a perjury conviction, a witness must actually willfully state a material matter that he does not believe to be true. It is insufficient that a witness willfully state a material matter that implies another material matter that he does not believe is true. While the perjury statute serves a valuable role in the adversarial fact-finding process, neither the Government (P) nor the jury is permitted to speculate on a witness's intent to mislead his questioner. Rather, the adversary process provides alert counsel ample opportunity to ensure his question is answered directly and truthfully. The burden is on the questioner, not the witness, to pin down the answer to the questioner's specific inquiry. Even when the witness shrewdly intends to evade an incriminating response, the better recourse is a follow-up question, not a perjury prosecution. Reversed.

Analysis:

A perjury charge sustained by negative implication would create a slippery slope of judicial and juror discretion. It would require courts and jurors to determine, first, whether the witness in fact lied under oath. If so, the witness committed perjury. If not, however, a judge or jury must actually delve into the mind of the witness to determine whether he or she understood the question asked and intentionally evaded the question by truthfully answering a related question._ Perjury by negative implication would also give crafty lawyers the opportunity to trap a witness with confusing or compound questions, hoping that they will be unresponsive.

■ CASE VOCABULARY

PERJURY: The act of an instance of a person's deliberately making material false or misleading statements while under oath.

United States v. Moore

(Prosecuting Authority) v. (Criminal Defendant)

612 F.3d 698 (D.C. Cir. 2010)

SIGNING A FICTITIOUS NAME ON AN EXPRESS MAIL DELVIERY SLIP IS A VIOLATION
OF FEDERAL LAW

■INSTANT FACTS Moore (D) signed a false name when a postal inspector delivered a package to him, and he was charged with making a materially false statement about a matter within the jurisdiction of the federal government; he appealed his conviction, arguing that there was nothing "material" enough about his signing a fake name to satisfy the statute under which he was charged.

■BLACK LETTER RULE A statement is material if it has a natural tendency to influence, or is capable of influencing, either a discrete decision or any other function of the agency to which it was addressed.

■ PROCEDURAL BASIS

Federal appellate court consideration of the defendant's appeal from his conviction.

■ FACTS

Postal Service workers intercepted a package containing powder cocaine addressed to a "Karen White," whom the Postal Service believed to be a fictitious person. The police and Postal Service worked together to organize a controlled delivery, whereby they delivered the package after replacing the cocaine with flour and enclosing a tracking device. When a postal inspector attempted the delivery, Moore (D) arrived at the residence address. Moore (D) told the inspector that White was not home, but that she was his girlfriend and he would sign for the package. He signed the name "Kevin Jones." Moore (D) was arrested when he attempted to leave the house with the package. Moore (D) was charged with making a materially false statement about a matter within the jurisdiction of the United States Postal Service. He admitted that he signed the delivery form using a false name, and was convicted. Moore (D) appealed, arguing that no rational jury could have found that the false name was material to any matter within the jurisdiction of the federal government.

■ ISSUE

Did Moore (D) violate 18 U.S.C. § 1001(a)(2) by making a "materially false" statement about a matter within the jurisdiction of the federal government?

■ DECISION AND RATIONALE

(Ginsburg, J.) Yes. A statement is material if it has a natural tendency to influence, or is capable of influencing, either a discrete decision or any other function of the agency to which it was addressed. To prove a violation of the statute, the government must show that Moore (D) knowingly and willfully made any materially false, fictitious, or fraudulent statement in a matter within the jurisdiction of the executive branch of the U.S. government. Section 1001 does not

---

define "materially false," but the Supreme Court has said that a statement is materially false if it has a natural tendency to influence, or is capable of influencing, the decision of the decision-making body to which it was addressed. Our sister circuits have adopted a broader approach, asking whether a statement might in any way affect the functioning of the agency to which it was addressed. We are combining the two approaches.

The question of materiality is not answered by reference only to the specific circumstances at hand. As the Supreme Court explained in *Gaudin*, a statement need only have a natural tendency, or be capable of, influencing a government agency's decision-making or functioning, which connotes qualities of the statement that transcend the immediate circumstances. Moore's use of a false name could have impeded the ability of the Postal Service to investigate the trafficking of narcotics through the mail. The inspector would not have delivered the package to Moore (D) if she had not received a signature from him. The jury could reasonably infer that one function of the Postal Service is to track certain types of packages and to identify the recipients thereof. Clearly, signing a false name on a delivery form may adversely affect the ability of the Postal Service to perform this function. Affirmed.

Analysis:

In the *Gaudin* case cited in the court's opinion, the defendant was charged with violating 18 U.S.C. § 1001 by making false statements on HUD loan documents. After instructing the jury that the government had to prove that the false statements were material to HUD's activities and decisions, the trial court added that the issue of materiality is a matter for the court to decide rather than the jury, and that the statements in question there were material. The jury convicted Gaudin, but the Ninth Circuit reversed, holding that taking the question of materiality from the jury violated the Fifth and Sixth Amendments. The Supreme Court agreed, holding that the trial judge's refusal to submit the question of "materiality" to the jury was unconstitutional.

■ CASE VOCABULARY

MATERIAL: Having some logical connection with the consequential facts; of such a nature that knowledge of the item would affect a person's decision-making; significant; essential.

Brogan v. United States

(Union Officer) v. (Prosecuting Authority)

522 U.S. 398 (1998)

AN "EXCULPATORY NO" IS CRIMINAL WHEN FALSELY STATED TO AN INVESTIGATING FEDERAL AGENT

■INSTANT FACTS Brogan (D) was charged with and convicted of knowingly making a false statement to a federal agent by merely denying the receipt of illegal cash payments from an employer.

■BLACK LETTER RULE A "false statement" under 18 U.S.C. § 1001 includes *any* false statement knowingly and willfully made within the jurisdiction of a federal agency, encompassing even a mere false denial of criminal wrongdoing.

■ PROCEDURAL BASIS

Certiorari to review a decision of the Second Circuit Court of Appeals affirming the defendant's conviction.

■ FACTS

Brogan (D) was a union officer who accepted cash payments from a real estate company whose employees were represented by the union. During an investigation of the real estate company, federal agents from the Department of Labor and Internal Revenue Service visited Brogan (D) at his home to seek his cooperation. Brogan (D) was told that if he wished to cooperate he could consult with an attorney, but Brogan (D) declined. When asked whether he had received any cash payments from the real estate company, Brogan (D) said "no." After telling Brogan (D) that company records indicated such payments, and informing him that lying to federal agents was a crime, Brogan (D) did not change his answer. Brogan (D) was charged with and convicted of accepting unlawful cash payments from an employer and of making a false statement to a federal agent in violation of federal statutes. The Second Circuit Court of Appeals affirmed. Brogan (D) appealed to the Supreme Court.

■ ISSUE

Is a false denial of wrongdoing to federal investigators sufficient to impose criminal liability under 18 U.S.C. § 1001?

■ DECISION AND RATIONALE

(Scalia, J.) Yes. A "false statement" under 18 U.S.C. § 1001 includes *any* false statement knowingly and willfully made within the jurisdiction of a federal agency, encompassing even a mere false denial of criminal wrongdoing. Such an "exculpatory no" perverts governmental investigations, as do more elaborate falsities, and invokes the same Fifth Amendment incriminations as do other statements. Yet, many federal court of appeals decisions have repeatedly excluded the "exculpatory no" from the criminal reach of the statute. Courts, however, are not free to fashion judicial exceptions to plain statutory language, no matter how strong the policy arguments may be. There is no statutory language in § 1001 to except the "exculpatory no." Affirmed.

■ **DISSENT**

(Stevens, J.) The "exculpatory no" exclusion is a well-settled exception to the statute that has been debated, considered, and recognized by legal scholars and experienced jurists for decades. The majority ought to pay the bench and the bar greater respect before casting their doctrine aside.

Analysis:

In theory, the abolition of the exculpatory-no exception vastly expands the law-enforcement weapons available to the Government. In practice, however, the Government is unlikely to prosecute every untruth told to a federal agent or settle for a § 1001 conviction when investigating a more serious offense. Even in this case, the federal agents did not arrest Brogan (D) immediately upon hearing his lie. Rather, they attempted to convince Brogan (D) to tell the truth so that they could collect evidence for their broader investigation. Of course, Brogan (D) may have been charged with the crime he lied about committing had he been truthful.

■ **CASE VOCABULARY**

EXCULPATORY—NO DOCTRINE: The principle that a person cannot be charged with making a false statement for falsely denying guilt in response to an investigator's question. This doctrine is based on the Fifth Amendment right against self-incrimination.

FALSE STATEMENT: An untrue statement knowingly made with the intention of misleading; any one of three distinct federal offenses: (1) falsifying or concealing a material fact by trick, scheme, or device; (2) making a false, fictitious, or fraudulent representation; and (3) making or using a false document or writing. 18 U.S.C. § 1001.

United States v. Aguilar

(Prosecuting Authority) v. (Federal Judge)

515 U.S. 593 (1995)

OBSTRUCTION OF JUSTICE REQUIRES A NEXUS BETWEEN THE ALLEGED CORRUPT ACT AND A PENDING JUDICIAL PROCEEDING

■INSTANT FACTS A federal judge was convicted of obstruction of justice when he lied to the FBI about the disclosure of a wiretap authorization to the targeted individual.

■BLACK LETTER RULE The utterance of a false statement to an investigating agent—who may or may not testify before a grand jury—does not constitute an endeavor to interfere with the due administration of justice.

■ PROCEDURAL BASIS

Certiorari to review a federal court of appeals decision reversing the defendant's conviction.

■ FACTS

Aguilar (D), a federal judge, sat in the same courthouse as Judges Weigel and Peckham, who presided over two separate cases. In the first, Judge Weigel presided over a case involving a union official accused of embezzling funds from the union. The official had asked two acquaintances, Solomon and Chapman, for their "assistance," since Solomon had attended law school with Judge Aguilar (D), and Chapman was related to Aguilar (D). Judge Weigel later testified that Aguilar spoke to him about the case, but did not attempt to influence the outcome.

In the second matter, the union official was under FBI investigation for labor racketeering. The FBI sought a wiretap from Judge Peckham after learning of meetings between Chapman and Aguilar (D). Judge Peckham told Aguilar (D) about the Chapman wiretap and suggested that Aguilar (D) avoid Chapman. Aguilar (D) disclosed the wiretap authorization to Chapman.

Thereafter, a grand jury investigated Aguilar's (D) alleged attempt to influence Judge Weigel. Aguilar (D) lied to the FBI about his contact with Judge Weigel and his knowledge of the Chapman wiretap. Aguilar (D) was indicted on charges of obstruction of justice based on his alleged attempt to influence Weigel and his lies to the FBI. The jury convicted Aguilar (D) based only on his lies to the FBI. Aguilar (D) appealed, contending that he did not interfere with a judicial proceeding because the grand jury had not authorized the FBI investigation, and merely uttering false statements did not "corruptly influence" within the meaning of the obstruction statute. The court of appeals reversed the conviction on these grounds.

■ ISSUE

Does the mere utterance of false statements to the FBI corruptly endeavor to interfere with the due administration of justice?

■ DECISION AND RATIONALE

(Rehnquist, C.J.) No. The utterance of a false statement to an investigating agent—who may or may not testify before a grand jury—does not constitute an endeavor to interfere with the due administration of justice. The relevant statute's omnibus clause, which prohibits persons from endeavoring to influence, obstruct, or impede the administration of justice, requires a nexus between the charged conduct and the actor's knowledge of a pending court proceeding. "In other words, the endeavor must have the 'natural and probable effect' of interfering with the due administration of justice." Here, although Aguilar (D) knew that a grand jury had convened, there was no proof that Aguilar (D) knew or should have known that his false statement to the investigating FBI agent would be submitted as evidence to the grand jury. Without that nexus, Aguilar's (D) statements cannot amount to an endeavor to interfere with the grand jury proceeding. Rather, an endeavor to interfere with the administration of justice requires an actual knowing intent to interfere with an official proceeding, whether successful in doing so or not. Affirmed.

■ DISSENT

(Scalia, J.) The statute prohibits not only successful acts of interference with the due administration of justice, but all "endeavors" to do so as well. While the statute has been construed to require purposeful attempts of interference, the Court's nexus requirement substitutes a "natural and probable effect" element for proof of the actor's intent. Under the Court's reasoning, one may set out to intentionally interfere with justice, but be exonerated because his obstructing actions are impossible or improbable to succeed. The Court's decision reads the word "endeavor" out of the statute.

Analysis:

Justice itself is a goal to be achieved through a defined process. It can exist only after that process has been carried out. In this sense, obstruction of justice is a misnomer, for the crime is not dependent on the particular outcome of a proceeding. Rather, as the statute suggests, obstruction of justice requires an interference with the *due administration* of justice. It is interference with the process, not the outcome, which must be the natural and probable effect of the interfering conduct to support an obstruction of justice conviction.

■ CASE VOCABULARY

CORRUPTLY: In a corrupt or depraved manner; by means of corruption or bribery. As used in criminal-law statutes, corruptly usually indicates a wrongful desire for pecuniary gain or other advantage.

OBSTRUCTION OF JUSTICE: Interference with the orderly administration of law and justice, as by giving false information to or withholding evidence from a police officer or prosecutor, or by harming or intimidating a witness or juror.

(Prosecuting Authority) v. (Attorney)

151 F.3d 620 (7th Cir. 1998)

ATTORNEYS MAY NOT ABUSE THEIR POSITION AS OFFICERS OF THE COURT

■**INSTANT FACTS** An attorney was convicted of obstruction of justice in connection with numerous court filings made on behalf of a criminal defendant.

■**BLACK LETTER RULE** Otherwise lawful conduct violates 18 U.S.C. § 1503 if employed with the corrupt intent to interfere, obstruct, or impede the due administration of justice.

■ **PROCEDURAL BASIS**

Appeal to review the defendant's conviction.

■ **FACTS**

Venezia, the owner of a vending and amusement business operating illegal video poker machines in southern Illinois bars and restaurants, hired Cueto (D) as counsel to his business. In 1992, the Illinois Liquor Control Commission (ILCC) appointed Robinson, an ILCC agent, to investigate illegal gambling activities in the area, and particularly Venezia's business. Eventually, the FBI got involved in the investigation and placed Robinson under cover as a corrupt liquor agent, in order to gather evidence. In this role, Robinson indicated to Venezia that the investigation could be discouraged if he would pay bribes, and he suggested that they meet to discuss it. Thereafter, raids were conducted, during which Venezia's gaming machines were confiscated. Venezia then consulted Cueto (D). In response, Cueto (D) drafted a letter to State's Attorney Robert Haida, accusing Robinson of corrupt conduct and accusing him of soliciting bribes. Cueto (D) also filed a complaint in state court against Robinson, seeking a preliminary injunction against all further corrupt activities that interfered with Venezia's business operations. Without permitting Robinson access to counsel or allowing him to put on a defense, the judge granted the injunction. Nonetheless, Robinson continued his investigation for the FBI and moved to remove the state-court case to federal court, where Robinson disclosed his undercover role. The injunction was dissolved, and Cueto (D) filed an appeal to the Seventh Circuit Court of Appeals, which affirmed. Cueto (D) then unsuccessfully filed a petition for writ of certiorari with the Supreme Court.

During Robinson's investigation of Venezia, he learned that Venezia and Cueto (D) enjoyed more than an attorney-client relationship. They jointly purchased and developed real estate to be used as a topless nightclub, jointly incorporated an asbestos removal company, and Venezia purchased Cueto's (D) office building and moved his corporate offices there. During this time, one of Venezia's customers was arrested for illegal gambling; Robinson testified at the hearing and Cueto (D) cross-examined him. After the hearing, Cueto (D) wrote to State's Attorney Haida demanding Robinson's indictment for perjury. Nothing came of the demand.

In 1994, a grand jury was empaneled to examine the evidence collected in the Venezia investigation. Cueto (D) unsuccessfully filed numerous motions to hinder the investigation and to discharge the grand jury. Venezia was ultimately convicted of racketeering by operating an illegal gambling enterprise. Seven months later, Cueto (D) was indicted on three counts of obstruction of justice under the omnibus clause of 18 U.S.C. § 1503, for corruptly endeavoring to use his office as an attorney to influence, obstruct, and impair the due administration of justice. Specifically, count 2 charged Cueto (D) with corruptly endeavoring to influence the due administration of justice by filing pleadings in the federal-court removal action, an appeal, and a petition for certiorari. Count 6 charged Cueto (D) in connection with his corrupt endeavor to influence State's Attorney Haida to indict Robinson for perjury. Finally, Count 7 charged Cueto (D) with obstruction of justice relating to the filing of various pleadings and motions in Venezia's racketeering case. Cueto (D) was convicted on all three counts.

■ **ISSUE**

Can an attorney be convicted of corruptly endeavoring to influence, obstruct, or impede the due administration of justice by filing court documents and otherwise acting on behalf of his client?

■ **DECISION AND RATIONALE**

(Bauer, J.) Yes. Otherwise lawful conduct—even acts undertaken by an attorney in the course of representing a client—violates 18 U.S.C. § 1503 if employed with the corrupt intent to interfere, obstruct, or impede the due administration of justice. The statute clearly prohibits a corrupt intent to interfere with the administration of justice, but does not address any specific means that may or may not be employed. The result is that the statute broadly covers any conduct falling within its prohibition. Contrary to Cueto's (D) argument, however, this breadth does not make the statute unconstitutionally vague. The statute plainly placed Cueto (D) on notice that any actions taken with the requisite corrupt intent are punishable. Here, Cueto (D) used his position as an attorney to protect his client's illegal activities and promote his own financial interests. His acts alone were permissible, but not when done for the purpose that he intended. The Government's (P) proof sufficiently demonstrated that there was a pending judicial proceeding, Cueto (D) know of the proceeding, Cueto (D) did or endeavored to influence, obstruct, or impede the administration of justice in that proceeding, and Cueto (D) acted corruptly. By filing frivolous petitions, motions, and appeals, and uncovering a covert FBI investigation designed to reveal his client's illegal activities, Cueto (D) violated § 1503. Moreover, Cueto (D) knew at the time he attempted to persuade State's Attorney Haida to charge Robinson with perjury that it was likely that the evidence from Robinson's investigation would be presented to the grand jury. This provides the sufficient nexus between Cueto's (D) conduct and the requisite judicial proceeding to support the conviction. Affirmed.

Analysis:

An obstruction of justice charge may be the penultimate attorney sanction. While courts may impose monetary sanctions for frivolous filings, and ethics boards may censure or disbar an attorney for misbehavior, criminal charges for obstruction of justice likely involve all three. Note, however, that the court was careful to point out the personal motives of Cueto (D) as strong support for the obstruction charge. Had Cueto (D) acted purely in his client's interests, though frivolously and inappropriately, there may have been less of a chance of criminal charges. Ethical sanctions, though, would remain likely.

(Auditor) v. (Prosecuting Authority)

544 U.S. 696 (2005)

DOCUMENT DESTRUCTION POLICIES, IF HONESTLY ENFORCED, DO NOT OBSTRUCT THE ADMINISTRATION OF JUSTICE

■**INSTANT FACTS** During an informal investigation of Enron's financial activities, Arthur Andersen (D) instructed its employees to destroy material documents pertinent to Enron when otherwise called for by its document retention policies.

■**BLACK LETTER RULE** One knowingly corruptly persuades another person with intent to cause that person to withhold documents from, or alter documents for use in, an official proceeding only when the person is conscious of his wrongdoing in contemplation of a particular official proceeding to which the documents might be material.

■ **PROCEDURAL BASIS**

Certiorari to review a decision of the Fifth Circuit Court of Appeals affirming the defendant's conviction.

■ **FACTS**

In the 1990s, Enron Corporation switched its business operations from natural gas pipelines to an energy conglomerate, which required aggressive accounting practices to achieve rapid growth. Arthur Andersen (D) provided audit and consulting services to Enron. In the early 2000s, Enron experienced financial difficulties and it became internally apparent that the company's accounting practices were questionable at best. In response to an August 2001 informal investigation by the Securities and Exchange Commission, Arthur Andersen (D) formed an Enron "crisis-response" team to prepare for a formal SEC inquiry. In October, a high-level Arthur Andersen (D) partner spoke at a meeting of ninety-nine company employees, informing them of the company's document retention procedures. At the meeting, the partner indicated that documents could be destroyed according to company policy until the day litigation began. In the months that followed, Arthur Andersen (D) frequently reiterated its document retention policy and insisted that employees comply with it. As a result, numerous documents relating to its accounting practices relative to Enron were shredded. On October 30, the SEC launched a formal investigation of Enron, yet the shredding continued. Not until September 9, however, did Arthur Andersen (D) receive a formal subpoena requesting its documents, at which time all document destruction ceased. Arthur Andersen (D) was indicted on one count of "knowingly, intentionally, and corruptly" persuading its employees with intent to cause them to withhold documents from, and alter documents for use in, an official SEC investigation under 18 U.S.C. § 1512. A jury convicted the defendant of the charges, and the Fifth Circuit Court of Appeals affirmed.

■ ISSUE

Was the jury correctly instructed on the elements of "corrupt persuasion" under 18 U.S.C. § 1512?

■ DECISION AND RATIONALE

(Rehnquist, C.J.) No. One knowingly corruptly persuades another person with intent to cause that person to withhold documents from, or alter documents for use in, an official proceeding only when the person is conscious of his wrongdoing in contemplation of a particular official proceeding to which the documents might be material. To emphasize this point, each element of the offense must be examined. Because it is not criminal to innocently persuade another to withhold documents from use in an official proceeding, such as when an attorney counsels his client to invoke his Fifth Amendment rights, only persuasion that corruptly convinces another to withhold documents falls within the statute. Because the statute also requires the persuasion to be knowingly as well as corruptly imposed, only those who persuade conscious of their wrongdoing face criminal liability. However, the jury was instructed that it could convict the defendant if its instructions to follow its document retention policy, although honest and sincere, nonetheless intended to subvert or impede the governmental fact-finding process. These instructions erroneously negated the "corruptly" element.

Likewise, the instructions suggested that the jury need not find any nexus between the defendant's persuasion and any particular governmental proceeding, because no proceeding need be pending at the time of the offense. While no proceeding need be pending when the offense occurred, it is essential to criminal liability that a proceeding be foreseeable to the defendant at the time of his persuasion. Without a foreseeable proceeding, the defendant cannot have knowingly persuaded another to interfere with it. Reversed and remanded.

Analysis:

The Enron collapse and the controversy over the Arthur Anderson document destruction prompted far-reaching congressional action. In 2002, Congress responded to the controversy by enacting the Sarbanes—Oxley Act, 18 U.S.C. § 1348 *et seq*. Under Sarbanes—Oxley, accountants are required to maintain "audit or review workpapers for a period of 5 years from the end of the fiscal period in which the audit or review was concluded." 18 U.S.C. § 1350. Administrative provisions require even longer holding periods for other such documents.